Approaches to popular film

Inside Popular Film

General editors   Mark Jancovich and Eric Schaefer

Inside Popular Film is a forum for writers who are working to develop new ways of analysing popular film. Each book offers a critical introduction to existing debates while also exploring new approaches. In general, the books give historically informed accounts of popular film which present this area as altogether more complex than is commonly suggested by established film theories.

Developments over the past decade have led to a broader understanding of film which moves beyond the traditional oppositions between high and low culture, popular and avant–garde. The analysis of film has also moved beyond a concentration on the textual forms of films, to include an analysis of both the social situations within which films are consumed by audiences, and the relationship between film and other popular forms. The series therefore addresses issues such as the complex intertextual systems which link film, literature, art and music, as well as the production and consumption of film through a variety of hybrid media, including video, cable and satellite.

The authors take interdisciplinary approaches which bring together a variety of theoretical and critical debates that have developed in film, media and cultural studies. They neither embrace nor condemn popular film, but explore specific forms and genres within the contexts of their production and consumption.

Forthcoming titles include

Harry Benshoff   *Monsters in the closet: reading gay and lesbian horror films*

Joanne Hollows   *The state of the heart: re-mapping the field of women's genres*

Bennet Schaber   *Everyday life and popular film*

Esther Sonnet   *Sexuality and popular film*

Ben Taylor   *Film comedy*

Approaches
to popular film

edited by
Joanne Hollows and Mark Jancovich

Manchester University Press
Manchester and New York

Distributed exclusively in the USA and Canada by St. Martin's Press

Copyright © Manchester University Press 1995

While copyright in the volume as a whole is vested in Manchester University Press, copyright in individual chapters belongs to their respective authors, and no chapter may be reproduced wholly or in part without the express permission in writing of both author and publisher.

Published by Manchester University Press
Oxford Road, Manchester M13 9NR, UK
and Room 400, 175 Fifth Avenue,
New York, NY 10010, USA

Distributed exclusively in the USA and Canada
by St Martin's Press, Inc;.,
175 Fifth Avenue, New York, NY 10010, USA

British Library Cataloguing-in-Publication Data
A catalogue record for this book is available from the British Library

Library of Congress Cataloging-in-Publication Data
Approaches to popular film / edited by Joanne Hollows and Mark Jancovich.
    p.   cm. —(Inside popular film)
   Includes bibliographical references and index.
   ISBN 0–7190–4392–1.—ISBN 0–7190–4393–X (pbk.)
    1. Motion pictures—Philosophy. 2. Film criticism. I. Hollows,
Joanne. II. Jancovich, Mark. III. Series.
PN1955.A66 1995
791.43,dc20   94–37371

ISBN 0–7190–4392–1 *hardback*
ISBN 0–7190–4393–X *paperback*

Typeset in Great Britain
by Northern Phototypesetting Co Ltd, Bolton
Printed in Great Britain
by Bell & Bain Ltd, Glasgow

Contents

Illustrations

Notes on contributors

Joanne Hollows is a Lecturer in Media and Cultural Studies at the Nottingham Trent University. She is currently preparing a book on women's genres for Manchester University Press and is also researching into discourses of romance in contemporary popular culture.

Peter Hutchings is a Lecturer in Film at the University of Northumbria at Newcastle. He is the author of *Hammer and Beyond: the British Horror Film* (Manchester University Press, 1993) and is currently working on the aesthetics of horror.

Mark Jancovich is a Lecturer in American Studies and Director of the Centre for Literary and Cultural Studies at the University of Keele. He is the author of *Horror* (Batsford, 1992), *The Cultural Politics of the New Criticism* (Cambridge University Press, 1993) and *Rational Fears: American Horror in the 1950s* (Manchester University Press, forthcoming).

Henry Jenkins is Associate Professor in Literature at Massachusetts Institute of Technology. He is the author of numerous publications, including *Textual Poachers: Television, Fans and Participatory Culture* (Routledge, 1992) and *What Makes Pistachio Nuts?: Early Sound Comedy and the Vaudeville Experience* (Columbia University Press, 1992), and editor (with Brunslova Karnack) of *Classical Hollywood Comedy* (Routledge, 1994).

Paul McDonald is a Senior Lecturer in Media Performance at University College, Salford. His current research is on masculinity and method acting in 1950s Hollywood.

Helen Stoddart is a Lecturer in Literature and Film in the Department of English, Keele University. She is currently working on the representation of carnivals and circuses within literature and film. She has also published on the contemporary Gothic.

Lisa Taylor is a Lecturer in Cultural Studies at Wolverhampton University. She is currently doing research on gender and consumerism. **Andy Willis** runs the Higher Education Programme in Media Studies at Wirral Metropolitan College.

For Duncan

Introduction   *Joanne Hollows and Mark Jancovich*

Popular film and cultural distinctions

This book aims to introduce the main approaches to the analysis of film and to provide students with clear and accessible accounts of the main theoretical debates. In the process, it examines the ways in which these approaches are shaped by their constructions of the 'popular' – that is, the ways in which distinctions between popular film and alternative film forms underpin their basic theoretical positions.

Each chapter situates the particular approach under discussion within the historical development of approaches to film, and relates its particular approach to other stages of development. However, it is important to bear in mind that these approaches are neither as discrete nor as historically fixed as this organization may imply. Approaches may survive long after they have been attacked or even superseded by later developments. For example, practitioners of auteur theory did not simply abandon this approach with the advent of genre criticism, star studies, or screen theory. Indeed, many auteur theorists were violently opposed to these later developments.

Furthermore, the book also seeks to illustrate how these approaches intersect one another. While one theory may reject certain features of another approach, it may also leave certain assumptions unquestioned and so reproduce aspects of the previous approach. In other cases, particular critics may draw upon a variety of different approaches and seek to resolve their differences so that they can be used in conjunction with one another. However, it should be pointed out that given the major disagreements between different approaches this is a very difficult and complex process.

As Raymond Williams has illustrated, one of the problems with the word 'popular' is that it has acquired two different, and often confused, meanings. The oldest sense of the term popular referred to that which was of 'the people' or belonged to them, but it has also acquired the meaning of that which is 'widely favoured' or 'well liked'.[1] The first meaning implies a distinction or opposition between sections of society – 'the popular' and 'the elite'. In this way, this definition of 'popular' depends upon the existence of something, which by implication, is 'not popular'. The second meaning corresponds to what Stuart Hall has called 'the "market" or commercial definition of the term'.[2] It refers to whether or not something is consumed or accepted by large numbers of people. However, these two meanings are quite different. For example, the film *Hudson Hawk*, which was a disaster at the box–office, would be classified as popular in the first sense, but not in the second. It may not have been consumed by large numbers of people, but it would still be defined by its difference from elite forms of culture.

Indeed, it is within this sense of 'the popular' that 'folk cultures' are defined as forms of popular culture. They may be the culture of a small, local community, but they are still defined by their relation to 'the common people', rather than an economic, political or cultural elite. However, with the emergence of modern mass media such as cinema, critics have frequently confused these two meanings of 'the popular'. The problem is that while folk cultures are usually seen as forms within which culture was both produced and consumed by 'the people' – and were therefore seen as 'authentic' – mass media forms are usually produced by large capitalist industries for sale to the common people. As a result, for many critics contemporary popular culture came to be seen as either (1) something which is not really 'of the people' because it is imposed upon them by others and is, therefore, deemed 'inauthentic' (see, for example, chapter one), or (2) something which is seen as akin to old 'folk' forms that is understood to be both produced and consumed by 'the people' for 'the people'.[3]

Stuart Hall has taken issue with both of these definitions of 'the popular'. The first, he claims, presents 'the people' as 'cultural dopes' who are 'purely passive', a position he refers to as 'a deeply unsocialist perspective',[4] (even though it is one which is common among socialists and left critics in general). The second definition he also describes as 'highly dubious' in so far as it 'neglects the absolutely essential relations of cultural power – of domination and subordination – which is an intrinsic feature of cultural relations'. As he goes on to argue:

> I want to assert on the contrary that there is *no* whole, authentic, autonomous 'popular culture' which lies outside the field of force of the relations of cultural power and domination. [This position] greatly underestimates the power of cultural implantation.[5]

Therefore although Hall is critical of the idea that people are passive objects who are controlled from outside by others, he stresses that all cultural forms are defined within conditions of power.

Hall also introduces a third definition of the popular, 'the descriptive', which he finds equally unsatisfactory. In this definition, 'the popular' is simply equated with 'all the things that "the people" do and have done'.[6] Hall's objection to this definition is not simply that it is tautological, but also that it simply provides a list or inventory. He claims that simply listing forms and practices ignores how 'the real analytic distinction' between 'the people' and those who are 'not the people' is made.[7] Indeed one of the major problems with this definition is that the 'meaning of a cultural form and its place or position in the cultural field is *not* inscribed inside its form. Nor is its position fixed once and for ever.'[8] As Hall puts it: 'The categories [popular and non-popular] remain, though the inventories change.'[9]

Hall's point is that most theories of the popular present the distinction between popular and non-popular forms as a 'condition' of specific texts and activities, rather than as the product of the ways in which texts and activities are appropriated by, or become associated with, specific social groups. In this way, for example, many approaches to film imply that popular films can be distinguished by certain characteristic features which produce certain characteristic effects. Such approaches fail to recognize that 'the popular' is simply part of the process by which texts are classified. As a result, any particular text is not inherently popular or elite in character, but may well move between the two as historical conditions change. As Hall claims:

> This year's radical symbol or slogan will be neutralised into next year's fashion; the year after, it will be theobject of profound cultural nostalgia. Today's rebel folksinger ends up, tomorrow, on the cover of *The Observer* colour magazine.[10]

Hall's examples describe the process by which radical, 'popular' forms are incorporated into the culture of dominant and elite groups, but it is also the case that the opposite happens; that a form previously defined as elite will lose its cultural status, and be incorporated into the culture of 'popular' or subordinate groups. For example, while Pavarotti's *Nessun Dorma* might have once been classified as elite, it has been incorporated into the 'popular' because of its associations with football. For this reason, Hall argues that popular culture should not be seen simply as either the means by which dominant groups impose their ideas on subordinate groups, or the way in which subordinate groups resist domination. Instead, he defines the popular as a site of struggle, a place where conflicts between dominant and subordinate groups are played out and distinctions between the cultures of these groups are continually constructed and reconstructed.

The work of the French sociologist Pierre Bourdieu, offers a particularly useful way of understanding how distinctions between popular and elite forms of culture are produced.[11] For Bourdieu, there are effectively three main categories of taste: legitimate (or elite); middlebrow; and popular.[12] These, he argues, are strongly linked to class formations. Indeed, he claims that class is not defined simply by the forms of economic capital which one possesses but also by the forms of 'cultural capital'. These forms of cultural capital are made up of both competences and dispositions, or specific forms of knowledge and particular predispositions.

Bourdieu argues that because different sections of society have different competences and dispositions, this means that different sections of society will 'perceive, classify and memorize differently'.[13] This means that different groups consume cultural forms in different ways – for example, Bourdieu claims that the ability to recognize legitimate cultural forms relies on specific dispositions. Therefore, in the visual arts, for example, where one person will see a picture *of* something, another sees a picture *by* someone (It's a Rembrandt); and yet another sees an example of a particular art movement (It's Impressionist). The same is also true in the area of film where one person will see a film of a particular genre (a western); another sees a film with a particular star (Burt Lancaster); and yet another sees a film by a particular director (John Sturges).[14]

The ability to recognize legitimate culture depends on what Bourdieu calls 'the aesthetic disposition' or 'the pure gaze' which is based on a rejection of 'the popular aesthetic' or 'popular taste'. Like Hall, he claims that these features are primarily ways of classifying objects rather than inherent features of the objects themselves. Therefore, as Bourdieu argues in his characterization of the aesthetic disposition or pure gaze:

> If the work of art is indeed, as Panofsky says, that which 'demands to be experienced aesthetically', and if any object, natural or artificial, can be perceived aesthetically, how can one escape the conclusion that it is the aesthetic intention [of the viewer] which 'makes' the work of art ... , that it is the aesthetic point of view that creates the aesthetic object?[15]

This mode of perception is preoccupied with form over function. Even the most mundane objects can be perceived as aesthetic – for example, someone with the 'pure gaze' might prefer an Alessi kettle, which is valued for its formal features, to the functional, energy-saving features of an electric kettle. Similarly, a discarded, 'out-dated' old dress in a charity shop may be used to create an aesthetic effect by an art student who buys it and wears it in a night-club.

However, for Bourdieu, this mode of perception is not innocent. Instead, it fundamentally depends upon the process by which the persons in possession of the pure gaze distinguish themselves from the common people. The pure gaze is inherently a refusal of popular tastes which are dismissed as natural, naive and simple: hence the common distinction between the self-evident, transparent and easy pleasures offered by popular culture, and the complex, difficult and active processes associated with the appreciation of legitimate culture.

However, for Bourdieu, the association between popular taste and the 'naive' and 'natural' does not mean that it isn't socially produced, nor that it is neutral. Just as the pure gaze is fundamentally based upon its refusal of popular taste, so popular taste is based on a refusal of that refusal. Thus, the working classes' hostility to legitimate forms, and their 'reluctance and refusal' to engage with them 'springs not just from a lack of familiarity but from a deep-rooted demand for participation'.[16]

For Bourdieu, subordinate groups recognize that legitimate forms are 'a sort of aggression [or] affront' to their way of life.[17] In contrast to the demand for participation within popular taste, Bourdieu claims that the pure gaze depends upon distance. Thus he argues that what is normally seen as the simple inability of subordinate groups to appreciate legitimate culture is, in fact, at least as much, a refusal of that culture.

Indeed, Bourdieu argues that the pure gaze is directly related to the economic situation of the bourgeoisie, a situation which is unavailable to subordinate classes and groups. His claim is that its refusal of 'simple' or 'natural' pleasures is the product of a 'distance from necessity'. The ability to think about form over function – for example, at its most basic, to eat food that is stylish rather than filling – or to engage in practices with no functional purpose, comes out of 'an experience of the world freed from urgency and through the practice of activities which are an end in themselves, such as scholastic exercises or the contemplation of works of art'.[18]

However, as should be clear, he also stresses that it is defined in reaction against the tastes of other classes. It is a mode of perception which asserts its 'superiority over those who, because they cannot assert the same contempt for ... gratuitous luxury and conspicuous consumption, remain dominated by ordinary interests and urgencies'.[19] However, what is most worrying about these distinctions is that, as Bourdieu illustrates, they are not only the most 'classifying' of all social differences, but also have 'the privilege of appearing to be the most natural'.[20]

However, it should be emphasized that, for Bourdieu, these distinctions are neither claims about the character of specific texts, nor about the actual activities of specific consumers. They are ways in which cultural distinctions are produced and maintained so as to reproduce the dominant order. It is not that popular audiences do not think when they consume texts, nor that they simply reject formal innovation, but that they reject the terms of the pure gaze. They require that they are engaged by the intellectual and formal features, rather than distanced. They require that these features have a purpose.

The end result of the ways in which cultural distinctions operate, is that opposing tastes are homogenized as they are rejected or defended. In the work of intellectuals such as film theorists, not only are the politics underpinning cultural distinctions often repressed, but also the 'popular' becomes an undifferentiated monolith. Not only are differences between contemporary popular films repressed, but so is any sense of changes in popular forms over time or in different national contexts.

Indeed the question of the relationship between national identity and popular culture is crucial for a number of reasons. One of the most striking is the way in which the popular is often defined as foreign with national contexts. For example, within Britain, the popular has often been associated with America and with Americanization.[21] This position is usually constructed around a conception of the national in which Britishness is associated with legitimate culture. Furthermore, as chapter one demonstrates, the 'threat' of mass culture in the USA during the 1950s was associated with the threat of totalitarianism in Europe. Indeed, in both British and American contexts, fears of a foreign threat to legitimate culture are often linked to the threat of the 'foreigners' within – for example, the working class and Afro-Americans.[22]

It is also the case that, as a result, specific popular texts can have very different meanings within different national contexts. As Cora Kaplan observes:

> In a sixties American left constellation, westerns and thrillers were seen
> as generically as well as ideologically right-wing. And so they were for

the American audience. But in Britain the genres and narratives of American popular culture acted as a kind of wedge, forcing open, through contrast and a wild dissonance, the class-bound complacency of the Great Tradition of British Culture.[23]

It is therefore essential that we acknowledge the different ways in which popular culture has been articulated within different historical moments, but it is also essential that we recognize conflicts and contradictions within any specific moment between different forms of popular culture. For this reason, if for no other, there is a need to re-evaluate popular culture in general, and popular film in particular, and the ways in which these have been discussed within academic approaches.

As should be clear, Bourdieu sees academic intellectuals as central to the production and reproduction of these cultural distinctions. Indeed he claims that they tend to legitimate the pure gaze and render popular tastes illegitimate. As Andrew Ross has argued:

> The intellectual's training in discrimination is an indispensable resource in such a process. For this is where the intellectual's accredited power of discrimination reinforces the power to subordinate even as it presents itself in the form of an objective critique of taste.[24]

For Bourdieu, this situation is not simply a 'reflection' of the interests of the bourgeois class, nor is it simply associated with liberal or conservative critics. Indeed, much of Bourdieu's fiercest criticisms are directed against supposedly radical and left-wing intellectuals.

For Bourdieu, it is the problematic situation of the bourgeois intellectual which produces this particular defence of the pure gaze. He claims that while intellectuals are still members of the dominant class (the bourgeoisie), they exist as a dominated section of that class. They are dependent upon those sections of the bourgeoisie which are involved in the realm of economic production. This gives rise to a struggle between the cultural bourgeoisie and the economic bourgeoisie in which the former attempts to increase the value of cultural activities in opposition to the economic activities of the latter. It is for this reason, Bourdieu claims, that cultural intellectuals not only tend to claim an autonomy for cultural activities in which they are distanced from economic and practical criteria, but also tend to adopt a political rhetoric which opposes the dominant economic and material interests of their own class. The result is an ironic situation in which bourgeois intellectuals often claim to be anti-bourgeois in their politics.

However, as should be clear, while these intellectuals claim an anti-bourgeois politics, the specific character of this opposition effectively reproduces the legitimacy of the pure gaze, and so maintains social and cultural distinctions.

The following chapters will therefore examine the ways inwhich different theories have reproduced distinctions between the pure gaze and popular taste, despite their apparent, and often violently contested, differences. The book also charts a general movement in approaches to film from a preoccupation with authorship (broadly defined), through a concentration upon the text and textuality, to an investigation of audiences.

In the first chapter, 'Mass Culture Theory and Political Economy', Joanne Hollows examines the ways in which mass culture theory analysed the industrial conditions in which popular cinema was produced, and its claim that these conditions resulted in 'the Built-In Reaction'. In the process, she illustrates how mass culture theory revolved around a distinction between popular and avant-garde film. The mass culture critics claimed that popular Hollywood films were so easy to consume that they required no effort on the part of the audience. In contrast to the conformity and passivity which mass culture critics believed that Hollywood films produced in their audience, they argued that the complexity of avant-garde art forced its enlightened audience to think for itself and so question existing social relations. Finally, she moves on to discuss more recent work on the political economy of culture, notably the work of Nicholas Garnham. This work, it is claimed, continues mass culture theory's interest in the industrial conditions of cultural production, but refuses to privilege the avant-garde as a form which is somehow freed from these conditions. This section also examines the new structures of cultural production associated with 'post-Fordism' and the 'New Hollywood'.

In the second chapter, 'Auteurism and Film Authorship Theory', Helen Stoddart discusses the way in which certain critics took issue with mass culture theory. In particular, auteur theorists rejected the claim that industrial production provided no room for the individual expression which was supposedly essential to the production of art. In response, auteurism pointed to a number of film-makers, all of whom were directors, who they identified as figures who had been able to express a rich complex and personal vision while making films within the Hollywood studio system. However, as Stoddart points out, it is necessary to question whether an individual author is either essential to the production of great art or even a theoretically defensible entity. Furthermore, this movement did not represent a defence of popular film – indeed, these critics still accepted the basic assumptions of mass culture theory. Therefore, the work of auteurs was not seen to exemplify popular film in general, but was privileged because of the ways it subverted and challenged the system. The auteur was not of popular film, but *against* it.

The next chapter, 'Genre Theory and Criticism', shows how many critics took issue with auteurism. Instead of privileging the individual author, these critics shifted their emphasis to the textual structures within which film-makers worked, and stressed the meaning and significance inherent in these forms. However, Peter Hutchings argues that this mode of criticism not only spent too long trying to track down the elusive, defining features or deep-structures which distinguished genres from one another, but was finally unable to answer this question, at least in part, because it tended to ignore the importance of the audience. This work was much less clear in its conception of the popular. Some critics did argue that certain popular genres were of such richness that they were on a par with great art, but as in many other theories, it was more common to see the popular represented as an ideologically conservative realm.

In chapter four, 'Star Studies', Paul McDonald examines the various different approaches to the analysis of stars and star images. These approaches he describes as semiotics; the analysis of intertextuality; psychoanalysis; and audience studies. The first two are mainly concerned with the analysis of texts, but the second two mainly concern the ways in which viewers identify with stars. Finally, McDonald discusses the work of Pierre Bourdieu and applies it to the analysis of stars in order to argue that it is necessary to comprehend how the distribution of cultural capital leads different audiences to identify with different stars.

In chapter five, 'Historical Poetics', Henry Jenkins considers the kind of work exemplified by David Bordwell and Kristin Thompson. While allowing some space for the auteur, this approach sets out to detail the norms which govern the stylistic construction of film and therefore stresses that any innovation can only be defined in terms of these norms, not as an instance of pure self-expression. However, he argues that despite its tendency to privilege 'defamiliarization' as an artistic practice, a concept criticized by Bourdieu as a legitimation of the pure gaze, this approach opens up important issues for the study of popular film, particularly through its willingness to accept popular norms as part of an aesthetic system. Finally, in the last part of the chapter, he demonstrates the usefulness of this approach through an analysis of contemporary, 'postclassical' or 'New Hollywood' cinema.

In the chapter 'Screen Theory', Mark Jancovich assesses the move from Althusserian Marxism to Lacanian psychoanalysis within film theory. In the process, he considers the concept of the classic realist text, theories of narrative pleasure, the concept of 'suture' and claims about cinematic constructions of sexual difference. He argues that not only is this approach unable to distinguish between competing ideologies, but despite its claim to consider the relationship between the spectator and the text, it still perpetuates a form of textual determinism. Within screen theory, the spectator is an abstract textual construct and there is no consideration of how actual social subjects might engage with the text. Furthermore, it is argued that this approach consigns the popular to the realm of the ideologically conservative and once more privileges avant-garde forms which are supposed to require an active spectator, rather than the passive viewer associated with popular film.

Lisa Taylor's chapter, 'From Psychoanalytic Feminism to Popular Feminism', explores the implications of psychoanalysis for feminism, and considers feminist approaches which have taken issue with psychoanalytic feminism, approaches which have been largely ignored within film theory. She examines how other currents in feminism – for example, debates about the practice of reading romantic fiction and about the sexual politics of pornography – might be useful in analysing popular film. In the process, Taylor highlights the limitations of psychoanalytic feminism and the usefulness of alternative approaches. Finally, her chapter examines Penny Marshall's *A League of their Own* in order to illustrate the ways in which feminism has developed within popular film, not simply as a critique of it.

In the final chapter, 'Cultural Studies and Popular Film', Andy Willis discusses the development of cultural studies and its usefulness in rethinking popular film. In the process, he discusses the early 'culturalist' approaches associated with Richard Hoggart, Raymond Williams and E.P. Thompson before moving on to examine the work associated with the Centre for Contemporary Cultural Studies at the University of Birmingham. This work, which developed in relation to screen theory, is argued to have a quite different conception of the popular to that available in earlier approaches, one that is exemplified by the work of Stuart Hall which was discussed earlier in this introduction.

As should be clear, the editors of this book share a sympathy with this approach and argue that it provides an alternative to the ways in which most of the other approaches discussed legitimate the pure gaze and render popular tastes and forms inadequate, illegitimate or even dangerous. However, while contemporary cultural studies provides a more satisfying account of the relationship between audiences and texts than that available elsewhere, it has often been accused of concentrating on audiences and, in the process, excluding the conditions of cultural production. While there is certainly some evidence to support this case, this criticism is not justified in relation to most of the work on popular media done within cultural studies. Indeed, as Henry Jenkins has argued in his work on fan cultures, *Textual Poachers*:

> For me, an interest in audience activism is perfectly consistent with work on the political economy of media ownership, showing two sides of the same power imbalance.No account of fan culture makes sense unless it is seen as responsive to a situation in which fans make strong emotional investments in programs and yet have no direct control over network decision–making.[25]

Indeed Henry Jenkins's work makes a number of points which significantly develop the field of cultural studies.

His criticism of Stuart Hall's 'encoding and decoding' model (discussed in chapter eight) makes a number of acute comments. He takes issue with the notion that the only positive decoding would be an oppositional one, and he argues that the encoding/decoding model ignores the processes by which the relationships between institutions and audiences change. As Jenkins claims:

> No single synchronic record of audience response can fully account for the constant shifts within the audience's relationship to the primary textual materials; rather, what is needed is a diachronic mode of ethnographic writing that traces over time the process by which audiences move in and out of harmony with textual ideologies and begin to assert their own interests upon broadcast content.[26]

Indeed, one of the advances made by this work is the way it acknowledges that audiences have profound investments in certain texts or groups of texts. This doesn't meant that they necessarily make oppositional readings but neither does their investment render them passive – for example, in fanzines and on the internet, fans actively exchange responses to their favourite texts.

Audiences actively appropriate specific materials, but not necessarily through a transgression of their dominant materials as was the claim of much 1970s cultural studies. As Jenkins argues:

> Fans have chosen these media products from the total range of available texts precisely because they seem to hold special potential as vehicles for expressing the fans' pre-existing social commitments and cultural interests; there is always some degree of compatibility between the ideological constructions of the text and the ideological commitments of the fans and therefore some degree of affinity will exist between the meanings fans produce and those which might be located through a critical analysis of the original story.[27]

As a result, Jenkins does not imply that popular texts can be seen as uniformly conservative or even uniformly anything.

Another strength of Jenkins's work is its particular conception of the critic as fan. This approach has often been attacked for an uncritical celebration of popular forms. However, Jenkins's work does not conform to this characterization. His work is not a defence of the popular in its entirety nor is he unaware of the conditions of power within which popular culture operates. While there are certainly tendencies towards this uncritical celebration of the popular in the work of certain writers,[28] Jenkins represents a new generation of critics who are attracted to cultural studies because of their investment in particular popular forms. An investment and engagement in popular forms and practices need not lead to the uncritical celebration of the popular *per se*. Instead, it can lead to an analysis of the popular which is based on a greater investment in, and a fan's knowledge about, the forms under discussion. Such forms of investment might not only lead to a better critical understanding of the pleasures of popular forms and practices (rather than simply dismissing or celebrating these pleasures) but also, in the process, to new ways of thinking about popular forms and cultural identities. Such forms of knowledge might also lead to a greater sensitivity to historical trends and changes within popular forms and practices. For example, in genre studies it is not uncommon for people to write an account of a genre based on the viewing of a handful of films, and, as a result, to mistake that which is conventional as innovative and that which is innovative as merely conventional.[29] Although this is not always the case – for example, many of those who wrote on the western in the 1970s were avid consumers of this genre – many critics have felt the need to maintain a 'critical distance' by rejecting their own pleasures and couching their discussions within the accepted oppositions of academic criticism.

Just because the critic is also a fan need not mean abandoning evaluation but instead making distinctions within the popular, rather than against the popular, based on new forms of cultural politics. As a result, Jenkins's work may well represent a generational shift in cultural studies or what Raymond Williams has referred to as a new 'structure of feeling'.[30]

Notes

1 Raymond Williams, *Keywords: A Vocabulary of Culture and Society*, Glasgow: Fontana, 1976, pp. 198–9.

2 Stuart Hall, 'Notes on Deconstructing "The Popular" ', in Raphael Samuel, ed., *People's History and Socialist Theory*, London: Routledge, 1981, p. 231.

3 Indeed, if there are multiple definitions of 'the popular', there are also important differences between definitions of 'the people'. As Tony Bennett puts it, 'In one sense "the people" consists of everyone ... In another sense ... , "the people" may be equated with the working class. In yet another sense ... "the people" refers neither to everyone nor to a single group within society but to a variety of social groups which, although differing from one another in other respects (their class position or the particular struggles in which they are most immediately engaged) are distinguished from the economically, politically and culturally powerful groups within society and are hence *potentially* capable of being united ...' (Tony Bennett, 'The Politics of the "popular" ' in Tony Bennett *et al.*, eds, *Popular Culture and Social Relations*, Milton Keynes: Open University Press, 1986, p. 20.

4 'Notes on Deconstructing "The Popular" ', p. 232.

5 'Notes on Deconstructing "The Popular" ', p. 232.

6 'Notes on Deconstructing "The Popular" ', p. 234.

7 'Notes on Deconstructing "The Popular" ', p. 234.

8 'Notes on Deconstructing "The Popular" ', p. 235.

9 'Notes on Deconstructing "The Popular" ', p. 234.

10 'Notes on Deconstructing "The Popular" ', p. 235.

11 Although Bourdieu's research was conducted in France, his work's analytical framework has struck a chord with critics working in many other national contexts.

12 There is debate about whether there are in fact three or four taste formations outlined in Bourdieu – even among the editors of this book! For an account that distinguishes four taste formations, see Dick Hebdige, 'The Impossible Object. Towards a Sociology of the Sublime', *New Formations*, 1(1), 1987.

13 Pierre Bourdieu, 'The Aristocracy of Culture' in Richard Collins, *et al.*, *Media, Culture and Society: A Reader*, London: Sage, 1986, p. 172. This article is taken from the introduction to Pierre Bourdieu's classic study of

French culture, *Distinction: A Social Critique of the Judgement of Taste*, London: Routledge, 1984.

14 'The Aristocracy of Culture', pp. 171–2.
15 'The Aristocracy of Culture', p. 173.
16 'The Aristocracy of Culture', p. 176.
17 'The Aristocracy of Culture', p. 177.
18 'The Aristocracy of Culture', p. 190.
19 'The Aristocracy of Culture', p. 191.
20 'The Aristocracy of Culture', p. 192.
21 See Duncan Webster, *Looka Yonda!: The Imaginary America of Populist Culture*, London: Comedia/Routledge, 1989 and Dick Hebdige, 'Towards a Cartography of Taste' in *Hiding in the Light: On Images and Things*, London: Routledge, 1988.
22 For an analysis of these debates see, for example, Iain Chambers, *Border Dialogues: Journeys in Postmodernity*, London: Routledge, 1990.
23 Cora Kaplan, 'The Culture Crossover', *New Socialist*, 43, (November 1986), pp. 38–40.
24 Andrew Ross, *No Respect: Intellectuals and Popular Culture*, London: Routledge, 1989, p. 61.
25 Henry Jenkins, '"It's not a Fairy Tale Anymore": Gender, Genre, *Beauty and the Beast*' in *The Journal of Film and Video*, 43: 1 & 2, (spring/summer, 1991), pp. 91–2.
26 ' "It's not a Fairy Tale Anymore" ', p. 92.
27 Henry Jenkins, *Textual Poachers: Television Fans and Participatory Culture*, New York: Routledge, 1992, p. 34.
28 For a critique of this tendency in the work of people such as John Fiske, see Meaghan Morris, 'Banality in Cultural Studies' in Patricia Mellencamp, ed., *Logics of Television: essays in Cultural Criticism*, Bloomington: Indiana University Press, 1990.
29 See, for example, some of the articles on *Alien* and *Blade Runner* in Annette Kuhn, *Alien Zone: Cultural Theory and Contemporary Science Fiction Cinema*, London: Verso, 1990.
30 Raymond Williams, *The Long Revolution*, Harmondsworth: Penguin, 1965, pp. 64–88.

Even Dwight MacDonald felt 'full of goodwill toward all humanity'after viewing *The Sound of Music* (1965).

Mass culture theory
and political economy

From the 1930s through to the late 1950s, American intellectuals were concerned with the analysis of the 'industrialization of culture'. They concentrated on the production and consumption of cultural forms which, they claimed, had become economic and industrial activities which were governed by commercial interests. The industrialization of culture, it was argued, was a process of cultural decline which brought about an insidious 'mass culture' and an equally insidious 'mass' of consumers. For these critics, mass culture and the masses threatened not only aesthetic standards but also political life. Popular film was often used as the exemplary instance of mass culture in this work. From its earliest moments, cinema was a product of 'technology' and mechanical reproduction, and, from an early stage, it was based on a system of industrial production and mass distribution.

Since the 1950s, many aspects of this work have been criticized but it has also laid the foundation for more recent work on the political economy of culture. This contemporary work on the political economy of culture is also highly critical of the mass culture critics. It has taken issue with their claims about the masses and the ways in which they privilege 'high culture' and the avant-garde. However, like the mass culture critics, they argue that popular films are the product of industrial and economic processes which shape their form, their content and the ways they are consumed by audiences. This approach goes against the grain of much of contemporary film studies which tends to privilege the analysis of film texts and regard the discussion of their economic context as reductive.

The mass culture debate

The 'cultural implications of the mass media'[1] became a crucial issue for American intellectuals in the post-war period. The debate about mass culture brought together writers from a range of disciplines – for example, politics, economics, psychology, sociology, literature and art criticism. This multi-disciplinary approach to cultural analysis would become an important element of contemporary cultural studies, although it was often forgotten in communications studies in the intervening period.

Many mass culture critics came from the American radical left. However, their nostalgia for a 'pre-modern Paradise Lost'[2] is reminiscent of nineteenth-century conservatives. The mass culture critics found little promise in the modern world and compared it unfavourably to 'traditional' societies. They treated the small-scale communities of the past as an 'ideal' which was infinitely preferable to the unseemly scale of mass production and urban life in the modern world. Often, the only hope that the mass culture critics could offer was to go 'back to the future'. The lack of faith that American radicals had in the promise of modernity stemmed from their loss of faith in Marxism. They no longer believed that a politically conscious working class would rise up and change the modern world for the better. Whereas Marx saw a contradictory promise in modernity, many American radicals argued that, by the mid–twentieth century, capitalism had overcome many of its contradictions. They pointed pessimistically to the failure of socialism to mobilize the working class in the USA and argued that class conflict was notable only by its absence.

The mass culture critics' loss of faith in Marxism corresponded with their belief that the American working class was virtually extinct. In its place had grown a politically dangerous mass which was a threat to democracy. They echoed the claims of nineteenth-century conservatives that democracy could only work in a society made up of thinking individuals, and would fail in a society dominated by ignorant masses. The mass culture critics claimed that the processes of industrialization and urbanization separated people from their roots and their traditional family ties. Alone in an urban mass, people were vulnerable to the appeals of authoritarian propaganda. American radicals claimed that the success of European dictators such as Stalin and Hitler was the inevitable and horrifying result of the spread of mass culture. Europe was a nightmare vision of America's future. Their only hope was that mass culture might be 'contained' in the USA.[3]

Whereas liberals claimed that the mass media might help bring about a cultural democracy, critics of mass culture saw the media as a threat to cultural stratification. These critics believed that, ideally, in a cultural democracy, intellectuals would bring high culture to the people. However, they claimed that in practice the masses were conditioned to prefer new popular forms such as cinema and broadcasting over the diet of traditional culture prescribed by intellectuals. The mass culture critics responded to their loss of cultural authority by turning their marginalization from cultural life into an asset. As 'outsiders', they could be safe from contamination by mass culture and maintain the 'purity' of their own culture. In fact, the notion of a degraded mass taste was necessary to legitimate the social position of these intellectuals. By pre-

senting popular taste as aesthetically and politically dangerous, intellectuals were able to justify and maintain their social authority by constructing a form of cultural distinction. They could present their own
cultural tastes as the only hope of salvation in the modern world.

The mass model of society proposed by radical critics challenged the
alternative view of American society in the post-war era which was put
forward by liberals. Although most American intellectuals had rejected
a class model of society, many liberals believed that classlessness led to
the freedom of individuals rather than domination by the mass. For
these critics, liberal pluralism was the 'ideal model of a fully democratic society'[4] – an ideal that was, or could still be, realized. The mass
media, claimed liberal intellectuals, were a potentially positive force in
a cultural and political democracy. They acted as a socializing agent and
offered increased freedom and choice. They also argued that mass culture critiques were based on European models which could not be
applied to American society and culture. In doing so, they reaffirmed
the claims of 'American exceptionalism' which maintained that American society and culture was founded on a break from the corruption of
European societies. America, it was claimed, was not troubled by the
barriers of class stratification, nor the concentrations of power which
characterized the 'Old World' of Europe.

Adorno and Horkheimer: European intellectuals in Hollywood

A group of German Marxists in exile in Hollywood would play a major
role in shaping American debates on mass culture. Indeed most American research on the media in the 1940s and 1950s either drew on, or
was a response to, the Frankfurt School's 'pessimistic thesis'.[5] The
Frankfurt School's influence on contemporary film and media theory is
often still acknowledged, while the work of American mass culture critics has been dismissed as simplistic and elitist. This is somewhat surprising given how much these two movements have in common.

The Frankfurt School's response to mass culture was a product of its
own historical context, although its analysis tended to be somewhat
ahistorical. Its agenda was influenced by a response to Americanization
and the 'cult of technology' in Weimar Germany. It was also moulded
by the rise of Fascism.[6] Mainly staffed by Jewish Marxists, The Frankfurt School's Institute for Social Research fled Nazi Germany in the
1930s, and relocated itself in Los Angeles. Here its members experi-

enced a profound culture shock. In this context, the two members of the school most closely identified with the mass culture critique, Theodor Adorno and Max Horkheimer, retreated into a 'self-imposed ghetto, clinging to their old-world prejudices like cultural life–preservers'.[7] Having developed their critique of American mass culture from a safe distance in Germany, they saw little need to refine it by giving it a closer inspection from first-hand. Given their experiences in Europe, it is unsurprising that Adorno and Horkheimer's work on American mass culture became an investigation into the conditions under which Fascism could take hold, or that, in America, they were to find a whole host of terrifying symptoms. Immersed in the values of the European avant-garde, it is also unsurprising that they related the political dangers of mass culture to what they saw as its aesthetic poverty.

In 'The Culture Industry: Enlightenment as Mass Deception', published in 1944 in *The Dialectic of Enlightenment*, Adorno and Horkheimer outlined their critique of mass culture. This critique needs to be understood in relation to their wider theoretical framework. They presented the pessimistic thesis that the promise of liberation offered by the Enlightenment project had not been fulfilled. In particular, they argued that although scientific rationality had liberated the world from superstition and traditional forms of authority, it had become a new, and more powerful, mechanism of domination. Furthermore, this domination was strengthened when scientific rationality was integrated within a capitalist economy. They claimed that 'the basis on which technology acquires power over society is the power of those whose economic hold over society is greatest'.[8]

Adorno and Horkheimer believed that the culture industry is incorporated within, and in turn incorporates, social relations in a capitalist society. They claimed that the culture industry is relatively 'weak' economically and depends on more powerful industries. For example, even the Hollywood studio system needed banks and the electronics industry and, in the process, was integrated into a wider system of control. Similarly, the studio system controls both the people who work within it and the consumers of its products. Adorno and Horkheimer claimed that by wanting to work in Hollywood in the first place, employees have already accepted the film industry's values. In the same way, they argued that the 'attitude of the public, which ostensibly and actually, favours the system of the culture industry, is a part of the system and not an excuse for it'.[9]

In this way, Adorno and Horkheimer claimed that the logic of a rationalized, technological society permeates all aspects of our lives, leaving us dominated, controlled and open to manipulation. It is the extent of this control that leaves the German critics in such a state of despair. Despite Marx's predictions, capitalism had 'refused' to collapse. Furthermore, they argued, the working class, whose members were supposed to be the active makers of a utopian future, had degenerated into a passive mass which masochistically desired domination by fascist regimes.

This highly abstract theoretical framework developed by Adorno and Horkheimer was applied to American society to make sense of mass culture. However, the main points of their argument were consistent with other mass culture critics, both radical and conservative. Like other critics, the Frankfurt School argued that the industrialization of culture had transformed culture into a commodity. The sole value of culture was to generate profit and therefore maintain the capitalist system. In the process, they claimed, older 'folk' or 'popular' cultures and most art was taken over by the culture industry. The mark of individuality that had characterized these forms was wiped out as 'culture now impresses the same stamp upon everything'.[10]

Adorno and Horkheimer claimed that the culture industry was characterized by standardized production and consumption, and this was a result of the fact that the culture industry, like all capitalist industries, was based on processes of mass reproduction and mass distribution. In the Hollywood studio system, they argued, films were mass-produced through the use of assembly-line techniques in a similar way to other commodities such as cars. All films were basically identical and therefore thoroughly predictable. 'As soon as a film begins, it is quite clear how it will end, and who will be rewarded, punished or forgotten.'[11] These critics also claimed that not only did economies of scale operate in a system of mass production, standardization also guaranteed profit. Having found a successful formula, the studios stuck with it. This, in turn, conditioned the audience into conformity – the audience were taught what to expect, and got more of the same. This fed back into the production process, it was argued: it became too risky to produce anything different, so there was 'a constant reproduction of the same thing'.[12]

However, as the Frankfurt critics argued, films must appear to be different so the audience can be persuaded to keep coming back for more. They believed that these differences were illusory, the product of marketing and distribution whose role was to differentiate between both undifferentiated products and audiences. The marketing process was concerned with 'classifying, organizing and labelling consumers' so that they could be controlled.[13] In this way, fans of musicals, for example, could be relied upon to pay to watch the latest one. This also motivates the consumers who believe they are expressing their own unique taste rather than being controlled by the marketing process. For Adorno and Horkheimer, the star system operated in a similar way. Stars are 'mass-produced like Yale locks whose only difference can be measured in fractions of millimeters'.[14] Therefore, when consumers prefer Mel Gibson to Arnold Schwarzenegger, they are merely responding to pseudo–individual differences which give them the illusion of having individual tastes.

The masses, claimed Adorno and Horkheimer, didn't even make individual responses to films. Hollywood films were not complex enough to give enough space for individual interpretation. Instead, 'the product prescribes every reaction' so that the passive audience reacts automatically.[15] For Adorno, the 'power of the culture industry's ideology is such that conformity has replaced consciousness'.[16] As a result, it was argued, films condition people to defer to authority and conform. In this way, for Adorno and Horkheimer, films are politically dangerous because they create the preconditions for a totalitarian society. Even Donald Duck is implicated in this process. When we watch Donald get knocked around in movies, we learn to take punishment in our own lives. These critics were also concerned that as film technology became increasingly sophisticated, the audience would find it harder to distinguish between movies and real life. It is the illusory realism of film which disguises the fact that it is actually only a construction.

This position invoked a 'hypodermic syringe' model of media effects in which a negative message is injected into a passive audience, and it was widely accepted in early research into media effects. The exceptions were the liberal theorists of the 1940s and 1950s who pointed out that just because production was standardized, this didn't mean that the audience's responses were also standardised. Instead, they argued, individuals made active choices about what they watched and how they watched it, choices that were based on their own particular needs and interests. But although the hypodermic model has been discredited as a highly simplistic model of how media messages work and highly patronizing in its view of the audience, it still underpins much contemporary 'common sense' about the media. For example, campaigns against 'video nasties' and 'pornography' often imply that people can't tell the difference between fantasy and reality and respond automatically to stimuli from the media. This can be seen, for example, in the feminist slogan 'porn is the theory, rape is the practice'.

For Adorno and Horkheimer, the only part of life that transcends the all-encompassing control of the culture industry is avant-garde art and its audience. Avant-garde artists, it was claimed, refused to let their work be commodified and maintained aesthetic and, therefore, political freedom. Art didn't reconcile its audience to the system but showed them the contradictions within it. Its audience of 'enlightened outsiders', including Adorno and Horkheimer themselves, were prepared to struggle to find meanings in art forms that refused to let themselves be easily consumed. In this way, Adorno and Horkheimer legitimated their own tastes as 'politically correct' and popular tastes as politically dangerous. In doing so, they also conferred a prestige upon themselves as 'outsiders', the very thing which they claimed the misguided mass was seeking when it chose between standardized products. At one point they argue:

> One simply 'has to' have seen *Mrs Miniver* just as one 'has to' subscribe to *Life* and *Time* ... No object has an inherent value; it is only valuable to the extent to which it can be exchanged ... the work's social rating becomes its use value.[17]

What Adorno and Horkheimer fail to admit is that avant-garde can be, and is, used for its 'social rating' so that a cultural elite can distinguish itself from the masses.

In Adorno and Horkheimer's analysis, there is no position from which good cinema can exist. Cinema is part of the culture industry and therefore its aesthetics have one ideological purpose – to reproduce the spectator as a consumer. There is no room for any alternative filmmaking practice. Furthermore, as cinema was rooted in the technology of mass reproduction and distribution, these critics believed that it was already implicated in the maintenance of ideological and economic domination. The more sophisticated the technology and the greater the spectacle, the more cinema dominates the audience. This argument explains why some contemporary left critics still maintain the idea that the most technologically innovative, big budget, spectaculars must be the most politically dangerous. From this perspective, a film like *Terminator 2* has been judged as aesthetically and politically corrupt despite the fact that it presents a critique of increasing technological control by capitalist industry! By the mid-sixties, Adorno did modify his position to suggest that low-tech films that deliberately courted imperfection were the most likely to have aesthetic merit.[18] In this way, some European avant-garde cinema could be legitimated.

Dwight MacDonald: film critic as mass culture critic

Despite a growing disenchantment with Marxism, which was exacerbated by revelations about practices in Stalin's Russia, American radicals such as Dwight MacDonald, Clement Greenberg and Irving Howe were influenced by the terms of Adorno and Horkheimer's critique. They not only reproduced many of the Frankfurt critics' central arguments but also grounded them in a more informed knowledge of American history and culture.

Adorno and Horkheimer's analysis proceeded from a high level of abstraction and a refusal to engage too closely with the products of mass culture. However, many radical mass culture critics in America proceeded from a closer engagement with changes in American cultural life and new popular forms. For example, Dwight MacDonald's mass culture critique developed out of his role as a film critic. His knowledge of both popular and avant-garde film allowed him to produce an informed critique of film forms and cinema history. If these American radicals produced an analysis that, at times, sounded like conservative responses to modernization, many of their reactionary and elitist assumptions are also present in Adorno and Horkheimer's analysis.

Like Adorno and Horkheimer, MacDonald argued that the process of capitalist industrialization scrambled all cultural forms and practices together both within and between nations. For MacDonald, industrialization wiped out cultural distinctions and pre-modern systems of cultural stratification. In pre-modern societies, he argued, cultural life was not an economic activity. Traditional high culture was supported by patrons. Therefore, artists were free to express their own unique individual style. Artists and audience formed an educated elite community who shared the same values. For non-elites, there was a separate 'folk culture' produced and consumed within a community of 'ordinary folk' to satisfy their own popular taste. MacDonald claimed that these two cultural spheres were able to coexist because folk culture knew its place.

These distinctions, it was claimed, were eroded by the industrialization of culture. Although high culture still had a tenuous foothold in the modern world, it faced a mounting assault from 'masscult'. (For MacDonald, culture was too good a word for this bastardized form.)

The rise of masscult was due to three factors. First, from 1750 onwards, the economics of cultural production and consumption changed. Culture was no longer supported by economic activity but became a commodity to be sold on the capitalist market-place. In this situation, MacDonald claimed, masscult became subject to the industrial values of popularity and profitability and pandered to the 'lowest common denominator'. Second, whereas the 'folk' had known their place, the masses didn't. The masses were literate and educated but weren't satisfied with high culture. They demanded their own culture and industry gave them masscult. Finally, MacDonald claimed that the industrialization of culture meant that culture was mass-produced using assembly–line techniques. As a result, masscult became homogeneous and standardized.

Like Adorno and Horkheimer, MacDonald believed that in industrial societies, cultural production had been taken over from above. Masscult was 'fabricated by technicians hired by business men'.[19] For MacDonald, it wasn't simply that masscult was poor art. As he put it, masscult

> doesn't even have the theoretical possibility of being good. Up to the eighteenth century, bad art was of the same nature as good art, produced for the same audience, accepting the same standards. The difference was simply one of individual talent. But masscult is something else. It is not just unsuccessful art. It is non-art. It is even anti-art.[20]

For MacDonald, masscult was structurally doomed to be awful.

MacDonald also argued that masscult respected quantity not quality, repetition not innovation. This can be seen in his analysis of popular film. Big-budget films which get big audiences and, therefore, make big profits were valued in the movie industry. He argued that Hollywood tried to guarantee profits by establishing formulas that would repeat previous successes. For example, he claims that the popularity and profitability of the box-office hit, *The Sound of Music*, was guaranteed in two ways. First, it took tried-and-tested ingredients: 'nuns'; 'children'; 'family drama, TV style'; 'Nazis'; and 'Salzburg'. Second, it reprised

> three consumer-tested properties: *Life with Father*, the record-run play … which first exploited the poor-dad-clever-mum theme; *The King and I*, by Rodgers and Hammerstein, which successfully transported the theme to Siam; and the stage version of *The Sound of Music* also by Rodgers and Hammerstein.[21]

He claims that the masses are happy with such formulaic films because they were not only 'satisfied with shoddy mass-produced goods', but also feel more comfortable with them due to the fact that they are thoroughly predictable and, therefore, 'easier to consume'.[22]

Formula films were also easier to produce as they used the mass-production techniques of the studio system and were easier to market as 'genres'. However, the logic of MacDonald's argument suggests that not only are all films within a genre the same, but he continually implies that all Hollywood films are the same. MacDonald does begin to acknowledge this contradiction. 'There's one little puzzle, however: how can both *Psycho* and *The Sound of Music* make box–office records? ... Perhaps we have *two* mass audiences ... each of them patronizing only its own kind of movie.'[23] Far from being a 'little puzzle', the acknowledgement that the audience for popular films might be fragmented not only undermines some of the generalizations of the mass culture critique, it is a crucial step to a better understanding of the film industry.

Like Adorno and Horkheimer, MacDonald identifies a further feature of standardization as the standardized response of the audience. According to MacDonald, popular films have a 'Built-In Reaction'. They include 'the spectator's reactions in the work itself instead of forcing him [*sic*] to make his own responses'.[24] Such is the power of popular film that after his trip to see *The Sound of Music*, even MacDonald felt 'full of goodwill toward all humanity'.[25] This power over the audience is again related to the claim that masscult is politically dangerous because it is argued that masscult trains people to defer to authority. In totalitarian states, it is argued, the masses had been manipulated to become a 'collective monstrosity'.[26] But similar tendencies were also claimed to be inherent within American culture. The Soviet form of masscult may have been seen seen as 'worse and more pervasive'[27] than American masscult, but only because it exploited people politically, rather than commercially, and was therefore self-consciously manipulative.

If masscult threatened to take over the world, MacDonald discovered a more ominous threat to cultural distinctions in the form of 'midcult', a 'hybrid' of masscult and high culture. Midcult masqueraded as art but had the 'essential characteristics of masscult – the formula, the Built-In Reaction, the lack of any standard except popularity'.[28] Increased affluence, college education and leisure time in America hadn't lead to an increased appreciation of art but to midcult. MacDonald saw midcult as the product of a middlebrow taste formation which wanted to distinguish itself from the masses. It obeyed the basic formal features of masscult, but passed itself off as high art. Film versions of great literary classics such as Shakespeare plays are an obvious example, but McDonald also directed his attack at well-respected and 'classy' works such as those directed by Elia Kazan.

In the process, midcult challenged the claims to distinction of high culture and its audience. In particular, midcult was a threat to the claims of intellectuals like MacDonald to legislate about cultural life. Drawing on the French sociologist Pierre Bourdieu, Andrew Ross argues that 'Cultural power does not inhere in the contents of categories of taste. On the contrary, it is exercised through the capacity to draw the line between and around categories of taste.'[29] The cultural power of intellectuals comes from their ability to identify what is legitimate 'and what can then be governed and policed as illegitimate or inadequate or even deviant ...'[30] The legitimate culture for MacDonald, as for Adorno and Horkheimer, was the modernist avant-garde which kept alive the values and standards of traditional high culture in the modern world. Like traditional high culture, the avant-garde formed a small sophisticated community the members of which were distinguished by their unpopularity and marginality.

Untainted by the market, like traditional artists, the artists of the avant-garde were free to express their own unique individual style. Similarly, they addressed an active audience of individuals who were prepared to work with the complexities of their texts and develop their own responses. In response to MacDonald, Gilbert Seldes argued that the avant-garde chose a marginal position rather than were pushed into it.[31] He claimed that the 'treason of the intellectuals' was their cultivation of the role of 'misunderstood' artists and their refusal to acknowledge popular tastes. Indeed, Seldes points out that Hollywood films in the 1950s responded to the refusal of intellectuals to understand popular taste by rejecting the legitimacy of intellectuals and making them into figures of fun.

Unlike Adorno and Horkheimer, MacDonald didn't see films as bad *per se*, but used his distinctions between the avant-garde and masscult to distinguish between good and bad films. MacDonald believed that cinema had the promise of being one of the great modern art forms but, for most of his career, he found this promise unfulfilled. He finds much to praise in what he identifies as the first major movie period, the 'classic silent period' (1908-29). In this period Americans like D. W. Griffith, Russians like Sergei Eisenstein and Germans like Fritz Lang produced work of individual genius. However, in the second period, 'early or medieval sound' (1930-55), cinema had regressed. Not only were directors unable to use sound innovatively, sound also helped to secure the 'Built-In Reaction' by exaggerating the emotions of the film. Therefore, like Adorno and Horkheimer, MacDonald associates developments in technology with decline.

In America, this period also coincided with the rise and fall of the studio system which promoted industrial modes of production and supposedly worked against individual expression. According to MacDonald, this period produced only two 'masters' in Hollywood, Orson Welles and Ernst Lubitsch. By the time of third period, 'Later or Renaissance Sound' (1956-), MacDonald claimed that film's early promise was being realized again as an 'esthetic of the sound film' developed.[32] However, he rarely found this promise in Hollywood, but in the 'art' cinema of directors such as 'Bergman, Fellini, Antonioni, Truffaut, Resnais, Bunuel and Kurosawa'.[33]

From MacDonald's work, it is clear that good, art cinema is the product of an individual genius or author. It is watched by a small audience who form a community of individuals able to understand the aesthetic codes and conventions of cinema. Bad, commercial cinema, he argues, is the product of an industrial system staffed by technicians. It is geared to a mass audience who are conditioned to want predigested entertainment. For MacDonald, a cultured audience chooses a film on the basis of its director because they recognize individual genius. The mass audience chooses films on the basis of stars who are but manufactured standardized personalities who give an illusory point of identification within a film. In this way, he legitimates the preferences of those with the cultural power to identify 'what is worthy of being seen and the right way to see it'.[34] Bourdieu's work makes it clear that there are consistent differences between the ways in which social classes select and watch films.[35] Those with cultural power maintain their distinction by distancing themselves from popular forms and audiences, and by asserting the legitimacy of their own culture.

Adorno and Horkheimer mask their distaste for popular culture, which arises from their own privileged position as members of the cultivated bourgeoisie, through an analysis that concentrates on economic inequality in a capitalist society. However, MacDonald admits to being an elitist and against a liberal cultural democracy, even if he hides the power relations that give him a position of authority from which to speak. He believes that having a 'great culture' and a culture for the masses is a contradiction. One solution to the problem of masscult offered by MacDonald is a vigorous defence of high culture by 'the few who care' against the attack of masscult, midcult and the masses.[36]

Although it may be tempting, it would be unwise to reject Mac-Donald's work as elitist if his analysis is accurate. However, some critics during the period challenged the idea that there can be a straightforward opposition between popular and high cultural forms. For example, Robert Warshow argued that although film genres are governed by specific sets of conventions, so are high cultural forms such as Restoration Comedy.

Warshow also claimed that although films within a genre may rely on the same conventions, they can still be of aesthetic merit. For example, he finds *Scarface* interesting because of the way in which Howard Hawks uses the conventions of the gangster film. Rather than assuming the distinction between Hollywood and art films, Warshow argues that it is possible to distinguish creative and politically progressive Hollywood films. For example, contrary to the claims of most mass culture critics that popular film offers a rose-tinted view of life, Warshow argues that some gangster films offer a 'current of opposition' by presenting a tragic, desperate side of life.[37]

Recently, more critics have followed this lead. The analysis of how different genres work suggests that all popular films are not, in fact, the same. Furthermore, some critics working on genres such as 1940s and 1950s melodrama and horror have found they contain a critique of the very system that the mass culture critics assumed they supported. However, some writers have been tempted to achieve this by legitimating certain popular forms over others, using the opposition between mass culture and art. Robin Wood argues that horror films offer an exposé of the contradictions of capitalism. For example, he claims that *The Texas Chainsaw Massacre* implies that the bourgeois institution of the family is monstrous and shows the horror of people (literally) living off other people. For Wood, certain horror films are 'apocalyptic texts' which share the critical spirit of 'authentic' art.[38] To do this, however, he differentiates radical horror films from the horror films of mass commercial cinema. As a result, he tends to privilege low-budget, independent horror such as *The Texas Chainsaw Massacre* over big-budget studio productions such as *The Omen*. A similar tactic is used by Carol Clover in her recent work on horror.[39] This kind of argument may account for the low-budget feature *The Terminator*, but would fail to account for the fact that the big-budget blockbuster *Terminator 2* shares the same politics.

If, as Stuart Hall argues, critics insist on seeing the products of the culture industry as 'purely manipulative and debased' then the people who use them will constantly be presented as either 'debased by these activities or living in a permanent state of false consciousness. They must be "cultural dopes" '.[40] These assumptions continue to exert an influence in film theory. For example, screen theory in the 1970s shared the Frankfurt School's concern with ideological properties of mass cultural forms and the passivity of their audience, and offered avant-garde cinema as the only hope of aesthetic and political salvation.[41] As Judith Williamson points out, 'oppositional' avant-garde films are the very films valued by the bourgeois culture to which they are meant to be opposed.[42] Furthermore, avant-garde film exists as a reaction to mainstream commercial cinema and therefore depends on the very practice it seeks to undermine.[43]

Also, mass culture critics' claim that art is the expression of a unique, individual style ignores the fact these ideas are a modern invention. Many of the pre-industrial cultural forms we now call art were in fact the product of communal activity, a point MacDonald himself acknowledges. However, the idea that art should be the expression of a unique individual style continues to exert an influence in film studies in auteur theory.

Another flaw in the mass culture critique is the 'little problem' raised by MacDonald when he discusses the possible existence of two mass audiences. Indeed, in 'Masscult and Midcult' he goes so far as to note, optimistically, that since 1945 it has been realized that 'the mass audience is divisible'.[44] In doing so, he acknowledges what the industry may have known all along: specialist audiences can be profitable. Just because cinema is a commercial enterprise doesn't mean it only addresses the audience as a mass. MacDonald's optimism stems from the hope that art cinema and Hollywood might coexist, rather like high culture and folk culture had in the past. Whether he was witnessing cultural change is debatable. Jim Collins argues that the rise of a reading public in the eighteenth century did not lead to the rise of a mass audience for mass-produced texts as the mass culture critics claim. Instead, it led to the fragmentation of a unitary cultural sphere into a 'series of reading publics' and competing forms of cultural expression.[45]

The political economy of cinema

Contemporary work on the political economy of culture continues the
project of analysing the industrialization of culture. However, critics
today claim that a far more complex understanding of this process is
needed than was offered by mass culture criticism. These theorists also
go against the grain of contemporary film studies which has tended to
avoid questions of industrial processes and practices, in order to legitimate film as an art form. Historically, film studies modelled itself on
other arts subjects such as literary studies and has tended to be located
within the arts or humanities, rather than social sciences. As a result,
film studies students have rarely been required to learn the research
skills necessary for economic and institutional analysis. In fact, the
humanities have often tended to oppose their own analytical approaches
to the 'empiricism' of the social sciences. The solution, however, is not
to opt for an either/or approach, or to privilege one mode of analysis
over the other. Instead, it is necessary 'to conceptualize the relation
between [the] two sides of the communications process – the material
and the discursive, the economic and the cultural – without collapsing
either one into the other'.[46]

Contemporary political economy suggests that film texts must be
understood in the context of the culture industries within which they
are produced and distributed. Nicholas Garnham argues that cultural
analysis must consider the practices of workers in the culture industries
and the industrial processes and practices which produce the films
which we get to see. For example, 'the budget available and the given
structure of the division of labour affects what you can say and how you
can say it'.[47] An analysis of popular film must also include an analysis
of how social and economic factors structure the access different audiences have to films and how they interpret them.

In this way, critics such as Garnham share some of the mass culture
critics' preoccupations. Garnham claims it is foolish to ignore the fact
that large-scale capitalist activity and cultural production are now insep-
arable. We only have access to film through this market. However,
Garnham does not maintain the distinction between high culture and
popular forms advocated by the mass culture critics. There is no space
outside a capitalist economic system for high culture to exist in a state
of splendid isolation from economic and material life. High culture also
has a political economy. Mass culture critics assert the legitimacy of
their own values, those of a high cultural tradition. But these values,

'far from being universal, are closely linked to the structural inequality of access to society's resources'.[48] Furthermore, Garnham argues, the views of a cultural elite affect the funding of culture. Patronage still exists in the form of state funding which is usually used to support traditional high culture or the 'legitimate' branches of newer cultural forms – for example, art films and art–house cinemas. In this way, alternatives to market provision tend to serve the existing tastes and habits of the middle class and ignore the popular audience.[49]

In his analysis of the culture industries, Garnham argues that they have three central characteristics. First, they use capital intensive technology as a means of mass production and/or distribution. This makes the cost of entry into the industries high, and so curbs diversity. Second, they are hierarchical organizations with a complex division of labour. Third, their main aim, like any other industry, is to maximize efficiency and make a profit.

Garnham argues that the culture industries also face specific problems. First, people only have a limited amount of time and money to spend on cultural pursuits. Second, it is difficult for the culture industries to pin down the 'use values' of specific cultural products. For example, although the film industry knows there is a market for films, it is difficult for it to predict which particular films people will pay to watch. As a result, it must offer what Garnham calls a 'cultural repertoire' of product. A wide variety of films must be produced in order to spread risks. If one film is unsuccessful, others may be successful enough to recoup the loss. The industry must also match the costs of production to the spending power and size of the audience. In contemporary Hollywood, blockbusters such as *Jurassic Park* may be expensive but they are also profitable because of the size of the audience which they can attract. They offer 'something for almost everyone'. The need to produce large audiences exerts a dual pressure to limit diversity and innovation, while still requiring some degree of diversity and innovation in order to continue to attract audiences.

In contemporary Hollywood, Garnham argues that distribution also exerts control over the industry. Film distribution is controlled by the major studios. Although these studios are directly involved in the production of a small number of films, the majority of films are produced by independents. However, most independent producers are not only dependent on the majors for distribution but also, in many cases, for film finance, finance which is given on terms favourable to the majors. In the contemporary film industry, it is in distribution rather than production that there are most opportunities to maximize efficiency and profit. As Garnham argues 'because of the limit on productivity in production, there … is always a premium on expanding the audience to the maximum possible for each unit of production'.[50] Therefore, distributors aim to maximize audience size and recoup their costs as quickly as possible. This puts an increasing emphasis on promotion within the film industry's practices.

The rise to dominance of the blockbuster in the new Hollywood needs to be understood in this context. Although the importance of the blockbuster had begun to be realized earlier, Thomas Schatz argues that it was the success of *Jaws* in 1975 that consolidated industrial trends and practices around the blockbuster. He claims that '*Jaws* was a social, industrial and economic phenomenon of the first order, a cinematic idea and cultural commodity whose time had come.'[51] For example, the emphasis on the summer hit, big-budget promotion, tie-ins with other media forms and the director-as-superstar were all features of *Jaws* and can also be seen in the recent blockbuster, *Jurassic Park*.

The contemporary majors not only make profit from film distribution but also generate profit from the duplication and distribution of pre-recorded videos and the sale of films to television, especially with the increasing importance of cable and satellite. In the contemporary industry, the majors are usually part of diversified conglomerates in which the studios may be tightly integrated with television, music and publishing industries. Therefore, for example, the music movie with its multi-media potential has become a dominant form in the past fifteen years since its potential was realized following the success of *Saturday Night Fever* in 1977.[52]

However, while the majors' profits depend on a few big blockbusters, these big-budget projects do not fulfil the public's demand for product. Therefore, Schatz argues that in the New Hollywood three types of film are produced: alongside the calculated blockbuster is 'the mainstream A–class star vehicle with sleeper-hit potential' such as *Pretty Woman*, and 'the low-cost independent feature targeted for a specific market and with little chance of anything more than cult-film status'.[53] This second group of films can generate new film forms and therefore play a part in the research and development process. For example, *The Terminator* with a small budget of approximately $6 million laid the foundations for a whole new science fiction sub-genre (the 'cyborg' movie). It also led to a sequel which cost more than ten times as much as the original and was one of the most expensive and profitable films ever made.

In this way, the film industry produces films for both a mass audience and specialized audiences. Far from being homogeneous, film production, film texts and film audiences are fragmented. Far from dismissing or eradicating differences within the audience, the film industry recognizes and exploits diversity (if the audience can pay). For example, Schatz argues that since the 1950s and 1960s the 'youth market' has been seen as crucial to the industry. Similarly, following the establishment of an audience for 'art' and 'European' film during the same period in US film societies and art-house cinemas, Hollywood responded by setting up 'quasi-independent' relationships with European directors to bring 'art cinema into the mainstream'.[54] More recently, as Jim Hillier argues, 'Hollywood's current enthusiasm for black subjects and black film-makers' is built on a recognition of the size and the purchasing power of the black audience, although films with a 'cross-over' potential are seen more favourably.[55]

A political economy of cinema is therefore necessary if we are to understand why and how certain types of films get produced and distributed; the industrial processes and practices that structure the form and content of these film texts; and how audiences select and interpret them. It offers a way of understanding the power relations involved in film production and consumption, and contributes towards a more historical analysis of cinema. Many critics, including Marxists, criticize this form of analysis, and claim that it presents cultural forms as a simple reflection of economic activities and interests. However, economic determinism isn't an automatic consequence of taking industrial and economic practices into account. Rather, political economy allows an analysis of the ways in which the relations of cultural production affect the formal properties of texts. Too often theorists anxious to avoid economic determinism have thrown the baby out with the bath-water, and overemphasized the autonomy of cultural forms. Furthermore, critics who dismiss political economy and focus on the ideological properties of film texts still tend to assume that these texts reflect dominant economic interests. They simply fail to investigate how they come to do so.

Indeed, both political economy theorists such as Garnham and theorists who see texts as ideological tend to share the belief that popular films support capitalism ideologically simply because they are a product of a capitalist economy. But to attract a large audience films must (at least to some extent) address the values and aspirations of social groups and classes other than the dominant classes. Although films are not produced outside a capitalist mode of production, they may challenge the system that their profits help to maintain. Indeed, not all workers within the film industry necessarily share the same values. There is a tension between different sectors of employment. For example, during the period of the classic Hollywood cinema many screenwriters felt under-valued and exploited by the managers of the studios. In such situations, the creative personnel frequently develop a hostility to economic capital. Therefore, although they must deliver commercial films to be employed, this doesn't mean that the films which they make will auto-matically support dominant economic interests. Indeed, it is quite common for the heroes and heroines in Hollywood films to be placed in opposition to exploitative economic interests as films such as *Termi-nator 2*, *Total Recall*, *The Big Knife*, and *Broadcast News* illustrate.

Notes:

1 B. Rosenberg and D. Manning White, *Mass Culture: the Popular Arts in America*, New York: Free Press, 1957, p. v.
2 M. Berman, *All that is Solid Melts into Air: the Experience of Modernity*, London: Verso, 1983, p. 15.
3 See A. Ross, *No Respect: Intellectuals and Popular Culture*, New York: Rout-ledge, 1989.
4 *Ibid.*, p. 42.
5 D. Morley, *Television, Audiences and Cultural Studies*, London: Routledge, 1992, p. 42.
6 See A. Huyssen, 'Introduction to Adorno', *New German Critique*, 6(4), 1975.
7 M. Davis, *City of Quartz: Excavating the Future in Postmodern Los Angeles*, London: Verso, 1990, p. 47.
8 T. Adorno and M. Horkheimer, 'The Culture Industry: Enlightenment as Mass Deception' in J Curran *et al.*, eds, *Mass Communication and Society*, London: Edward Arnold, 1977, p. 350.
9 *Ibid.*
10 *Ibid.*, p. 349
11 *Ibid.*, p. 353.
12 *Ibid.*, p. 359.
13 *Ibid.*, p. 351.
14 *Ibid.*, p. 354.
15 *Ibid.*, p. 361.
16 T. Adorno, 'Culture Industry Reconsidered', *New German Critique*, 6(4), 1975, p. 17.
17 'The Culture Industry', p. 377.
18 See M. Hansen, 'Introduction to Adorno, "Transparencies on Film"

(1966)', *New German Critique*, 24–5, 1981–82.

19 D. MacDonald, *Against the American Grain*, London: Victor Gollanz, 1963, p. 14.
20 *Ibid.*, p. 4.
21 D. MacDonald, *Dwight MacDonald on Movies*, Englewood Cliffs, NJ: Prentice Hall, 1969, p. 41.
22 *Against the American Grain*, p. 29.
23 *Dwight MacDonald on Movies*, p. 42.
24 *Against the American Grain*, p. 29.
25 *Dwight MacDonald On Movies*, p. 42.
26 *Against the American Grain*, p. 9.
27 *Ibid.*, p. 14.
28 *Ibid.*, p. 37.
29 *No Respect*, p. 61.
30 *Ibid.*
31 G. Seldes, 'The People and the Arts' in *Mass Culture: the Popular Arts in America*.
32 *Dwight MacDonald on Movies*, p. xviii.
33 *Against the American Grain*, p. 56.
34 P. Bourdieu, *Distinction: a Social Critique of the Judgement of Taste*, London: Routledge, 1984, p. 28.
35 *Ibid.*, p. 271.
36 *Against the American Grain*, p. 73.
37 See C. Brookeman, *American Culture and Society since the 1930s*, London: Macmillan, 1984.
38 J Collins, *Uncommon Cultures*, New York: Routledge, 1989, p. 20.
39 C. Clover, *Men, Women and Chainsaws: Gender in the Modern Horror Film*, London: British Film Institute, 1992.
40 S. Hall, 'Notes on Deconstructing "The Popular" ', in R. Samuel, ed., *People's History and Socialist Theory*, London: Routledge, 1981, p. 231.
41 P. Brantlinger, *Crusoe's Footsteps: Cultural Studies in Britain and the United States*, New York: Routledge, 1990, p. 167.
42 J. Williamson, 'Two Kinds of Otherness', in *Deadline at Dawn*, New York: Marion Boyars, 1993.
43 F. Jameson, 'Reification and Utopia in Mass Culture', *Social Text*, 1, 1979, p. 134.
44 *Against the American Grain*, p. 73.
45 *Uncommon Cultures*, p. 4.
46 G. Murdock, quoted in *Television, Audiences and Cultural Studies*, p. 4.
47 N. Garnham, *Capitalism and Communication: Global Culture and the Economics of Information*, London: Sage, 1990, p. 15.
48 N. Garnham, 'Towards a Political Economy of Culture', *New Universities Quarterly*, (summer 1977), p. 347.

49 See N. Garnham, 'Concepts of Culture: Public Policy and the Cultural
   Industries', *Cultural Studies*, 1(1), 1987.
50 *Capitalism and Communication*, p. 185.
51 T. Schatz, 'The New Hollywood' in J. Collins *et al.*, eds, *Film Theory Goes
   to the Movies*, New York: Routledge, 1993, p. 19.
52 *Ibid.*, p. 23.
53 *Ibid.*, p. 35.
54 *Ibid.*, p. 14.
55 J. Hillier, *The New Hollywood*, London: Studio Vista, 1992, p. 148.

The director as star and brand-name: a poster for Hitchcock's *The Birds*
(1963)

Auteurism and film authorship theory

Whereas mass culture theory was centrally concerned with the relationship between popular forms and their industrial and commercial conditions of production, authorship theorists began by side-stepping the influence of commercial practices on popular film. This early effacement of the market place was part of a project to indicate film's importance as a form of individual expression. In this chapter, however, I shall be tracing the changes in authorship theory from this initial Romantic[1] removal from the demands of commerce to its contemporary return, under the umbrella of postmodernism, to a newly 'globalized' market place. Indeed, what makes the examination of theories of authorship at once so perplexing and so rewarding is that, as Pam Cook confirms, 'the history of auteur criticism can be seen as the history of different methods of reading films, and of the shifting and complex relationship between spectator, critic and film'.[2] The debate on authorship has been the arena in which many of film theory's most productive breakthroughs, as well as some of its greatest embarrassments, have been played out. Yet because the question 'Who is the author of the text?' always implies another, 'Who defines what the text means and for whom?', this is also a debate which is of central importance in film theory and one which touches on all aspects of film discussion and analysis.

A look at the roots of film authorship theory reveals the fundamental significance of certain key contextual circumstances. Perhaps the most important of these was a certain long-harboured insecurity and doubt among both film-makers and critics from the 1930s onwards about the social status of film as an art form. This of course needs be seen against the backdrop of the 'mass culture' debate of the 1950s discussed in the previous chapter. Far from demonizing the cinema as a threat to cherished high cultural values, however, the first writings on film authorship constituted an attempt by French intellectuals to recuperate film from its designation as merely a commercial and industrial enterprise, and to incorporate it within the ranks of 'classical art'.[3] Although some 'serious' European film criticism had already been established by the late 1940s, the work of its principal figures, André Bazin in France and the German film historian Siegfried Kracauer[4] had mainly been driven by an enquiry into the relationship between film aesthetics and reality, to which concerns about the director were secondary. While some films may have been deemed better than others, and some even 'great', what was lacking at this stage was a consistent critical approach to the process of establishing what made a film 'great'.

The *Politique des auteurs*

'*La politique des auteurs*' (auteur policy), as it came to be known, provided such a consistency. It did so primarily by referring back to an
essentially literary and Romantic conception of the artist as the central,
even the sole source of meaning in a text.[5] Within what is now taken to
be one of the first expressions of this Romantic view of film authorship,
Alexandre Astruc's claim that 'cinema is quite simply becoming a means
of expression, just as all the other arts before it, and in particular painting and the novel'[6] underpins what would become three of the important assumptions in the *politique des auteurs*. These were, first, that
cinema has obtained an equivalence to literature, or any other art form
of 'profundity and meaning'.[7] Second, that it is constituted through a
new and unique language; and third, that this situation affords directors a means of personal expression, that is, a form within which an
artist may 'translate his (or her) obsessions' and is not simply a mass art
form which deals only in popular pleasures.[8]

The *politique* must also be seen as the result of a French response to
a sudden influx of the backlog of Hollywood cinema which had been
held up during the German Occupation in World War II. Film-goers
at the Cinémathèque in Paris were able to watch several films by the
same director all at once and so perhaps were better primed to spot con-
necting styles and themes across a director's work. A great deal of popular and genre-based American film permeated the *Cahiers du Cinéma*
writings. Certainly its influence is discernible in François Truffaut's
highly influential manifesto for film-making in France, 'Une Certaine
Tendence du Cinéma Français'.[9]

Truffaut had two main gripes. The first problem was the overemphasis in French cinema on the 'school of psychological realism', which
was perpetuated through the second problem in what he labelled the
'tradition de la qualité' of French cinema. This was the practice of
making film adaptations of French literary classics as though film lacked
artistic sophistication or cultural prestige in itself. Instead Truffaut
pushed for a shift in critical and practical focus which emphasized an
attention to, and a faith in, the cinematographic specificity of film, most
particularly its use of *mise-en-scène* (the theatrical aspects of the image
– lighting, scenery, acting style, sets) or, in other words, precisely all
those visual aspects of the cinema which Truffaut terms 'audacities'[10]

which make it *not* literature. The real artists, or 'auteurs', of the cinema, he proclaimed, were its directors, not its 'scenarists' (screenplay writers). Though the *Cahiers* critics were just as absorbed in European cinema as they were in popular American film, the latter became a favoured model because Hollywood directors, unfettered by issues of literary fidelity, were seen as having more freedom to develop personal visual styles within which their own particular 'world-view' might be apprehended, as was the case with French cinema in the work of directors like Jacques Tati, Jean Cocteau, Jean Renoir, Abel Gance, Max Ophuls and Robert Bresson.

Ironically, in the end, the *politique* served to introduce a new critical hierarchy into film criticism which this time revolved around the distinction between directors who were real 'auteurs', and those who were merely 'metteurs-en-scene'. The latter were seen as craftsmen rather than artists, (William Wyler and Fred Zinnemann are cited) and the choice of these two terms indicates an important distinction within auteurism between industrial production or 'manufacturing' and artistic creation. Though the metteurs-en-scène may have displayed considerable technical 'competence', crucially their work appeared to lack consistency of style, purpose and theme across their films. A true auteur, it was argued, was distinguished by the presence in each film, above and beyond generic variations, of a distinctive personality, expressed as a world-view or vision, which would thereby constitute a trace or 'personal stamp'[12] of the director's presence in the film and therefore within their *œuvre*.

It was always within the visual style of the film that the auteurs left their characteristic mark. Orson Welles, for example, was applauded extensively by Bazin for his combined use of deep focus cinematography and long takes, Nicholas Ray was declared the 'poet of nightfall' by Truffaut for his repeated use of night-time scenes and Jacques Rivette delighted in Otto Preminger's 'starkness' of sets and in the apparently 'improvised quality' of his photography.[14] Violence was a particularly cherished emotion within films because, in typically Romantic form, it was taken to be the state of being which most readily facilitated the 'bursting through' of previously repressed aspects of personality into the visual language of the film, preferably through formal techniques which 'account[s] for and share[s] in the primary emotion of the auteur'.[15]

From the outset, however, the price paid for the early *Cahiers*' selective declarations of auteur status was their neglect of the commercial and industrial origins of popular film production. Attention was paid to what made a director's film personal and thereby unique, rather than what made films popular. Though popular cinema is produced precisely to attract as wide an audience as possible, *Cahiers* critics appeared to fly in the face of this imperative in their selection of auteurs who were great artists despite their being popular. By the same token, auteurs were rare birds and as such they were invariably the exceptions and not the rule of popular cinema.

However, it is also important to bear in mind that, as John Caughie points out, the writing of *La Politique* displayed both 'variety and dissension'[16] and never existed as any kind of collective statement. For example, although Bazin was certainly involved in auteurist criticism, its central tenets sat very uncomfortably with his fundamental and persistent insistence on the director's role as one who mediates but does not reconstruct reality; hence his fear that auteur criticism might lead to 'the negation of the film to the benefit of praise of its auteur'. Bazin had also always stressed that cinema, especially American cinema, was impure because it was 'an art which is both popular and industrial', a fact which was often elided by others in the name of auteurism.[17]

Neither was the emergence of the *politique* in this period, together with the critical scandal which ensued, an isolated critical phenomenon by any means and it needs to be placed alongside comparable movements of male artists and critics in Britain (the 'Angry Young Men') and the United States (the 'Beat' generation) who, frustrated by what they regarded as a climate of cultural stagnation in the post-war period, were eager to kick over the traces, questioning received wisdom and celebrating change. There was a general emergence of more oppositional cultures in the late 1950s which can now be characterized in terms of a rebellion of youth against traditional values.

The auteur theory

The high point of the *politique* in France was between 1951 and 1961, by which later date the same critics who had declared its terms now announced its passing.[18] The baton had already been passed on to Anglo-American film criticism, however, and was picked up for a brief time in two places. First, *Movie*, a British periodical, edited by Victor Perkins, Mark Shivas and Ian Cameron from 1962–72, found a correspondence between the *Cahiers* line and a Leavisite literary tradition which valued the 'detailed criticism'[19] of a sensitive 'ideal reader' more highly than theoretically based analysis. Not only did Leavis outline a specific approach to textual analysis, but implicit within this outline was, as John Caughie points out, 'a view of culture and tradition [which defined it as that which had] not been debased by mass industrial society'[20] and a series of critical values which perpetuate this view: moral integrity, honesty, depth, unity and personal vision. Whereas the *Cahiers* critics had mostly ignored the industrial basis of the American film industry, it is noted by Ian Cameron in *Movie*, yet with some unease:

> Hollywood films are not so much custom-built as manufactured. The responsibility for them is shared, and the final quality is no more the fault of the director than of such parties as the producer, the set designer, the cameraman or the hairdresser. Only by a happy accident can anything good escape from this industrial complex.[21]

Later in the same article, however, Cameron shifts ground slightly by identifying the director as the figure most likely to determine the final form of the film. 'Happy accidents' are thereby revised as consistent artistic achievements/interventions.

Second, in the United States, Andrew Sarris, who wrote for a radical journal of the avant-garde, *Film Culture* shaped a much more influential attitude to authorship in a series of articles in the late 1950s and early 1960s which came to be known as auteur theory. Fundamental to Sarris's work was a refusal of the separation between artists and their work. Interpretation, under these conditions, constituted a search for a 'meaningful coherence' between the two. Ultimately this led to the establishment or disputation of 'auteurs', based on their ability to display, over a series of films, 'certain recurring characteristics of style which serve as [their] signature'.[22] Sarris also ushered back into thinking on authorship the idea that Hollywood was a commercial industry. Where he differed from the *Movie* writers, however, was that, rather than seeing American film directors as disadvantaged by commercial restrictions and the 'maze of conventions' within Hollywood, Sarris chose to see these as enabling structures and indeed as a test of character:

> The auteur theory values the personality of a director precisely because of the barriers to its expression. It is as if a few brave spirits had managed to overcome the gravitational pull of the mass of movies. The fascination of Hollywood movies lies in their performance under pressure. Actually no artist is ever completely free, and art does not necessarily

thrive as it becomes less constrained.[23]

These 'barriers', as well as the necessary involvement of collaborators in film production (cinematographers, producers, editors and so on) were conceived of as so much background 'noise' (Wollen)[24] above which the voice of the auteur's 'brave spirit' would always be heard.

On the whole Sarris comes across as a critic with a rather mathematical mind who was obsessed with forms of schematization, ordering and tabling as antidotes to what he saw as critical amateurism. He illustrates his auteur theory, for example, through a visualization of three 'concentric circles' which stand for the intersection between an auteur's technique, style and 'interior meaning'. It was perhaps this pseudo-objective methodology which spurred him on to make the apparently arithmetically-based claim that 'American cinema was the only cinema in the world worth exploring in depth' because, 'film for film, director for director' it was 'consistently superior to that of the rest of the world'.[25] Unfortunately, for Sarris, this claim simply boils down to an defensive assertion of taste and value. Most notoriously Sarris's tabling impulse resulted in his construction of a critical 'pantheon' of great auteurs within which directors were ranked hierarchically on a sliding scale of the more or less 'great', the criteria for entry on to which remained entirely personal to Sarris. While, unlike previous auteurist critics, Sarris widely acknowledges that Hollywood cinema is a commercial enterprise, the value he places on certain directors none the less depends wholly on the way in which they defiantly transcend this cluttered environment.

In summary, the *Politique*, mainly because of the Romantic grounding of its main precepts, seems less than radical now. It was quickly absorbed within a mainstream critical orthodoxy itself, one which reinforced the Romantic cult of the individual as one who transcends the demands of the market place and effaces those very cultural and economic conditions which mark popular film production. None the less, two significant developments in criticism were achieved. First, auteurism provided a systematic method which was more concerned with the cinematic qualities of films than their sociological implications, and this method was used to produce enormous amounts of research into film-makers who were previously unknown or dismissed within film criticism – for example, Samuel Fuller, Nicholas Ray, Howard Hawks, John Ford. Second, as John Caughie has argued, 'auteurism did in fact produce a radical dislocation in the development of film theory,

which has exposed it progressively to the pressures of alternative aesthetics and "new criticisms" '.[26] In other words, the *Politique*, and sub-
sequently the auteur theory, by forcing the contradictions immanent in
the application of a Romantic, literary theory of authorship on to an
industrial, mass art like film, pressed film theory into opening itself
up to 'new criticisms' which moved beyond this unsustainable Roman-
ticism.

Auteur- (or cine-) structuralism

It is hardly surprising that auteur-based criticism, in its reliance on the
perceptive, neutral critic who draws out implicit textual meanings,
inevitably produced highly personal readings, which continually ran the
risk of blocking off a film's social significance from the process of interpretation. Lapsley and Westlake justly argue, however, that 'in opting
for structuralism as a defensive tactic, the auteurists could hardly have
made a worse choice'.[27] The move towards structuralism in film criticism extended well beyond authorship theory, seeping steadily into
genre theory also, and crucially coincided with a new radicalism in the
social sciences during the late 1960s. By introducing apparently scientific principles into the arts, structuralists hoped to generate new
forms of analysis which would probe beyond the surface of things as
they 'seem' to reveal the hidden and therefore more significant 'deep'
structures. Whereas auteurist criticism had mainly carried out impressionistic readings under veiled agendas, it became important for structuralists to lay their cards on the table in statements of critical and
political positions (usually Marxist), precisely because the function of
their readings was to rewrite, challenge and expose the unstated but
nevertheless ideological underpinnings of existing orthodoxies.

    Auteur-structuralism took its methodological framework from the
French anthropologist Claude Lévi-Strauss[28] who had attempted to
account for the repetition of certain patterns of behaviour across different cultures (mainly in Africa and North and South America) and
historical moments. An important informing influence on his work was
Saussurian linguistics, a discipline which carried two fundamental pre-
suppositions into the study of film.

    First, Saussure argued that language terms are both arbitrary and dif-
ferential. Meaning is not something simply inherent in the world and
waiting to be expressed through language, but is rather created in and

through the relationship between different language terms:

> Language is a system of interdependent terms in which the value of each
> term results solely from the simultaneous presence of the others.[29]

> Whether we take the signified or the signifier, language has neither ideas
> nor sounds that existed before the linguistic system, but only conceptual
> and phonic differences that have issued from the system ... Proof of this
> is that the value of a term may be modified, without either its meaning
> or its sound being affected, solely because a neighbouring term has been
> modified.[30]

The relationship between the signifier (language term) and the signified
object/concept is therefore merely an arbitrary one. The meaning of the
signifier comes not from the object or concept itself, to which it has no
necessary connection, but from its relationship to other language terms
from which it will, to degrees, differ. As a result, any meanings which
are produced necessarily constitute part of social and political (rather
than private) processes and may signify unconscious or unintentional
meanings beyond the control of an individual speaker. It is not difficult
to see how, as Pam Cook has pointed out, this understanding of the
workings of language completely undermines the three fundamental
Romantic premises on which the auteur theory rested: 'individuality',
'presence' and 'intention'.[31] In other words, how could a critic hope to
elucidate the precise and intended meaning of an auteur when all the
terms (visual or linguistic) used by the artist only obtain meaning
through their relation to a whole system of other terms and, equally,
when each speech act must be suspected of having been interrupted by
the unconscious or the unintentional?

Second, the practice of structuralism involved locating patterns of
'structuring oppositions' or antinomies within and across texts. Peter
Wollen was probably the most influential of the British structuralists,
though shades of variation may be discerned between his writing and
that of other notable proponents.[32] Wollen drew on the work of
Vladimir Propp, whose study of Russian folk- and fairy-tales had
revealed that, beneath the apparent diversity of character and theme, at
the core of each tale lay a common 'archi-tale'[33] or what Lévi-Strauss
would call a 'deep structure' or unconscious. Crucially, however, the
structuralist (film) critic

> cannot rest at the perception of resemblances or repetitions ... but must
> also comprehend a system of differences and oppositions. In this way
> texts can be studied not only in their universality (what differentiates

them from each other). This of course means that the test of a structural analysis is not in the orthodox canon of a director's work, where resemblances are clustered, but in films which at first sight may seem eccentricities.[34]

While Wollen paraphrases and concurs with Renoir's claim that 'a director spends his whole life making one film', he claims that this film can only be apprehended by the meticulous critic who does not simply name the 'resemblances and repetitions' of antinomies across a director's *entire* work but, more importantly, who uses these antinomies to tease out the 'esoteric structure' within an *œuvre*; that is, its moments of variation, innovation or 'eccentricity'. In John Ford's films, for example, Wollen argues that there is 'a shift from an identity between civilised versus savage and European versus Indian to their separation and final reversal, so that in *Cheyenne Autumn* (1964) it is the Europeans who are savage, the victims who are heroes'.[35] It is the moments of variation, then, which lend the repetitions their significance. Equally, the significance of a repetition is not to be contained by genre boundaries. Films previously derided by critics, such as *Donovan's Reef* (1963), with its repetition of the 'vagrancy versus home antinomy', now provide revealing connections to more revered or diverse texts such as *The Searchers* (1956) and *Wings of Eagles* (1957) and indicate the necessary presence of 'a whole complex of meaning'[36] in and across texts.

Evaluation, however, was not jettisoned in the process of Wollen's analysis. He cast his structuralist eye on Howard Hawks only to find his work wanting in comparison with Ford:

My own view is that Ford's work is much richer than that of Hawks and that this is revealed by a structural analysis; it is the richness of the shifting relation between antinomies in Ford's work that makes him a great artist, beyond simply being an undoubted auteur.[37]

The legacy of the 'pantheon' continues. Here, however, Wollen replaces Sarris's checklist of techniques and styles, moving instead to go along with Geoffrey Nowell-Smith's suggestion that a 'structural hard core of basic and often recondite'[38] or hidden motifs may reveal an auteur, but that the work of 'great directors' needs to be marked not only by 'shifting relations' across films, but by 'singularity' and significant eccentricity or exception. While he believes this to be the case for Ford, it is not so with Howard Hawks, who may offer 'a systematic series of oppositions', but Wollen finds them too 'near the surface'. In addition, the dynamic between antinomies which should operate within films is visible only between the two genres within which, broadly speaking, Hawks worked; the 'adventure drama and the crazy comedy'.[39]

Importantly, however, Wollen later published a significant supplement to this work as part of a 1972 reprint of *Signs and Meanings* in an attempt to distance his auteur theory (later dubbed auteur- or cine-structuralism) from previous versions of the theory which assumed the auteur was a 'creative personality' who filmed an original and 'coherent message or world-view'.[40] Rather, auteur-structuralism, through Wollen, introduced a new metaphor – that of the auteur as 'unconscious catalyst'.[41] Just as Lévi-Strauss argued that societies, as groups, bear and pass on myths without individuals necessarily being aware of their full implication, so too, Wollen claimed, it was with film directors. It is for this reason that he placed the names of directors in inverted commas; when he uses the names 'Hitchcock' or 'Ford', he is labelling the set of structures, the 'auteur code', named after them (retroactively), not the men themselves.

Directors are catalysts in so far as they facilitate the coming together of culturally important structuring motifs, the full weight of which may be quite beyond them. None the less, of all the component parts of any film's production (studio interests, genre conventions, star performances and so on) it is the director who, above all others, remains the preferred principle of consistency in the equation. They are imagined to be a neutral agent (rather than agency), through which wider social meanings are simply refracted. In John Ford's films it may be possible to trace a 'master antinomy' of 'the garden and the desert', but for Wollen (and for Jim Kitses) this was the marker of an American cultural opposition which predated Ford and which is simply confirmed through its restatement and reworking. Even here, it was still clear that structuralism never really questioned why it should be that the director remains the chosen catalyst figure at the centre of the text. S/he appears not to be a neutral element at all, but a very specific, individualizing component.

The important advance secured by this significant footnote to auteur-structuralism was its placing of the director as a textual indeterminacy which then takes shape in the reading process. It was no longer necessary, therefore, to refer to some predetermined, often self-pronounced, version of the director's intentions to validate a film's reading. At the same time, Wollen led criticism to consider that the apparent coherence of Hollywood films was a 'secondary revision'. In other words, films manufacture narrative and ideological coherence for spectators, thereby concealing actual conflicts which then become buried in the film 'unconscious'.[42] He stopped short, however, of opening out and questioning the moments where gaps, silences and contradictions are masked. This work was (now famously) undertaken by the *Cahiers du Cinéma* 'collective' in their analysis of Ford's *Young Mr Lincoln* (1939). Under the influence of French Marxist ideology criticism from writers such as Pierre Macherey and Louis Althusser, *Cahiers* concentrated, not on completed (or completing) structures of meaning, but on the instants of 'masking' what is contradictory, what cannot be said or what is silenced, so that the 'concealed order of the work is thus less significant than its real determinate disorder (its disarray)'.[43]

In the end, the crucial flaw in the application of structuralist analysis was that, as Brian Henderson indicates, structuralist readings were founded on a less than meticulous application of Lévi-Strauss who, in the first place, held that individual subjects could not be the bearers of myths, which have 'no origin, no centers, no subjects and no authors'.[44] Auteur-structuralism fatally went against the grain of the very structuralism it invoked by tracing back from repeated structures to the names of distinctive individual directors (as opposed to Lévi-Strauss's interchangeable subjects). Henderson also charges auteur-structuralism with being a stifling critical twosome, in that by making 'the study of films as myths dependent on the fusion of auteurism and structuralism' it 'effectively rules out other modes of study' while 'constituting itself as a discourse which does not ask fundamental and foundational questions, above all about itself'.[45] His sympathies lie more with the Cahiers critics who had refused this empiricist and reductivist structuralist tendency of accepting texts as a given from which a core meaning may simply be dug out (leaving a 'de-mystified' shell behind), rather than something which is produced out of certain material conditions to which it must then be related.

Post-structuralism and beyond

A further blind spot for structuralism was the concept of spectatorial pleasure. As an approach to popular Hollywood cinema it could only account for repeated core structures, but not for how or why spectators engage with films and what kinds of textual strategies secure their pleasures. This change of emphasis towards a need to investigate the role of the subject in the interpretation/reading process is reflected in post-structuralism's use of semiotics and can best be illustrated with reference to Roland Barthes's essay 'The Death of the Author',[46] itself a significant rebuff to Romantic theories of authorship and a cornerstone of post-structuralist thought, both in literary and in film studies.

Barthes, a member of the influential Tel Quel group in Paris, placed a new emphasis on the way meaning is produced through the process of signification – a process in which the reader is as important as the text itself. This so-called 'birth of the reader' was to be at the 'cost of the death of the Author',[47] or at least the death of previous conceptions of the author as a being who is placed behind (or above) the text and whose meaning (intentional or not) may be revealed through well-honed critical rendering. Again the influence of Saussure is legible here in the way Barthes's rhetoric places a continual stress on emptiness and loss of origins. Enunciation, the act of speech or writing, is conceived of as an 'empty process' in which 'it is language which speaks, not the author'. In the moment of speech, the speaking subject 'slips away' or 'enters into his own death' as 'writing begins'. In this way 'the body writing' (person) is substituted by the subject within language ('inscription') which therefore inevitably 'traces a field without origin.' For Barthes there is nothing at all 'behind' or before the text. It exists, of necessity, only in the present moment of its performance, in the 'here and now'. In so far as there is authorship of meaning, it lies wholly in the shifting relationship between the text and its reader. As a result, there can be no supreme, final or scientific ('authorized') reading of a film because it is 'a multi-dimensional space in which a variety of writings, none of them original, blend and clash', always marked by its 'intertextuality'. If there is a place where meaning temporarily inheres, it is not in its origins, but in the text's destination (its reader), and in the 'disentanglement', not 'decipherment' of the text.

One of the most glaring problems with Barthes's thesis was that, in his rush to jump on the author's grave, he neglected to outline fully the role of his or her successor. His call was for the reader to be regarded as 'without history, biography, psychology; he is simply that someone who holds together in a single field all the traces by which the written text is constituted'.[48] As Lapsley and Westlake point out, this was an omission more troubling for film than it was for literary studies, because of the sharper emphasis on the political effectiveness of texts on subjects which had evolved within film studies. However, in the wake of the political changes which followed May 1968, art practices of all kinds became highly politicized. Much post-structuralist writing became involved, not just in accounting for the dynamic between texts, subjects and social change but, like Barthes who held up Proust, Mallarmé, Valéry and the surrealists as models, it sought to champion particular kinds of modernist and avant-garde cinematic practice – specifically those which challenged or partially effaced authorial presence. So although Barthes overlooked the determining influences on reading subjects, he did reopen questions of authorship to discussions of textuality, reading and pleasure; and hence to the possibility of incorporating studies of the subject (the political, linguistic, sexual and psychoanalytic subject).

It was Michel Foucault who recentred debate with his account of the discourse of the 'author function'.[49] It is one thing, he argues, to declare that the author as a person is absent from a text, but it is quite another to suggest that the institution of authorship does not exist in Western society, although certainly it has changed and developed in historically determined ways. While, for Foucault, an author's name is not simply 'a proper name amongst others', neither is its function to be determined by the person to whom it refers. Rather, it indicates 'a speech that must be received in a certain mode and that, in a given culture, must receive a certain status'.[50]

First, authors' names perform a 'classificatory function' in enabling us to associate a particular group of texts under a heading such as 'John Ford westerns' and hold them up against another group which might be 'Howard Hawks westerns'. The name functions at once to mark off the types and numbers of discourses to which the author's name refers (which may extend beyond simply the volumes of books they have written, which is the case, for example, with Marxism) and to codify the cultural status which they hold as they circulate under this name. Second, there is also a legal function which both holds the author responsible for their work ('penal appropriation'), and likewise confers ownership rights. Finally, what is most interesting to Foucault is not so much what is expressed in the discourses circulated under a particular author's name, but how these discourses come to exist and undergo changing processes of 'valorisation, attribution and appropriation'.[51] The 'author function' works ideologically through these turns as 'the principle of thrift in the proliferation of meaning'.[52] Foucault argues, within a post-Saussurian understanding of linguistic signification in which the speaking or writing subject has been removed from the position of originator of meaning (behind the text as it were), that Western culture, in its apprehension of the potentially subversive uses to which texts might be put, insists on a conservative maintenance of the author in his or her place as source and 'regulator of the fictive'.[53]

John Caughie, though his primary cue appears to have been taken from Barthes, in some ways skates among various other linguistically and psychoanalytically-based theories of spectator/text relationships (Christian Metz and Emile Benveniste, as well as Foucault), to provide an interesting and influential new position. He sees the author not as a figure behind but within the text. While the main point of identification for the spectators, he argues, will usually be the subject of the film, there may also be moments of rupture in which they are temporarily dislocated from this fictional centre. Nevertheless, this loss of identification 'is not experienced as a loss of pleasure, because it is accompanied by a recognition – a recognition of the figure of the author which I reconstruct precisely to fill the subject position of the film's performance'.[54] Therefore, at these moments the spectator recognizes, and thereby admires and enjoys, what is taken to be the performance of the author – for example, the characteristic use of certain kinds of editing, acting, music. Thus, although Caughie acknowledges his reanimation in this account of the auteurist hunt for intertextual consistencies, he does stress that these are not then to be hailed as the markers of the author's creative genius. Instead, 'we return them to the question of discourse, of how they produce an authorial subject for the discourse, and of how that production relates to the production, positioning and continual repositioning of spectating subjects'.[55] In this way, Caughie has combined Barthes's concept of the film as 'performance' with Foucault's argument that we need to account for the pleasures within this performance as discourses which produce authorial and spectatorial subjects. None the less, as Stephen Crofts points out, all this would still leave us wondering precisely how to identify and define such moments of rupture and whether films which displayed none were then to be classified as 'unauthored'.[56]

During the 1980s, because questions of authorship were rarely debated in film journals, it may have seemed as though post-structuralism had won the day. However, as Andy Medhurst points out,[57] on the review pages of newspapers and in film magazines, auteurism still reigned supreme with a whole series of new directors being crowned as auteurs – Martin Scorsese, Alan Rudolph, Ridley Scott, Spike Lee, Robert Altman, Kathryn Bigelow and Woody Allen, to name a few. Furthermore, theories of authorship are beginning to be re-examined, partly in response to the challenge posed by the new kinds of cinema being produced outside Hollywood by some of the directors named above, but partly also to accommodate new historicism as well as theories of postmodernism and postmodernity.

Medhurst's own return to authorship theory, which focuses on *Brief Encounter* (David Lean, 1945), is driven by the imperative that Noel Coward's homosexuality be acknowledged not simply as an incidental biographical detail, but as a significant influence on his screenplay, into which it has been codedly written. Whereas post-structuralist criticism had vilified any such moves to incorporate biography into textual interpretation, Medhurst sees this injunction as a dangerous effacement of a marginalized identity – an authorial identity which, in Coward's case, gives way to 'a sort of subcultural authorship, a collective 'special thrill', a method of analysis based on a recognition of shared structures of feeling'.[58] In other words, the retrieval and reinsertion of biography may be justified if its function is the political one of empowering socially marginalized groups through recovering evidence of the contribution of some suppressed aspect of an artist's identity (race, gender, sexuality, religion) to his or her art and, through this, accounting for a common pleasure or feeling experienced by the group through the art. Indeed perhaps these moments of 'thrill' can be linked back to Caughie's identification of the ruptures in a film in which the spectator takes pleasure in the recognition of the figure of the author, except that this performance now takes on a specific cultural and group significance. It also leads us to regard Foucault in a new way in that although he describes how the author has, for the most part, been an ideologically reactionary 'regulator of the fictive', here we have an example of an author being used to valorize a previously hidden or unofficial version of the text.

As Medhurst seems to acknowledge, however, as many questions are suggested by this argument as are answered. What, for example, constitutes a 'socially marginalized' group, and which one is the critic 'politically justified' in supporting with biographical evidence? Medhurst chooses not to pursue the more unacceptable aspects of Coward's identity such as his class snobbery, racism and xenophobia in his analysis, but how should such omissions be monitored? Clearly not all marginalized groups are ones whose identity many would want to reaffirm through such readings. Indeed many artistic figures are likely to belong to more than one such group, though there may be considerable tension between different aspects of their identity – for example Leni

Riefenstahl is both a woman and a Nazi film-maker. Also this argument assumes a unity of identity in marginalization – that through such information about a writer or director's life one facilitates group identification and thereby empowerment – when in fact the result could be to provoke dissent and dispute among groups which may themselves contain many diverse subgroupings. That Spike Lee is an African–American may be a politically important piece of information for African–American spectators, both in terms of his films and of the economics of American film production, yet critical responses to his films, especially from women, often indicate dissent rather than fulfilment.[59]

The final, and to date most recent, contribution to authorship debates has been made by two American critics, Dudley Andrew and Timothy Corrigan. Caught up in a whirlwind of postmodernist theory and commercial metaphors, they are primarily interested in spectators as 'consumers'.[60] Each writer seems to hold on to the auteur theory as the only preceding model of film authorship and thereby transforms this into a straw dog to be beaten by a new, postmodern, version of the auteur. Corrigan, for example, in some ways convincingly, argues that film directors are self-consciously styled and marketed as auteurs with their own particular 'star images'. Rather than being a critical category with any influence on the way his or her 'products' are read, however, the auteur is simply to be seen as 'a commercial strategy for organising audience reception, as a critical concept bound to distribution and marketing aims that identify and address the potential cult status of an auteur'.[61]

While Corrigan is right to signal the influence of such commercial strategies, the danger is that they may be overemphasized as determinants of the way the texts are read rather than as one of many influential factors in the production of meaning. The excess weight placed on commercial strategies for audience influence is reflected in the way both writers fail to investigate the role of the spectator beyond an image of passive consumerism. Corrigan for example depicts an unpleasantly smug 'movie buff' viewer:

> To respond to a movie as primarily or merely a Spielberg film is, after all, the pleasure of refusing an evaluative relation to it – a pleasure that might equally be true of the standard reception of Herzog movies – and much of that pleasure lies in being able to already know, not read, the meaning of the film in a totalising image that precedes the movie in the public images of its creator.[62]

In some ways, again, this carries an echo of Caughie's account of the spectatorial pleasure of recognizing authorial figures in the text as patterns and consistencies are recognized (equally Andrew celebrates the reduction of the auteur to 'a cinematic effect'),[63] yet it is without the concomitant recognition that these moments also work to offer spectators particular positions and meanings. Corrigan's throwaway line about the 'standard reception of Herzog movies' also both indicates that his conception of audiences is as an undifferentiated (and undifferentiating) mass and marks his difference from Medhurst's intervention. In the long term, however, it is the latter which would seem to be eminently the more useful in its redirection of debate towards the tangible emotional and often political effects of popular films as well as in its recognition of spectatorial communities.

Conclusion

This review of the various modifications of, and transmutations within, film authorship theory reveals a persistent unease with the category of the popular in film. Auteurist critics either drew a curtain around Hollywood's roots in the market-place (*Cahiers*) or else they conceived of these as a quagmire out of which the true auteur would heroically rise (Cameron, Sarris). In both cases, the 'popular' constitutes a negative term which is explicitly defined (in much the same way as it had been by the mass culture theorists) as something synonymous with the formulaic, cliché-ridden and the politically or formally conservative. Though later structuralist and post-structuralist critics took issue with many of these earlier positions, none the less the application of their critical methods still privileged 'exceptional directors' over popular film in general. Implicit in ideology criticism such as the *Cahiers* analysis of *Young Mr Lincoln* and in Wollen's notion of popular films as 'secondary revisions', for example, is the understanding that popular texts are indeed conservative and that it is only the critic who exposes the film's ideological unconscious. Any subversion or radical potential, therefore, lies in the reading and not in the film itself. Corrigan and Andrew's postmodern approach may have attempted to level distinctions between European art cinema and Hollywood, yet in many ways their contribution to the debate looks like the flip side of the mass culture theorist's coin in that it promotes an acceptance of the wholesale commercialization of culture. However, in its reversion to auteurist principles and its perpetuation of a critical interest in exceptional or 'star' directors, it fails to provide a more general approach to the question of which figures constitute the shaping influence(s) over the meaning of popular films.

Notes:

1 The term used to describe the literary, artistic, critical and philosophical movements of the late eighteenth and early nineteenth century which were characterized by an emphasis on the expression of strong personal feelings, and on the necessary links between nature (rather than society), imagination and the creative individual. See Raymond Williams, *Keywords*, London: Fontana, 1983, pp. 274–6; and M. H. Abrams, *The Mirror and the Lamp*, Oxford: Oxford University Press, 1953.

2 Pam Cook, *The Cinema Book*, London: British Film Institute, 1985, p. 183.

3 'The American cinema is a classical art, but why not admire in it what is most admirable, i.e. not only the talent of this or that film-maker, but the genius of the system, the richness of its ever-vigorous tradition, and its fertility when it comes into contact with new elements', (André Bazin, 'On the *Politique des Auteurs*', (1957), trans. Peter Graham, in Jim Hillier, ed., *Cahiers du Cinéma: The 1950s*, London: Routledge, 1985, p. 258.

4 See Siegfried Kracauer, *The Theory of Film: The Redemption of Physical Reality*, Oxford: Oxford University Press, 1960. However, Jim Hillier also stresses the importance of *Revue du Cinéma* in providing valuable film criticism from 1929–31 and 1946–49 in his introduction to *Cahiers du Cinéma: the 1950s*, pp. 1–27.

5 See M. H. Abrams's summary of Romantic conceptions of authorship in 'Literature as a Revelation of Personality', in *The Mirror and the Lamp*, pp. 226–56.

6 Alexandre Astruc, 'The Birth of a New Avant-Garde: Le Caméra-Stylo', (1948), reprinted in Peter Graham, trans. and ed., *The New Wave*, London: Secker and Warburg, 1968, p. 17.

7 *Ibid.*, p. 20.

8 *Ibid.*, p. 18.

9 First published in *Cahiers du Cinéma*, no. 31, January 1954, and reprinted in Bill Nichols, ed., *Movies and Methods*, Berkeley: California University Press, 1973, pp. 224–36.

10 *Ibid.*, p. 234.

11 Jacques Rivette, 'Six Characters in Search of Auteurs', in *Cahiers du Cinéma: the 1950s*, pp. 31–46.

12 'On the *Politique des Auteurs*', p. 255.

13 Francois Truffaut, 'A Wonderful Certainty' (1955) in *Cahiers du Cinéma: the 1950s*, p. 108.

14 Jacques Rivette, 'The Essential' (1954) in *Cahiers du Cinéma: the 1950s*, p. 132.

15 Jacques Rivette, 'Notes on a Revolution' (1955) in *Cahiers du Cinéma: the 1950s*, pp. 94–7.
16 John Caughie, ed., *Theories of Authorship*, London: Routledge, 1981, p. 38.
17 'On the *Politique des Auteurs*', pp. 258, 251.
18 See Claude Chabrol, Jacques Doniol-Valcroze, Jean-Luc Godard, Pierre Kast, Luc Moullet, Jacques Rivette, François Truffaut, 'Questions about American Cinema: A Discussion' (1963–64) in Jim Hillier, ed., *Cahiers du Cinéma Vol. II: the 1960s*, London: Routledge, 1986, pp. 172–80.
19 Ian Cameron, 'Films, Directors and Critics' (1962), in *Theories of Authorship*, pp. 58.
20 *Theories of Authorship*, p. 49.
21 'Films, Directors and Critics', p. 52.
22 Andrew Sarris, 'The American Cinema' (1963) reprinted as 'Towards a Theory of Film History', in *Movies and Methods*, p. 246.
23 *Ibid.*, p. 247.
24 Peter Wollen, 'The Auteur Theory', in *Signs and Meanings in the Cinema*, London: Secker and Warburg, 1972, p. 104.
25 Andrew Sarris, 'Notes on the Auteur Theory in 1962' (1962–63), reprinted in Gerald Mast and Marshall Cohen, eds, *Film Theory and Criticism*, Oxford: Oxford University Press, 1979, pp. 663, 660. Also see Pauline Kael on Sarris's use of formulae in 'Circles and Squares' (1963), in *Film Theory and Criticism*, pp. 666–79.
26 *Theories of Authorship*, p. 11.
27 Robert Lapsley and Michael Westlake, *Film Theory: An Introduction*, Manchester: Manchester University Press, 1988, p. 108.
28 See Claude Lévi-Strauss, *Structural Anthropology*, London: Allen Lane, 1968; and *The Raw and the Cooked*, London: Jonathan Cape, 1970.
29 Ferdinand de Saussure, *Course in General Linguistics*, London: Fontana/Collins, 1974, p. 114.
30 *Ibid.*, p. 120.
31 *The Cinema Book*, p. 170.
32 See Geoffrey Nowell-Smith, *Luchino Visconti* (1967), New York: Doubleday, 1968; Charles Eckert, 'The English Cine-Structuralists', *Film Comment*, Vol. 9, no. 3, May–June 1973, pp. 46–51; and Jim Kitses's study of the western, *Horizon's West*, London: Secker and Warburg, 1969.
33 'The Auteur Theory', p. 93.
34 *Ibid.*, p. 104.
35 *Ibid.*, pp. 95–6.
36 *Ibid.*, p. 102.
37 *Ibid.*
38 *Luchino Visconti*, p. 10.
39 'The Auteur Theory', p. 102–4.
40 *Ibid.*, p. 167.

41 *Ibid.*, p. 168.

42 *Ibid.*, p. 167.

43 Pierre Macherey, *A Theory of Literary Production*, (1966), London: Routledge, 1978, p. 155. Also see Louis Althusser, *Lenin and Philosophy and Other Essays*, London: New Left Books, 1971; and the editors of *Cahiers du Cinéma*, 'John Ford's *Young Mr Lincoln*', Screen, Vol. 13, no. 3, 1972; and *Film Theory: An Introduction*, pp. 115–17, which provides a useful assessment of this work.

44 Brian Henderson, 'Critique of Cine-Structuralism' (Part 1, 1973), in *Theories of Authorship*, p. 176.

45 *Ibid.*, p. 178.

46 Roland Barthes, 'The Death of the Author' (1968), in *Image/Music/Text*, London: Fontana/Collins, 1977, pp. 142–8.

47 *Ibid.*, p. 148.

48 *Ibid.*

49 Michel Foucault, 'What is an Author?' (1977), in Paul Rabinow, ed., *The Foucault Reader*, Harmondsworth: Penguin, 1984, pp. 101–20.

50 *Ibid.*, p. 107.

51 *Ibid.*, p. 117.

52 *Ibid.*, p. 118.

53 *Ibid.*, p. 119.

54 *Theories of Authorship*, p. 204.

55 *Ibid.*, p. 205.

56 Stephen Crofts, 'Authorship and Hollywood', *Wide Angle*, Vol. 5, no. 3, 1982, pp. 16–23.

57 Andy Medhurst, 'That Special Thrill: *Brief Encounter*, Homosexuality and Authorship', *Screen*, Vol. 32, no. 2, 1991, p. 197.

58 *Ibid.*, pp. 204–5.

59 Though commenting from a British context, see Felly Nkweto Simmons, 'She's Gotta Have It: The Representation of Black Female Sexuality on Film', in Terry Lovell, ed., *British Feminist Thought: A Reader*, Oxford: Blackwell, 1990, pp. 314–24.

60 Dudley Andrew, 'The Unauthorised Auteur Today', in Jim Collins *et al.*, ed, *Film Theory Goes to the Movies*, London: Routledge, 1993, pp. 77–85; and Timothy Corrigan, *Cinema Without Walls*, London: Routledge, 1991.

61 *Cinema Without Walls*, p. 103.

62 *Ibid.*, p. 106.

63 'The Unauthorised Auteur Today', p. 84.

In search of Factor X! Ethan Edwards (John Wayne) goes wandering in *The Searchers* (1956).

Genre theory and criticism

G enre first becomes a focus for significant theoretical and critical activity in film studies in the late 1960s and then on into the 1970s. Much of this work dealt with Hollywood cinema and, initially at least, placed itself in relation to the auteurist debates which had been so important in film criticism since the 1950s. For some genre critics, the study of particular genres provided the opportunity to situate the auteur more systematically (and perhaps more credibly) within the Hollywood set-up. For others who wanted to question the notions of creativity embodied by the figure of the auteur, the stress on genre represented, in Anthony Easthope's words, 'a tactical attempt to think beyond auteurism'.[1]

While this proliferation of critical activity around genre did not mark an unequivocal break with the past, it did enable new ways of thinking about film in general, and Hollywood cinema in particular, to emerge. However, an overall survey of the various articles and books associated with 1970s genre study gives one a sense of unrealized or thwarted potential, of perceptive and insightful work which eventually fades away into nothing. It has been suggested by Paul Willemen that the virtual disappearance of genre from film criticism's agenda was caused by the dominance of *Screen* theory, with its rather more generalizing concerns, from the mid-1970s onwards.[2] Certainly there is some truth to this claim. But it can also be argued that the particular critical questions and issues which genre critics identified as being important proved in the end incapable of being sustained, and perhaps even blocked any substantial and long-lived enquiry into the subject.

This chapter will record the positive achievements of 1970s genre study (which included contributions from, among others, Tom Ryall, Ed Buscombe, Colin McArthur, Douglas Pye, Steve Neale and Will Wright) and also identify some of the reasons why it foundered when it did. Also discussed will be the influential early work on film genres produced by André Bazin, Robert Warshow and Lawrence Alloway. It will be shown that while the insights of these pioneers of genre study often anticipated developments in the 1970s, certain other lines of enquiry opened up by their work were largely ignored by these later critics, arguably much to the detriment of their work. Finally, the chapter will look briefly at some important studies of specific genres (for example, 1970s and 1980s work on film noir and melodrama). It will be argued that accounts like these, which generally lacked the specific theoretical ambitions of much of the work mentioned above, often have a clearer sense of the historical and/or national specificity of genres, and offer an alternative way of thinking about genre to that offered by the 1970s theorists.

It is worth mentioning at this point that genre as a subject for discussion has always transcended the traditional boundaries of film studies (in much the same way as issues relating to stars have done). While in the history of film studies genre theory comes after auteurism, it is also true to say that as far as the film industry and its audiences are concerned genres preceded any notions of highlighting the director/author as a meaningful way of ordering and classifying the cinematic experience. While the auteur seemed to exist in spite of the structures of the industry and his or her presence was only detected (or perhaps constructed) by critics after the event, genres have always existed because of the nature of the industry. They offer a means by which the industry can seek to repeat and capitalize upon previous box-office successes. This connects with the way in which genres also provide audiences with particular sorts of knowledge which they can use to organize their own viewing (although the terms of this relationship are not at all clear). Of course, this is a rather basic way of putting it, but, nevertheless, underpinning much academic writing is the sense that, when it comes to genre, the industry and the audience need to be held together in the same equation. (Compare this with the more classical forms of auteurism where the industry tended to be that which had to be transcended and the audience was usually absent.) In fact, part of the appeal of studying genre is that it offers the opportunity to deal with cinema, and Hollywood cinema in particular, as both an industrial and a popular medium. What needs to be done now is to explore the various ways in which critics set about this task, beginning with some of the earlier forays into the field. As will become clear, certain problems quickly became apparent which would preoccupy genre studies for years to follow.

Genre's pioneers

The three distinguished critics to be discussed here are André Bazin, Robert Warshow and Lawrence Alloway. All shared the belief that genres carried an intrinsic meaning or significance, but each adopted a different way of thinking about this.

André Bazin is perhaps the best known of the three. Closely associated with the French journal *Cahiers du Cinéma* and the auteurist school of criticism, his writings on genre – notably 'The Western, or the American Film par excellence' and 'The Evolution of the Western' – need to be located within this context. (Indeed, in the latter piece, Bazin identifies authors/auteurs as a key factor in the evolution of the western genre.)[3] For Bazin, one of the key things that needed to be explained about the western, the American film par excellence in his own words, was its international popularity (an appropriate task, perhaps, for a non-American critic).

> What can there possibly be to interest Arabs, Hindus, Latins, Germans, or Anglo-Saxons, among whom the western has had an uninterrupted success, about evocations of the birth of the United States of America, the struggle between Buffalo Bill and the Indians, the laying down of the railroad, or the Civil War![4]

For Bazin, the answer to this question did not lie in the western's formal qualities, which Bazin identifies as specific settings, objects and scenarios: 'the western must be something else again than its form. Galloping horses, fights, strong and brave men in a wildly austere landscape could not add up to a definition of the genre nor encompass its charms.'[5] Rather, the western's formal attributes 'are simply signs or symbols of its profound reality, namely the myth.'[6] Myth, as Bazin understands it, is universal and timeless, and manifests itself in the western through the portrayal of Manichaean struggles between the forces of evil and 'the knights of the true cause'. This mythic quality, according to Bazin, stands in a dialectical relationship with the western's very specific historical settings, and because of this conjunction the genre takes on further epic and tragic qualities (both of which Bazin defines vaguely).

In 'The Western', the article in which these ideas are featured, Bazin is obviously painting in rather broad strokes and many of his general ideas about the western are, to say the least, questionable (although his recognition of the international dispersal of the genre is important). In 'The Evolution of the Western', however, he is much more specific about what he sees as the historical development of the western form. He argues that the western had attained a 'classical' perfection in the late 1930s, and that subsequent westerns, while not necessarily inferior, were, variously, 'baroque', 'novelistic' or 'superwesterns', 'a western that would be ashamed to be just itself, and looks for some additional interest to justify its existence'.[7]

For our purposes, two particular points of interest can be isolated in Bazin's writing on genre. First, there is the focus on the western (also apparent in the near-contemporaneous work of Warshow), a genre which would also preoccupy 1970s genre critics. In Bazin's case, his remarks refer to the western only; there is no attempt to relate these films back either to the conditions of their production or to a more general theory of genre. However, in the case of the 1970s work, the western (and, to a lesser extent, the gangster film) was often used as an exemplar of genres in general. As will be shown, this caused rather more problems than it solved, as did the concentration on identifying the formal components of the western, a task dismissed by Bazin as an unsatisfactory way of defining the genre.

Second, there is a clear awareness running beneath Bazin's periodizing 'classical' and 'baroque' terminology of the fact that specific genres do actually change as time passes, with these changes most apparent in the formal organization of the genre in question. A rather banal point perhaps, but later accounts of genre often shied away from a historical awareness of generic forms.

As Tom Ryall has noted, Robert Warshow's writings on the western and the gangster film offer a more ideological analysis than that offered by Bazin.[8] What one takes from Warshow's work is a sense of the cultural and historical specificity of these groups of films (which immediately sets his approach apart from Bazin's universalizing tendency), the way in which they provide answers to, and seek to resolve in imaginary terms, particular needs and contradictions within American society. For example, Warshow argues that the fascination with the film gangster entails an ambivalence about certain dominant American values: 'the gangster is the "no" to that great American "yes" which is stamped so big over our official culture and yet has so little to do with the way we really feel about our lives'.[9]

At the same time, Warshow does not see genres merely as mirroring a pre-existing social reality. Again and again, he stresses, like Bazin, the aesthetic significance of genres but, unlike Bazin, links this with the organization of the film industry and with audience expectations:

> the gangster film is simply one example of the movies' constant tendency to create fixed dramatic patterns that can be repeated indefinitely with a reasonable expectation of profit ... One goes to any individual example of the type with very definite expectations, and originality is to be welcomed only in the degree that it intensifies the expected experience without fundamentally altering it ... It is only in an ultimate sense that the

type appeals to its audience's experience of reality; much more immediately, it appeals to previous experience of the type itself: it creates its own field of reference.[10]

Finally, Lawrence Alloway, writing in the 1960s and early 1970s (and thereby overlapping with but considerably different in his approach from other 1970s genre critics), placed far more emphasis than either Bazin or Warshow on an understanding of the audience's experience of movies. 'The proper point of departure for a film critic who is going to write about the movies is membership in the large audience for whom they are intended.'[11] Importantly, Alloway was also one of the first critics to use the term 'iconography' as a means of analysing generic identity. Borrowing the term, and the critical practice it suggests, from art history (in particular, the work of Erwin Panofsky), Alloway sought to apply this concept to movies by identifying recurrent character types and situations which would become familiar to the audience through repetition and could be used by film-makers as a kind of shorthand.[12] For Alloway, genres could be considered as preliminary iconographical groupings:

> In this way we can indicate typical patterns of recurrence and change in popular films which can be traced better in terms of iconography than in terms of individual creativity. Indeed, the personal contribution of many directors can only be seen fully after typical iconographical elements have been identified.[13]

As with Bazin and Warshow, there is a reliance here on traditional notions of authorship, but elsewhere Alloway is far more interested in notions of collective authorship within the Hollywood studio set-up. For this reason, he does not try to identify any genre as a coherent whole but instead prefers to present a more fragmented picture of 'sets' and 'cycles' of films. One might argue here that Warshow's ideas about the 1930s gangster cycle of films could be framed within such an approach, as indeed could Bazin's periodization of the western when shorn of its evaluative rhetoric.

What one takes generally from these three critics is a sense of some of the possibilities of looking at American film in terms of genre. (The notable absence of European cinema from these and many later discussions of genre arguably derives from the highly questionable approach which associates Europe with art and America with commerce.)[14] In particular, these early genre critics provide us with ideas about how genres might be dealt with critically, and with discussions of icono-

graphy and generic themes which were especially pertinent to what was
to follow in the field. Equally important, although it is rather more
difficult to pin down, is an awareness in all three writers of what might
be termed here the 'liveliness' and changeability of genres, with this
awareness taking the form of a sense of genres' historical mutability,
their geographical dispersion or their cultural specificity. As will
become apparent, these latter insights were not always taken up in subsequent work.

Looking for Factor X: genre studies in the 1970s

'To say a film is a Western is immediately to say that it shares some
indefinable 'X' with other films we call 'Westerns'
Andrew Tudor, *Theories of Film*[15]

One of the more striking things about 1970s work on genre is how much
of it is British in origin. It is likely that the development of genre theory
and criticism throughout this period was influenced by concurrent
attempts to establish film studies as a recognizable discipline within the
British educational establishment (not least because of the fact that
much of this work was published by *Screen* and *Screen Education* and/or
generated within the British Film Institute, all of which had a clear educational brief). Hence there were numerous methodological discussions
of the problems involved in defining and analysing film genres, with
these surely functioning in part to locate the insights of Bazin and
Warshow within the particular academic institutions and discourses of
the period. At the same time, however, one also finds the now familiar
belief that auteurism is a critical imposition on Hollywood in a way that
genre studies is not, and that the turn to genre was a means of engaging with cinema as a popular medium. For example, Ed Buscombe,
writing in 1970, notes that 'anyone who is at all concerned with education must be worried at the distance between much of the criticism now
written and the way the average audience reacts to a film. For them it
is not a new Hawks or Ford or a new Peckinpah; it is a new western.'[16]

In the 1975 article entitled 'Teaching through Genre', Tom Ryall
sets out what he sees as the parameters of genre study.

When we suggest that a certain film is a Western we are really positing
that a particular range of meanings will be available in the film, and not
others. We are defining the limits of its significance. The master image
for genre criticism is a triangle composed of artist/film/audience. Genres

may be defined as patterns/forms/styles/structures which transcend individual films, and which supervise both their construction by the film maker, and their reading by an audience.[17]

Ryall's article was later to be criticised by Steve Neale for, among other things, the vagueness of its notion of a supervisory relationship between genres, film-makers and audiences.[18] But the point I want to address derives from Ryall's insistence that genre studies takes the form, in his words, of 'defining the limits' of a genre's significance. The identification of a genre (or genres generally) as a legitimate object of study here involves authorizing particular readings of the genre and, as a necessary by-product of this, marginalizing or ignoring others. What this meant in effect at this time, not only in Ryall's article but in most of the other 1970s genre work, was that the 'meaning' of a genre tended to be read out from the films which comprised that genre – this was where the 'truth' of the genre was seen to lie. This was often accompanied by an acknowledgement of the active role of the film-maker in relation to this, but rarely by any clear sense of what audiences – the third element of Ryall's triangle – were supposed to be doing in this generic relationship. Clearly audiences were important – their presence in part served to legitimize genre studies, and distinguished it from an elitist auteurism – but did they bring anything to genres other than a particular knowledge and competence (to do with familiarity with generic conventions) which enabled them to interpret genre films 'correctly'? (This is certainly how the audience is figured in Ryall's article, which concludes with an authoritative analysis of *The Searchers*, an analysis punctuated by references which imply that this reading is available to an audience if they have the appropriate knowledge.) One consequence of this film-centred approach is that the role of the audience within these critical discourses is often to serve as a rhetorical guarantor of the 'rightness' of the analysis offered by the critic. Real audiences (rather than Ed Buscombe's 'average audience') sometimes seem a million miles away.

Bearing all this in mind, it is perhaps not surprising that so much of 1970s genre work was concerned with defining particular genres, and the methodological problems involved in this process. One of the key problems was identified by, among others, Andrew Tudor:

> To take a *genre* such as a 'Western', analyse it and list its principle [*sic*] characteristics, is to beg the question that we must first isolate the body of films which are 'Westerns'. But they can only be isolated on the basis of the 'principal characteristics' which can only be discovered *from the*

films themselves after they have been isolated. That is, we are caught in a circle which first requires that the films are isolated, for which purpose a criterion is necessary, but the criterion is, in turn, meant to emerge from the empirically established common characteristics of the films.[19]

There seems to be a consensus at this time that Bazin and Warshow's tactic of using 'classic' genre films to provide a baseline for genre definition was impressionistic and generally unsatisfactory (although I have already suggested that Bazin and Warshow's writings do involve an awareness of the historical development of genres, an aspect of their work largely ignored in the 1970s). Tudor himself proposed two solutions to what he called the 'empiricist dilemma'. The first, rather arbitrary option was to classify films 'according to *a priori* chosen criteria'. The second option was 'to lean on a common cultural consensus as to what constitutes a "Western" and then go on to analyse it in detail.'[20] In other words, '*Genre* is what we collectively believe it to be.'[21] In a sense, the latter dissolves the empiricist dilemma by pointing out that the western (or other genres) is defined already via a shared set of beliefs and expectations, and, to a certain extent, places the critic in an Allowayesque position amid the audience (although, significantly, later in his argument Tudor insists that such an approach in itself is an unsatisfactory basis for a genre theory). At the same time, however, it merely replaces one problem with another, namely how does one identify the 'common cultural consensus' which 'defines' a genre?

Douglas Pye offers a rather more sceptical account of the whole business of genre definition in his 1975 article, 'Genre and Movies':

> In fact terms like 'definition' and 'classification', which seem almost unavoidable in genre criticism, are probably misleading: they suggest a greater precision of method than is in fact possible, and also tend to imply that genre criticism exists to establish territorial boundaries. It seems more likely that the outlines of any genre will remain indistinct and impossible to chart and that genre criticism should concern itself with identifying *tendencies* within generic traditions and placing individual works in relation to these.[22]

Like Alloway, Pye sees genres as offering resistance to any unitary or essentialist definition of their nature. However, unlike Alloway, his remarks are made within the context of a revisionary auteurism where an understanding of genre enables the critic to place the film-maker more successfully in relation to (in Pye's words) 'the immense fertility of convention in the American cinema',[23] and which also bestows upon the audience, rather less excitingly, 'the necessary experience to enter into the conventional relationship'.[24]

In general, and despite widespread discussion of the problem of 'definition', most critics accepted – for pragmatic reasons if no other – that there were readily identifiable entities such as 'the western' and 'the gangster film' and proceeded to elaborate on those elements which they saw as binding together the respective genres. An important influence on this activity was the work of literary theorists Rene Wellek and Austin Warren who in their book *Theory of Literature* argued that literary genres 'should be conceived ... as a grouping of literary works based, theoretically, upon both outer form (specific metre or structure) and also upon inner form (attitude, tone, purpose – more crudely, subject and audience)'.[25] Clearly literary genres are not the same as film genres, but Wellek and Warren's distinction between outer and inner form was quickly translated by critics into filmic terms so that a film genre's outer form was its iconography and its inner form its thematic identity.

One of the first to develop this idea (after Alloway of course) was Colin McArthur who in an unpublished article, 'Genre and Iconography', suggested that an iconographic study of genre would aid a semiological understanding of cinema. Focusing on the gangster film, he offered the following as a means of grasping the iconographic identity of that genre:

> The recurrent patterns of imagery can be usefully divided into three categories: those surrounding the physical presence, attributes and dress of the actors and the characters they play; those emanating from the milieux within which the characters operate; and those connected with the technology at the characters' disposal.[26]

Ed Buscombe was also influenced by Wellek and Warren's ideas. In 'The Idea of Genre in The American Cinema' he stresses the importance of an iconographic approach, and argues: 'Since we are dealing with a visual medium we ought surely to look for our defining criteria at what we actually see on the screen.'[27] However, he is less concerned than McArthur to schematize the distribution of iconographic elements across films. Instead he lists what he sees as the constitutive iconic elements of the western (which include settings, props, costumes, etc.) and suggests that 'these things operate as formal elements. That is to say, the films are not "about" them any more than a sonnet is about fourteen lines in a certain metre.'[28] He then goes on to argue that these formal elements will predispose a genre towards certain themes: 'a start can be made by saying that because of the physical setting a Western is likely to deal successfully with stories about the opposition between man and nature, and the establishment of civilisation'.[29]

Much of this iconographic work can and has been criticized for its unquestioning acceptance of a form/content distinction (something that is clearly apparent in the quotations above). However, inasmuch as it focuses on the ways in which films can be meaningful without the presence of an auteur figure, there are many useful insights to be gleaned from this material. That most of these accounts eventually turn back to a form of auteurism and away from some of the other avenues they have opened up – most notably, the ways in which audiences might relate to this site of meaning – should not detract unduly from their significance.

If for 1970s critics iconography provided the outer form of a genre, the underlying thematic preoccupations constituted its inner form. One important example of thematic genre analysis is provided in *Horizons West*, Jim Kitses's book on the western. Kitses argues that the idea of the West within American culture is 'an ambiguous, mercurial concept' which held together a number of ambivalent feelings and ideas about the progress of white American civilization. In order to illustrate this 'philosophical dialectic', Kitses sets out in tabular form a series of opposed values and ideas which, for him, identify the essential focus of thematic concerns for the western.[30]

THE WILDERNESS	CIVILIZATION
The Individual	The Community
freedom	restriction
honour	institutions
self-knowledge	illusion
integrity	compromise
self-interest	social responsibility
solipsism	democracy
Nature	Culture
purity	corruption
experience	knowledge
empiricism	legalism
pragmatism	idealism
brutalization	refinement

savagery	humanity
The West	The East
America	Europe
the frontier	America
equality	class
agrarianism	industrialism
tradition	change
the past	the future

The deliberate looseness of Kitses's defining thematic parameters enables him to describe the western as 'a loose, shifting and variegated genre with many roots and branches' and to chastise those critics who 'have ever tried to freeze the genre once and for all in a definitive model of the "classical" Western' (although in Kitses's reading of the genre, most of this variety and vitality is seen to be provided by auteurs such as John Ford, Anthony Mann and Sam Peckinpah).[31] Of course, whether a comparable table of polarities could be drawn up for other genres is another matter entirely, and this problem in turn raises the question of the applicability of Kitses's approach to genre definition in general.

Unlike Kitses, Will Wright's *Sixguns and Society: A Structural Study of the Western* will have no truck with auteurs, but, as with Kitses, one is left wondering about the effectiveness of the proposed methodology outside the relatively limited confines of the western. In his account, and in a manner strikingly reminiscent of André Bazin's account of different types of western, Wright seeks to identify particular structural formats and types within the historical progression of the western form and then attempts to relate these to broader shifts in American society. Wright argues that the western is a myth (although his notion of myth, which draws heavily upon the work of anthropologist Claude Lévi-Strauss, is very different from that proposed by Bazin) or rather a set of myths which bind the viewer/audience to a particular social order: 'the structure of the myth corresponds to the conceptual needs of social and self-understanding required by the dominant social institutions of that period; the historical changes in the structure of the myth correspond to the changes in the structure of those dominant institutions'.[32] Wright's four principal western types – the classical plot, the vengeance variation, the transition theme and the professional plot – are identified through a listing of narrative functions which, according to Wright, each film of a particular type must by definition share.

Wright's book is certainly detailed (and, in parts, dense to the point of laboriousness) and probably represents the most ambitious attempt to define once and for all a particular genre. Despite its exhaustiveness, however, this account of the western often feels rather sketchy, as if, even with all the details given here, further variants and more functions are required. In many ways, Wright's approach lives up to Tom Ryall's claim, discussed above, that genre studies should be about the defining of limits. However, it seems that in reality such an ambitious project finds it very difficult, if not impossible, to incorporate all the variations available within a particular genre into anything more than a provisional critical model. It is the combination of this approach with his mechanistic notion of how cultural production relates to dominant social institutions that finally makes Will Wright's *Sixguns and Society* an intriguing, but decidedly problematic, intervention in the field of genre criticism.

Some of the difficulties that dogged 1970s genre studies in its attempts to pin down the identity and meaning of genres can also be seen to have derived from an overinvestment in the western, which to a certain extent was figured at this time as the 'typical' genre, an understanding of which would eventually lead to an understanding of all genres. With its very specific historical and geographical setting (which in turn delimited the iconographic and thematic resources available to film-makers), the western offered an apparently hospitable terrain for 1970s genre critics to start their work. However, as it turned out, even with the western the whole business of definition was not at all straightforward; and this was even more the case with genres which did not figure prominently in this debate. For example, both horror and melodrama lacked the visual and iconographic unity of the western. It might be argued that many of the ideas and models developed within genre criticism at this time really only worked for the western (and then only to a limited extent), and when it came to constructing a broader understanding of other genres and genre in general, genre studies as it stood was relatively ill-equipped for the task.

Linked with these problems, and implicit in the very notion that genre studies was or should be about defining and analysing particular individual genres, was a tendency to see genres as being more or less discrete entities. There was little awareness of how they might relate either to each other or to the structures and conventions of Hollywood cinema generally. Douglas Pye (along with Kitses) was one of the few critics of this period to point out that 'What is needed is a sense that all these films belong to the traditions of the American narrative film, a fact that is on the whole treated as unproblematical.'[33] Unfortunately, this question did not occupy critics to any great extent throughout the first part of the 1970s and genre studies itself, when it came to the moment when it needed to move away from the western and address some of the broader issues, more or less faded away.

In 1980 Steve Neale reassessed the subject of genre, although he did so from a very different perspective to that adopted by earlier critics. Instead of beginning with and lingering over discussions of individual genres, Neale's book, *Genre*, outlined a much more wide-ranging theory of genre in terms of its particular function within classical narrative cinema. Influenced by Screen theory (to which Neale himself had been a contributor), Neale's approach involved seeing genres not 'as forms of textual codifications, but as systems of orientations, expectations and conventions that circulate between industry, text and subject'.[34] For Neale, Hollywood cinema demanded the production of films which were, to a limited extent, *different* from each other, and genres provided a means of regulating this: 'they [genres] can function to provide, simultaneously, both regulation and variety'.[35] Neale also relates these ideas to an understanding of Hollywood as an institution which seeks to position the spectator in such a way that his or her experience of cinema will be characterized by feelings of mastery and fullness. This is never achieved once and for all but is rather a process, one which involves a constant moving back and forth between moments of equilibrium and control and moments of flux and instability. For Neale, genre provides one of the means by which this process can be managed: 'genres function to move the subject from text to text and from text to narrative system, binding these instances together into a constant coherence, the coherence of the cinematic institution'.[36]

This is not the place to consider the theoretical issues raised by this model of cinema. As far as genre theory and criticism is concerned, Neale's account successfully identifies the need to think about genres in terms of the role they play within Hollywood cinema. At the same time, however, this account operates on a very abstract level, and generally seems incapable of incorporating any sense of the ways in which individual genres – or even the genre system itself – might change and develop through time. This is arguably because of the inherent idealism of the theory of cinema upon which the book depends for many of its founding assumptions. As a result, while some of the inadequacies of previous accounts of genre are usefully addressed by Neale, some of the strengths of earlier work – in particular, the close attention paid to the ways in which particular films are meaningful – are also lost.

One area of Neale's work which perpetuates one of the difficulties of 1970s genre theory is its conceptualization of the audience. Characteristically for an approach deriving from 1970s Screen theory – which, in Jim McGuigan's words, left 'virtually no conceptual space for the audience as a social rather than textual construct'[37] – Neale's account tended to see the genre audience(s) as, to all intents and purposes, an effect of textual and institutional processes. As already noted, earlier critics had constantly acknowledged the importance of the audience but had generally seemed unwilling to think about that audience (or audiences) in any systematic way, preferring as they did to focus on the relationship between film-maker and genre. This omission was all the more striking inasmuch as one of the key issues in 1970s genre studies – namely, the problem of definition – was mainly an issue for critics alone, not for the audiences for whom the genre films were intended. It could have followed from this – but did not in the period under discussion here – that audiences, and what Ed Buscombe referred to rather grudgingly as 'the aesthetic criteria of the man in the street', were rather more important in the 'meaningfulness' of genres than critics had supposed. Indeed, the problem of genre criticism was, at least in part, that the search for the identity and meaning of genre – the elusive Factor X – was being conducted in the wrong place.

Other accounts

In contrast to these approaches to genre, there are numerous studies of particular genres which largely take the existence of the genre in question (and genres in general) for granted and proceed to analyse them in terms of their relation to a socio-historical context, their ideological and political significance, or their development from their origins to the present day. Examples include work on the American horror film and feminist-orientated studies of film noir and melodrama.[38] These accounts usually incorporate discussions of what horror/film noir/melodrama as genres actually do and are about, but there is little or no discussion of the issues which so preoccupied the critics and theorists discussed elsewhere in this chapter, issues such as definition and other theoretical and methodological problems associated with thinking about film in terms of genre.

In her article '"Cinema/Ideology/Criticism" Revisited: The Progressive Genre', Barbara Klinger points out some of the dangers courted by such approaches, particularly those which seek to identify any genre as being in itself 'progressive', that is to say disruptive of Hollywood's norms.[39] As both Neale and Klinger have argued, disruption is in a sense built into the Hollywood system (with genre a means of regulating this), and any account which misses this point risks overvaluing or misreading the genre with which it is dealing (although some of the accounts criticized by Klinger are – very explicitly – rereadings of genres which seek to place the genre in relation to a particular political or cultural agenda rather than attempts simply to identify what the films are 'really' about).

Despite these dangers, however, this work has been very beneficial to an understanding of particular genres. In part, this contribution is to do with the ways in which empirical material has been amassed which has clarified the historical development of genres.[40] In part, it has taken the form of very detailed analyses of how genre films have addressed issues deriving from the context within which they were produced. Generally, we have a clearer view of the contours of genres and what goes on in them than we would have had without this work.

In a 1990 article entitled 'Questions of Genre' Steve Neale was rather more sympathetic to the notion of genres having particular histories and, importantly, also addressed the need to think about the often fluid boundaries between genres and the generic regime in which they are located.[41] He was also willing to pay far more attention to elements which had been seen as extraneous to the business of genre study in the past, namely the journalistic and trade discourses which surrounded the films in question.

This move away from an exclusive focus on the films is helpful, but it could be taken further. As Neale himself acknowledges, genres exist not only in American cinema but also in other national cinemas and for non-American audiences. The more one considers this geographical dispersal, the more genres seem to become rather fragmented entities. For example, as far as the horror genre is concerned, it arguably makes more sense to interpret British/Italian/Spanish horror films in relation to those institutions and practices which characterize the local cinematic regime rather than to lump them all together into a unified whole (with much the same to be said for other 'international' genres – melodramas, thrillers and, to a certain extent, even the western).[42] Similarly, it is unlikely that the response of American audiences to, say, the western is going to be identical with the response of European audiences, and any study of the western should take this into account. This is particularly so given that recent work both on fan culture and on European popular cinema has alerted us to some of the ways in which specific audiences can produce readings and interpretations that are not immediately available through a traditionally academic textual analysis.[43] At the very least, it is worth considering what role such readings might have in the constitution of genres.

What this would mean for genre studies in effect is a certain amount of disruption. In particular, the triangular (and in retrospect rather hermetic) relationship between film-maker, film and audience drawn by 1970s genre theory would have to be pulled apart so that other issues – to do with national cinemas and the role of audiences – could be addressed. This does not mean that broader patterns or relationships could not be drawn, but they would need to be built upon a sense of the proliferation of genres across different contexts and institutions. It is arguably only through an awareness of the 'liveliness' of genres – or their resistance to the fixed and exclusive definitions which proved so troublesome for 1970s writing on genre – that an understanding of this important area of film can be further developed.

Notes:

1 Antony Easthope, 'Notes on *Genre*', *Screen Education*, 32/33, autumn–winter, (1979–80), p. 39.
2 Paul Willemen, 'Presentation' in Steve Neale, *Genre*, London: British Film Institute, 1980, pp. 1–4.
3 André Bazin's *What is Cinema: Volume 2* (Berkeley: University of California Press, 1971) includes both 'The Western, or the American Film par excellence' and 'The Evolution of the Western' (both of which were originally published in the 1950s).
4 'The Western, or the American Film par excellence', p. 141.
5 *Ibid.*, p. 142.
6 *Ibid.*
7 'The Evolution of the Western', pp. 150–1.
8 See Robert Warshow, *The Immediate Experience*, New York: Atheneum, 1971, which contains both 'The Gangster as Tragic Hero' (originally published in 1948) and 'Movie Chronicle: The Westerner' (originally published in 1954).
9 'Movie Chronicle: The Westerner', p. 136.
10 'The Gangster as Tragic Hero', pp. 129–30.

11 Lawrence Alloway, *Violent America: The Movies 1946–1964*, New York: Museum of Modern Art, 1971, p. 19.

12 Lawrence Alloway, 'Iconography and the Movies', *Movie*, no. 7, (Feb–March 1963), pp. 4–6. Also see Erwin Panofsky's essay, 'Iconography and Iconology: An Introduction to the Study of Renaissance Art', in his book, *Meaning in the Visual Arts*, New York: Overlook Press, 1974 (originally published in 1955), pp. 26–54.

13 Alloway, *Violent America*, p. 41.

14 Andrew Tudor discusses European art cinema as a genre in *Theories of Film*, London: Secker and Warburg, 1973, pp. 145–7: also see Steve Neale, 'Art Cinema as Institution', *Screen*, vol. 22, no. 1 (1981), pp. 11–40.

15 Tudor, *Theories of Film*, p. 132.

16 Ed Buscombe, 'The Idea of Genre in the American Cinema', *Screen*, vol. 11, no. 2 (March–April 1970), p. 43.

17 Tom Ryall, 'Teaching Through Genre', *Screen Education*, no. 17 (1975), pp. 27–28.

18 See Steve Neale, *Genre*, pp. 7–17 for a discussion of 1970s genre theory.

19 Tudor, *Theories of Film*, p. 135–8.

20 *Ibid.*, p. 138.

21 *Ibid.*, p. 139.

22 Douglas Pye, 'Genre and Movies', *Movie*, no. 20 (1975), p. 29.

23 *Ibid.*, p. 30.

24 *Ibid.*

25 Quoted in Buscombe, p. 36.

26 Colin McArthur, 'Genre and Iconography', British Film Institute seminar paper, p. 2. Some of the ideas included here were incorporated into McArthur's book, *Underworld USA*, London: Secker and Warburg/British Film Institute, 1972. For a critique of McArthur, see Neale, pp. 11–13.

27 Buscombe, p. 36.

28 *Ibid.*, p. 38.

29 *Ibid.*

30 Jim Kitses, *Horizons West*, London: Thames and Hudson/British Film Institute, 1969, p. 11.

31 *Ibid.*, p. 17.

32 Will Wright, *Sixguns and Society: A Structural Study of the Western*, Berkeley: University of California Press, 1975, p. 14.

33 Pye, p. 31.

34 Neale, *Genre* p. 19.

35 *Ibid.*, p. 51.

36 *Ibid.*, p. 49.

37 Jim McGuigan, *Cultural Populism*, London: Routledge, 1992, p. 62.

38 Andrew Britton, *et al.*, eds., *The American Nightmare: Essays on the Horror Film*, Toronto: Festival of Festivals, 1979; E. Ann Kaplan, ed., *Women and*

Film Noir, London: British Film Institute, 1978; Christine Gledhill, ed., *Home is Where the Heart Is: Studies in Melodrama and the Woman's Film*, London: British Film Institute, 1987.

39 Barbara Klinger, '"Cinema/Ideology/Criticism" Revisited: The Progressive Genre' in Barry K. Grant, ed., *Film Genre Reader*, Austin: University of Texas Press, 1986, pp. 74–90.

40 For example, see David J. Skal, *Hollywood Gothic*, London: Andre Deutsch, 1992, for an invaluable historical account of the passage of Dracula from novel to screen.

41 Stephen Neale, 'Questions of Genre', *Screen*, vol. 31, no. 1, (spring 1990), pp. 45–66.

42 On European horror – still an under-researched area – see Peter Hutchings, *Hammer and Beyond: The British Horror Film*, Manchester: Manchester University Press, 1993; Leon Hunt, 'A (Sadistic) Night at the Opera: Notes on the Italian Horror Film', *Velvet Light Trap*, no. 30 (fall 1992), pp. 65–75; Kim Newman, 'Thirty Years in Another Town: The History of Italian Exploitation Part I', *Monthly Film Bulletin*, no. 624 (January 1986), pp. 20–4; David Pirie, *A Heritage of Horror: The English Gothic Cinema 1946–72*, London: Gordon Fraser, 1973; on Italian westerns see Christopher Frayling, *Spaghetti Westerns*, London: Routledge, 1981.

43 For a discussion of fans, see Henry Jenkins, *Textual Poachers*, London: Routledge, 1992; and Lisa Lewis, ed., *The Adoring Audience*, London: Routledge, 1992. For discussions of European genre cinema, see Richard Dyer and Ginette Vincendeau, eds, *Popular European Cinema*, London: Routledge, 1992.

A *big* star Arnold Schwarzenegger in *Terminator 2: Judgment Day* (1991)

Star studies

If genres have tended to be a more important category than directors for both the industry and the audience, the same is true of stars. As a result, when star studies emerged during the 1970s, it did so at least in part as a reaction against auteurism. Stars promised to be a more appropriate subject than the study of directors because they were central to the concerns of both the industry and the audience. The marketing of stars is one of the ways in which the industry attempts to ensure the stability of box-office returns, but a star's financial success is also dependent upon his or her ability to give the audience pleasure. The promise of star studies, like the promise of genre theory, was that it might allow one to address the organization of the industry, the properties of individual texts, and the experiences of the audience, and to relate all three within a small and coherent focus. Unfortunately, this promise has been barely realized. If genre theory made reference to the industry but tended to ignore the audience, star studies has made reference to the audience but tended to ignore the industry.

The star is not simply a performer, but a figure with particular associations of glamour and charisma. Not everyone in a film, therefore, is a star (though this is often forgotten even within star studies where the search for new objects of study has led to the analysis of more and more minor performers as though they were stars). Indeed, a star's status is not directly related to his or her acting ability, and as a result, it has become commonplace for certain critics of popular film to claim that stars cannot act, that they are bad actors, or that they only play themselves. Not only are such claims often misleading, but they are one of the ways in which distinctions between the star and the actor are used to reject popular tastes and privilege the tastes of more dominant groups.

In fact, this tendency can even be identified within star studies. Despite the fact that it only rarely operates around explicit distinctions between popular culture and more legitimate forms, star studies has often presented popular film as inherently conservative and claimed that the star's function is to reproduce the dominant ideology. It is therefore implied, though never explicitly stated, that popular film can somehow be distinguished from other forms of film where the performers do not necessarily fulfil ideological functions.

None the less, the main task of star studies has been to explain the appeal of stars, and it has done so through four main approaches; semiotics, intertextuality, psychoanalysis, and finally, audience studies. The first two concentrate mainly on the star as text, while the latter two concentrate on the ways in which audiences relate to stars. In the process, these approaches raise four fundamental questions: how do stars come to have meaning; how is this meaning historically produced; why do audiences identify with stars; and finally, in what different ways have audiences identified with stars.

Stars as ideological images

Probably the most significant departure in star studies was Richard Dyer's *Stars*.[1] For Dyer, the appeal of a star could not be explained by the charisma of a particular individual, but was a product of the particular meanings which that star signified. He was concerned to study stars as texts whose images were formed out of a series of signs which carried particular ideological meanings.

There are several benefits from this semiotic approach to the analysis of stars and star images. First, semiotics allows one to study the differences between stars through an analysis of the precise signs deployed in their star image. Second, it allows one to see that the appeal of stars is not the product of some unique, 'magical' quality inherent in the individual star but of the ways in which a star works in relation to certain ideological issues such as issues of class, gender or race. Finally, the relationship of the audience to the star need no longer be viewed as simply an issue of industry manipulation, but as a product of certain constructions of cultural identity. In this way, Dyer's work is able to present audience responses as the product of certain ideological processes, rather than purely individual tastes.

During the period in which Dyer was writing, it was commonly argued that one of the major effects of ideology was to suppress contradictions and present an apparently unified and coherent view of the world. As a result, Dyer argued that the appeal of stars lay in the way in which their image could resolve ideological contradictions for the audience. For example, Dyer uses the example of Marilyn Monroe who, he argues, resolved certain contradictory notions of femininity and female sexuality, particularly the meanings of sexiness and innocence. However, while he argued that the stars' image was a construct, not a pure expression of their 'real' personality, he also points out that the signs which construct this image are still deployed by someone, the actual performer. This fact is important as it is part of the way in which stars act to resolve ideological contradictions. First, the star's image resolves its contradictory elements partly because they are signified as the property of one person.[2] Second, as these meanings become attached to that person, they become naturalized. They appear to be a natural and inherent aspect of the star's individual identity rather than socially constructed. In this way, the star image achieves a double ideological closure. It reconciles contradictions, and it presents that which is social as though it were natural.

The purpose of this kind of study is therefore to open up these ideological closures in order to find out what is contradictory and arbitrary in what appears to be coherent and natural; it is the task of making visible that which seems invisible. John O. Thompson's use of the 'commutation test' is valuable in this respect.[3] This test relies on Saussure's proposition that the sign can be divided into the signifier (the material component such as the markings that make up a written word) and the signified (the concept which is associated with those markings).[4] It also relies on Barthes's extension of this proposition in his work on mythologies.[5] Barthes argues that while a particular signifier will denote a particular meaning, there will be further meanings which are connoted by that sign. He refers to a particular photographic image which signifies (or denotes) a black soldier saluting the French flag. However, he argues that this literal meaning also connotes another meaning; that blacks are loyal to France. As a result, while a particular photograph (signifier) may denote a film star, say, Arnold Schwarzenegger (signified), this image will also connote further meanings such as masculinity, Americanness, etc.

The usefulness of the 'commutation test' is that it makes the different connotations of particular stars visible through the substitution of one star for another. Many substitutions are immediately available through remakes: for example, Bridget Fonda in *The Assassin* (US, 1993) for Anne Parillaud in *Nikita* (France, 1990); Richard Gere and Jodie Foster in *Sommersby* (US/France, 1993) for Gérard Depardieu and Nathalie Baye in *Le Retour de Martin Guerre* (The Return of Martin Guerre) (France, 1982); Robert Donat, Kenneth More and Robert Powell in the three versions of *The Thirty-Nine Steps* (GB, 1939; 1959; 1978); or Dick Powell and Robert Mitchum in the two versions of *Farewell My Lovely* (US, 1944; 1975). Equally, historical decisions made in the casting of films provide examples which highlight the different ways in which star images can relate to narrative roles:[6] for example, Kim Basinger instead of Sherilyn Fenn in *Boxing Helena* (US, 1993); Jeff Bridges instead of Robert De Niro as Travis Bickle in Taxi

Driver (US, 1976); Bette Davis, Lana Turner, Tallulah Bankhead, Joan Crawford, Katherine Hepburn, etc., etc., instead of Vivien Leigh as Scarlett O'Hara in *Gone With the Wind* (US, 1939).

Stars in context

The study of stars as texts should not, and indeed cannot, be limited to the analysis of specific films or star performances. Star images are the product of intertextuality in which the non-filmic texts of promotion, publicity and criticism interact with the film text.[7] Although the star's name and body anchor the image to one person, the process of inter-textual associations is so complex that the meaning of a star's image is never limited, stable or total. The star's image is not one thing, but many things. As a result, this intertextuality is not simply an extension of the star's meaning, but is the only meaning that the star ever has. In other words, the star's image cannot exist or be known outside this shifting series of texts.

Dyer's later work on stars, *Heavenly Bodies*, examines this intertex-tuality and extends it beyond those texts which directly refer to the star.[8] Instead, he studies the star's meaning within the context of a broader network of other texts which were in circulation during the same period. These other texts are used to construct the historical con-text in which a star's image became intelligible. For example, in extended studies of Marilyn Monroe and Paul Robeson, Dyer seeks to historicize the meaning of each star's image by examining them in rela-tion to the complex of intertextual discourses on the respective issues of sexuality and ethnicity.

The aim of each study is to analyse how each star's image sought to produce a sense of individual identity within the context of modern capitalist society:

> Stars articulate what it is to be a human being in contemporary society; that is, they express the particular notion we hold of the person, of the 'individual' ... they articulate both the promise and the difficulty that the notion of individuality presents for all of us who live by it.[9]

One of the ways in which star images achieve this is by continually jux-taposing the public image of on-screen appearances (the performer) with the publicized private image of the star's off-screen life (the 'real person'). Either the two seamlessly correspond to one another, or antag-onistically conflict. In Western societies, the separation of public and private spheres which developed with the rise of capitalism, has resulted in a massive preoccupation with identifying the truth of ourselves, a truth which is supposedly hidden behind appearances.[10] In this history it is possible to understand that stars fascinate because their performances make the private self into a public spectacle, as they seem to reveal the truths of their selves within a public forum.

This notion of a 'true' self which is hidden or repressed by social life has been criticized by the French philosopher Michel Foucault.[11] In his work on the history of sexuality, Foucault suggests that we commonly think of sexuality as something which we possess, but which is repressed or distorted by society. He refers particularly to psychoanalysis as an example of this way of thinking. This position, which he refers to as 'the repressive hypothesis', he sees as misunderstanding the workings of power within society. For Foucault, the interesting thing about the periods which were supposed to be particularly repressive of sexuality was that they witnessed a massive proliferation of texts which took sexuality as their central concern. This mass of texts, he suggests, rather than simply acting to repress sexuality, combined to form a discourse of sexuality which produced the very object which it sought to study. Prior to this period, there was no real concept of sexuality. People may have engaged in sexual acts, but there was no sense that they had a particular sexual identity, a sexuality. As a result, Foucault argues that power does not work in relation to sexuality through its repression, but through active and creative processes in which the concept of sexuality is produced and acts to regulate and define specific constructions of subjectivity. In this way, sexuality and subjectivity are intimately bound together in relations of power which produce them both simultaneously. In the contemporary world, a sense of self is intimately connected to a sense of one's own, private sexuality, a thing which is seen as natural rather than social; innate rather than constructed.

In his study of Marilyn Monroe, Dyer examines the ways in which Monroe's star image served to redefine female sexuality in 1950s America. Dyer reads across a series of texts from the period in order to establish the discourse of sexuality and femininity which was circulating in the period. With references to *Playboy* and *Reader's Digest*, among other texts, a context was reconstructed in which women were encouraged to attain the quality of 'desirability', a quality which it was suggested would make both men and women happy. In this context, Monroe's public and private image 'conforms to, and is part of the construction of, what constitutes desirability in women'.[12] Monroe's blondeness and vulnerability offered a construction of female sexuality which is unthreatening and willing.

At the same time, in a context where the popularization of psychoanalysis in America had made sex a hot public issue, and in which the Kinsey report on women had addressed the question of whether American women had satisfying sex lives, Monroe's image coincided with a discourse on the psychosexual constitution of the female orgasm. To summarize Dyer's argument, the vaginal orgasm was discussed at the time as the peak of female sexual satisfaction. In this context, Monroe presented a quivering, wriggling, submissive sexuality which appeared as the visual analogue of the vaginal orgasm. She represented what was mysterious and enigmatic and made it seem visible and concrete. As Dyer points out, while women in the 1950s were encouraged to be sexually desirable, there were also more general fears concerning the emergence of a female sexuality which might exist independently from male sexuality. In this context, the vaginal orgasm was prized over the clitoral orgasm because the former defined female sexuality in terms of male sexuality in so far as it made women's pleasure dependent on penetration. This indicates the difficulty with Monroe figuring as a positive image of female sexual freedom.

The intertextual reconstruction of history faces the problem recognized by Fredric Jameson, that 'history is *not* a text' but 'is inaccessible to us except in textual form, or in other words, ... it can be approached only by way of prior (re)textualization'.[13] Texts return history in a tangible form, yet there is a need to recognize that the history which is so constructed can never be exhaustive or final. The intertextual construction of history omits the non-textual ephemera of everyday practices, which can only be imagined with reference to the textual record. Second, in constructing a context out of texts, historical analysis is faced with a basic problem. How do we tell which texts are significant and which are not, and how many texts do we need to reconstruct a context convincingly? History does not become unknowable, but it only becomes knowable in certain ways.

However, the intertextual approach is valuable in that it enables us to reconstruct the meanings which specific stars acquire at specific historical moments. Even an analysis of the present requires a work of reconstruction. Yet there is a need always to see such reconstructions as partial and provisional. In reconstructing these readings and readers, it must always be remembered that these are *hypothetical* readings and readers. The networking of texts is an endless task, and the results can only provide the possible conditions within which a star's image may have been intelligible. There may have been other ways in which a star was read. None the less, such tentative conclusions may be the best we can hope for.

Objects of desire

Both the semiotic and intertextual approaches to star images clearly imply a spectator or audience for whom these images become meaningful. However, these approaches concentrate on the meanings of texts, rather than the effect of such meanings upon the subjectivity of the audience. As a result, Dyer's work on stars has been criticized for neglecting the ways in which human subjectivity is constructed through meaning and language, and the ways in which stars figure in this process.[14]

Like Dyer, John Ellis regards stars as intertextual constructions, but he also distinguishes between the primacy of the film performance and the subsidiary texts of journalism and gossip.[15] For the spectator, the star image emerges from the fragments of subsidiary texts, but it does so as a 'incomplete image' which is only completed in the film performance.[16] As a result, Ellis argues that audiences are motivated to go to see stars by the desire to complete the puzzle of the star's image.

In his work, Ellis is drawing on psychoanalytic theories of subjectivity in order to explain why spectators are fascinated by stars and wish to identify with them. Psychoanalytic film criticism relates the cinema to a theory of desire. Christian Metz, for example, argues that the cinema was an institution for the commodification of desire.[17] The industrial economy of film production, it is argued, is reproduced by the psychic economy of the spectator's pleasure. In other words, films make their money so long as they provide pleasure, and in this process, stars play a crucial role in attracting audiences to regular cinema-going.

For Ellis, the spectator's desire to see the star image completed in performance is the result of a problem within subjectivity – its necessary incompleteness. For psychoanalytic film theory, the formation of the subject creates division and lack, and this motivates its desire. Desire is seen as the pursuit of that which will fill the lack, and so make the subject whole and complete. For Lacan, from whom much of this theory is derived, the formation of desire is also centrally bound up with the act of looking, and gives rise to what Metz calls the 'perceptual passions' of narcissism, voyeurism and fetishism.[18] As a result, psychoanalytic criticism regards the act of viewing film as fundamentally bound up with issues of desire which are related to the figure of the star.

The film text is organized around three types of looks: the spectator who looks at the screen; the camera which 'looks' at the action; and the characters within the film who look at one another. These looks create the conditions within which the spectator relates to stars, particularly through a process of identification. According to Lacan, infants go through the 'mirror stage' between the ages of six and eighteen months.[19] During this stage of their development, they anticipate a sense of autonomy by identifying with an image of self-independence which is perceived as though through a mirror.[20] In contrast to the powerlessness of the child's actual body, which Lacan refers to as the 'body-in-pieces', this 'mirror-image' appears complete and masterful. It is an object of narcissistic identification which presents an ego-ideal (or ideal self) which is believed to be the self. Cinema, it is argued, echoes this moment of the child's development, but substitutes the screen for the mirror. It replays the narcissistic process of identification. The audience identifies with stars who appear to them as complete in their idealized construction; stars become ideal selves for the audience.

The spectator also derives a sadistic pleasure in relation to stars. The star is presented as an object for the spectator who views him or her voyeuristically. The star has an exhibitionist aspect, and the spectator's sadistic sense of pleasure is derived from a position of control over the star who is presented as a spectacle which is presented for the spectator's pleasure. This voyeurism also takes on an 'illicit' quality. Unlike the theatre, where the spectator and performer are in the same room, cinema separates the spectator and the star in both time and space. The star is absent, though the cinematic image gives an impression of presence. As a result, the star's image exists for the spectator's pleasure and cannot respond to the spectator who surveys it. As Ellis puts it, the 'film photograph constructs the possibility of a voyeuristic effect of catching the star unawares',[21] as if one is spying on someone who is unaware of being watched. For this reason, it also acquires the qualities of a 'revelation' because the star's performance appears to provide the spectator with a glimpse of what the star is really like and so gives the appearance of completeness.

Fetishism also figures in the spectator's relationship to the star. For psychoanalysis, fetishism originates in the child's Oedipal anxieties when it perceives the sign of sexual difference as the mother's symbolic castration. This situation is supposed to result in a 'splitting of belief'; the child unconsciously knows that the mother lacks the phallus, but fetishizes other objects so that they will compensate for that lack. These objects acquire 'magical' qualities for the child who is then able to disavow the mother's castrated state.

The cinematic image and the image of the star are also seen to work through a similar process of fetishistic disavowal. In both cases, the spectator chooses to believe that what is absent is in fact present. The spectators may know that they are simply watching a series of light patterns upon a screen, but they choose to believe that they are actually watching real people in real locations. They may know that the star is just another person, but they choose to believe that he or she is somehow magical and special.

These concepts have particular relevance in feminist film theory. Laura Mulvey argues that in cinema pleasure is also related to issues of sexual difference and sexual politics.[22] The spectator's look, and that of the camera, are both mediated by the ways in which male characters look at female characters. It is the male star who acts as the spectator's ideal self. He is a point of identification rather than an object of desire. The female star, on the other hand, is defined as the object of his gaze. She is defined as a passive sexual spectacle. The subject of the look is defined as male, and woman is defined as the object of that look. In this way, cinema centres pleasure in male heterosexual desire, and defines the female as the passive object of male desire.

However, the viewer is held in a state of tension between fetishism and voyeurism. While looking at the woman's body involves a pleasure of voyeuristic control, the sight of that body always threatens to reawaken castration anxieties. As a result, popular cinema is said to fetishize the female body in order to avoid the threat of castration anxiety. Parts of the female body are invested with 'magical' qualities which disavow castration. The most often used examples of this process are Marilyn Monroe's breasts, Rita Hayworth's shoulders and Betty Grable's legs, although one might also include Julia Roberts's hair. All of these bodily parts are invested with power and significance. They become full of meaning as they operate to deny or disavow that which is absent. Heath uses the term 'intensities' to suggest the significance of these fetishised bits of bodies:

> The body in films is ... moments, intensities, outside a simple constant

unity of the body as a whole, the property of a some *one*; films are full
of fragments, bits of bodies, gestures, desirable traces, fetish points – if
we take fetishism here as investment in a bit, a fragment, of its own sake,
as the end of the accomplishment of a desire.[23]

This is also true of the gestures and movements which are part of a performer's performance.

However, while Ellis sees the star's performance as completing the
star image, this completion is never as total as it at first appears. The
apparent completion only provides more fragments and thereby reproduces the spectator's desire to return to the cinema in the expectation
of finally, once and for all, completing the star image.

Many critics have criticized Mulvey's tendency to neglect the pleasures of female spectatorship. As should be clear, she suggests that
spectators are addressed as though they were male, and that, as a consequence, women are only in a position either to assume an
identification with the male protagonist or else identify with the position of passive sexual object.

As a result, some psychoanalytic film critics have turned to Joan Riv-
ière's theory of 'womanliness as masquerade' as a way out of the problem. For example, Mary Ann Doane proposes that women can find
pleasure in popular cinema through their recognition of, and
identification with, the artificiality of femininity. Gender power, like all
ideological constructions, is supposed to claim legitimacy by presenting
gendered differences as though they were natural and unchanging,
rather than socially constructed and historically specific. However, the
masquerade reveals femininity as a performance; as something which is
socially constructed rather than natural and inherent. In contrast to the
taken-for-granted naturalness of the fetishized female image, Doane
suggests that the masquerade, 'in flaunting femininity, holds it at a distance ... resistance to patriarchal positioning would therefore lie in its
denial of the production of femininity as closeness, as presence-to-itself,
as, precisely, imagistic'.[24] In a similar way, as Barbara Creed suggests,
the hypermasculine bodies of Schwarzenegger and Stallone flaunt a per-
formative masculinity and so reveal masculinity to be a sign, not an
innate property of being male.[25] Rather than being a celebration of male
power, the masculine masquerade implied 'the ultimate threat ... that
under the mask there is *nothing*'.

This application of the masquerade to cinema brings together star
performances and gender performances, and implies that both are social

constructions. It also indicates another problem with Mulvey's hypothesis on male spectatorship. First, it illustrates that popular cinema continually defines men, and not just women, as the object of the look. If the body of the male action hero does progress the narrative and provide a point of identification, it is also clearly presented as a body to be looked at. As Paul Willeman and Steve Neale have suggested, looks between male characters are often sadistically motivated in order to displace the homoerotic implications of such looks.[27] Even so, popular films still include moments where there is a direct, and for that reason eroticized, contemplation of the male body. The fetishistic fragmentation of Schwarzenegger's body in the title sequence of *Commando* (US, 1985) is not justified by any sense of narrative agency and stands as a moment of pure contemplation. Likewise, the display of male torsos in the volleyball sequence of *Top Gun* (US, 1986) is prolonged without narrative purpose. It exists to display the male body. The forms and pleasures of bodily display are in fact far more various than Mulvey's account even begins to suggest.

Second, as Ian Green has suggested, cinema offers the possibility of cross-gender identification for male spectators as can be seen in the many films which feature female protagonists, unsympathetic male characters or de-eroticized female characters.[28] Spectatorship is far more complex than the easy association of male or female spectators with 'masculine' or 'feminine' positions. In the terminator films, for example, is the terminator (Arnold Schwarzenegger) really the only object of male identification? Is there really no identification with the character of Sarah Conner (Linda Hamilton)?

As a result, recent psychoanalytic film theory has seen a move away from the assumption that the spectator only identifies with a single narrative figure, and towards the claim that he or she engages in a more complex identification with the overall narrative. It has developed a theory of fantasy which suggests that any narrative provides the spectator with multiple and shifting points of identification. In this theory of fantasy, star identifications can either be of less significance than in previous forms of psychoanalysis – because the individual star is no longer seen as the defining point of the spectator's pleasure – or of more significance – because identifications are established with more than one star. Desire, then, is played through the progression of the narrative, with the spectator seemingly within the scene, occupying many and various associations with the stars.

Devotion and pretending

However, psychoanalytic theories of spectatorship have several problems. First, the spectator does not refer to actual social subjects, but to a position which is constructed and defined by the formal features of a text. This results in the second problem: psychoanalysis has tended to presuppose that it can simply deduce a text's effect upon the audience from an analysis of the ways in which the text constructs the position of the spectator. This tendency has assumed that audiences are essentially passive; that they submissively accept or adopt the position which the text constructs for them. It also, as a result, tends to present the audience as a homogeneous mass in which responses are unified and undifferentiated.

Unfortunately for these theories of spectatorship, actual audiences are not simply effects of the films which they watch. Indeed, audience members are better thought of as movie-goers because they are already historically constructed subjects who go to see movies. For the movie-goer, movie-going is only one activity alongside others such as work, education, family relations, sex, shopping, watching TV, etc. This suggests that social subjects are formed through multiple different practices, and as a result it suggests that their responses to a film are shaped by their previous history, not simply through their encounter with the film text, as psychoanalytic criticism tends to suggest. Indeed, the identities of movie-goers are differentiated in relation to a whole range of categories including class, gender, sexuality, race, nation and age, and these identities will differentiate the meaning and appeal of stars for specific movie-goers.

But such a recognition presents problems for the semiotic, intertextual and psychoanalytic traditions of star studies. First, star images can no longer be seen as closed texts with a single meaning, but must be rethought as the focus of competing readings.[29] This does not invalidate the semiotic project, but rather it requires that attention be paid to the social and historical contexts within which audiences make sense of stars. The historical and intertextual approach may hypothesize the possible conditions within which stars become intelligible, but they cannot simply stand in the place of actual audience readings.

Second, while the theory of fantasy accepts that the spectator establishes multiple identifications in relation to a text, its foundation in psychoanalytic theory still prevents its analysis of actual social subjects; it still concentrates on the analysis of texts rather than audiences. It is not just that psychoanalysis privileges inner psychic processes to the exclusion of 'external' social processes – a distinction which is dubious to say the least – but rather that the psychic processes are regarded as being formed in infantile encounters in a manner that is final, definitive and, ultimately, reductive. It also tends to universalize subject formation so that it becomes virtually impossible for one to account for the broad range of responses to stars. Psychoanalysis may offer an explanation of why we like stars in general, but it fails convincingly to account for the reasons why particular social groups like or dislike particular stars.

As a result, the dominance of semiotic and psychoanalytic approaches within contemporary film theory has meant that little work has yet been done on the study of film audiences and their relation to stars. One particularly significant exception is the work of Jackie Stacey, who has studied women's responses to Hollywood stars of the 1940s and 1950s.[30] Answering advertisements in two women's weekly magazines, her respondents revealed a variety of different types of identification. The first of these Stacey refers to as 'cinematic identificatory fantasies' and they involve the ways in which women related to stars while in the cinema. From an analysis of her respondents' letters, Stacey categorizes these trends as:

(i) 'Devotion', 'adoration' and 'worship'. These describe situations in which women movie-goers praise a star's difference from themselves. Stacey suggests that to greater and lesser degrees, such relations are based on homoerotic attachments.

(ii) 'Transcendence'. This describes the movie-goer's wish to overcome the difference between herself and the star so that she can become more like the star.

(iii) 'Aspiration' and 'inspiration'. Here the movie-goer values the personality and behaviour of the star, and sees the star's power and confidence as providing her with a positive role model. This differs from transcendence, in which the 'inspired' movie-goer wishes to replace her own identity with that of the star, because she only wishes to become like the star in certain specific respects.

Stacey's second set of categories concern 'extra-cinematic identificatory processes'. These categories relate to activities performed outside the cinema in which the movie-goer acts upon her identification with a particular star. If the previous categories were often about the sense of difference between the movie-goer and the star, the second set of categories often concern the identificatory pleasures of similarity to the star, whether or not this similarity results from the attempt to highlight

certain pre-existing traits or the acquisition of new traits. These categories are divided into the following:

(i) 'Pretending'. This describes child-like games where the partici-
pant acts out the fantasy of being the star in the full recognition of
the fact that the act is make-believe.

(ii) 'Resembling'. This describes how an actual physical similarity to
the star may be selectively emphasized in order to assume an association with the star's image.

(iii) 'Imitating'. In this case, the movie-goer's similarity is not actual
but acquired. Unlike pretending, imitation only involves assuming a
part of the star's identity, such as his or her style of singing or danc-
ing.

(iv) 'Copying'. This is another case in which similarity is not actual
but acquired, but it involves the copying of appearances, such as
hair-styles, rather than the imitation of particular styles of behaviour.

One of the strengths of this kind of work is that it offers a sense of the
distinctions between different types of identification, and in the process
it illustrates that audiences' identifications with stars are the product of
active practice, rather than passive acceptance. However, as Stacey
warns, this should not automatically lead to an uncritical celebration of
women's identifications with stars. It may suggest that such
identifications are not simply forms of ideological domination, but also
require a consideration of the ways in which women negotiate a place
for themselves between a simple acceptance or rejection of dominant
definitions of femininity. These identifications still take place within
conditions of power.

However, there are limitations to this work which prevent a thorough
consideration of the issues. First, the analysis of these identifications is
not related to a more detailed exploration of these women's everyday
lives. Despite the fact that Stacey's work does take the readings of
actual movie-goers into account, the fantasies and practices of these
movie-goers' star identifications still remain isolated from many of the
other social practices which make up their lives. What remains is a
typology of different, active positions which must consider the lives of
movie-goers in more far detail if it is to answer the questions of why,
and with what effect, these identifications are formed.

Second, while this work does show that there are many different
types of identification, it does not really explain why specific viewers
may like, dislike or remain indifferent to particular stars. The fact that
Marilyn Monroe's star image worked in relation to certain ideological

constructions of gender and sexuality does not mean that all movie-goers identified with her or even liked her as a star. Indeed, which star one likes is often highly important to movie-goers and the subject of debates and arguments between them.

Nor are such preferences innocent or individual. On the contrary, as Pierre Bourdieu has claimed, tastes are socially constructed and differentially distributed.[31] Bourdieu argues that different classes have different taste formations. Indeed, class membership, for Bourdieu, is not simply defined by the possession of specific forms of economic capital, but also by the possession of specific forms of cultural capital. But cultural capital is also related to economic capital in other ways. Its acquisition requires the investment of economic capital, as when parents decide to pay for private piano or dance lessons for their children. The investment of economic capital is made in the anticipation of some future gain, whether that be status or prestige.

However, Bourdieu is not simply suggesting that some social groups have more cultural capital than others, but that different groups will also have different forms of cultural capital. He claims that different groups develop different competences and dispositions which enable them to 'perceive, classify and memorize differently'.[32] In the area of film, for example, he notes that while some social groups classify films according to genres or stars, middle-class audiences tend to select films according to their directors.[33] But such differences are also given further significance. They are often used to make social distinctions. This even happens with regard to performers; for example, when people voice their preference for an obscure performer from European art cinema – Jean-Pierre Léaud, for example – they are usually implicitly distinguishing themselves from others who prefer more popular performers. They may be implicitly stating that 'my tastes are rarer than yours'. Indeed, it is here that the distinction between stars and actors is often made. It is often implied that the appreciation of actors requires 'rarer tastes' than the appreciation of stars. This is even true in the case of Hollywood cinema where there is a blurring between the two. For example, a preference for Robert De Niro is seen as far more legitimate and has far more cultural status than a preference for Sylvester Stallone or Arnold Schwarzenegger. But even in the, least legitimate, areas of popular cinema, preferences for one star or another are based upon cultural differences within the audience. Arnold Schwarzenegger, Mel Gibson, Bruce Willis and Harrison Ford have all made their names as the stars of action movies, but have very different star images. Certainly some viewers will like all four, but many viewers will have a particular fondness for one while also hating another. These different stars represent very different types of masculinity which may appear similar to those without the competences and disposition necessary to distinguish between them, but to other viewers they will look very different indeed. As a result, star studies needs to pay more attention not only to actual audiences, but also to the differential distribution of taste.

Conclusion

However, this question still focuses upon the star's relationship to the audience, and there is still a need for work on the place of stars within the context of film production. This chapter has reviewed the main currents within the analysis of star studies as they are manifested within film and cultural studies. These remain dominated by issues of the text-spectator relationship in which cultural consumption is studied to the exclusion of economic production. The relative absence of studies which examine stars as industrial commodities is indicative of the broad structure of debate within film and cultural studies. As Meaghan Morris comments on the current state and direction of cultural studies,

> the term production in cultural theory has atrophied instead of being re-theorized. These days it is often used as a shorthand for 'talking economics'.
>
> 'Consumption' means talking about sex, art, 'cultural politics', and fun. Before completely relegating the former to the realm of *déjà vu*, however, it may be as well to consider that in the late twentieth century, after a century of romanticism, modernism, the avant-garde, and psychoanalysis, economics, in fact, may be considerably more enigmatic than sexuality.[34]

Surprisingly, the economics of stardom and the employment of stars has seen little attention.[35] There is a need to integrate the industrial contexts of stars into analysis, not in order to give them economic pre-eminence, but merely to explain more fully the star images which we consume. It is less a question of *why* star images are produced – which assumes that producers can manipulate consumption with the intention of controlling the market – but *how* they are produced. After star studies has effectively tackled the meaning of stars in the 'big secret' discourse of Western sexuality, there still remains a need to understand where that discourse is produced.

Notes:

1 Richard Dyer, *Stars*, London: British Film Institute, 1979.
2 *Stars*, p. 30.
3 John O. Thompson, 'Screen Acting and the Commutation Test', *Screen*, 19: 2, (1978), pp. 55–69.
4 F. de Saussure, *Course in General Linguistics*, London: Fontana/Collins, 1974.
5 Roland Barthes, *Mythologies*, London: Paladin, 1973.
6 See L. Rosenkrantz, 'The Role that Got Away', *Film Comment*, 14: 1, (1978), pp. 42–8.
7 *Stars*, pp. 68–72.
8 Richard Dyer, *Heavenly Bodies*, London: British Film Institute, 1987.
9 *Heavenly Bodies*, p. 8.
10 Richard Sennett, *The Fall of Public Man*, London: Faber and Faber, 1986.
11 Michel Foucault, *The History of Sexuality: An Introduction*, Harmondsworth: Penguin, 1984.
12 *Heavenly Bodies*, p. 42.
13 Fredric Jameson, *The Political Unconscious*, Ithaca: Cornell University Press, 1981, p. 82.
14 Pam Cook, 'Star Signs', *Screen*, 20: 3/4 (1979–80) pp. 80–8.
15 John Ellis, *Visible Fictions*, London and New York: Routledge, 1982.
16 *Visible Fictions*, p. 91.
17 Christian Metz, *Psychoanalysis and Cinema: The Imaginary Signifier*, Basingstoke: Macmillan, 1982.
18 *Psychoanalysis and Cinema*, p. 58.
19 Jacques Lacan, 'The Mirror Stage as Formative of the Function of the I as Revealed in Psychoanalytic Experience', in *Ecrits*, London: Tavistock Press, 1977.
20 *Psychoanalysis and Cinema*, p. 49.
21 *Visible Fictions*, p. 100.
22 Laura Mulvey, 'Visual Pleasure and Narrative Cinema', *Screen*, 16: 3 (1975), pp. 6–18.
23 Stephen Heath, *Questions of Cinema*, London: Macmillan, 1981, p. 183.
24 Mary Ann Doane, 'Film and the Masquerade: Theorizing the Female Spectator', *Screen*, 23: 3 (1982), pp. 81–2.
25 Barbara Creed, 'From Here to Modernity: Feminism and Postmodernism', *Screen*, 28: 2 (1987), pp. 47–69.
26 C. Holmlumd, 'Masculinity as Multiple Masquerade: the "Mature" Stallone and the Stallone Clone', in S. Cohan and I. R. Hark, eds, *Screening the Male*, London and New York: Routledge, 1993, p. 218.
27 Paul Willeman, 'Antony Mann: Looking at the Male', *Framework*, 15–17 (1981) pp. 16–20; and Steve Neale, 'Masculinity as Spectacle: Reflections on Men and Mainstream Cinema', *Screen*, 24: 6 (1983), pp. 2–16.

28 Ian Green, 'Malefunction: A Contribution to the Debate on Masculinity in the Cinema', *Screen* 25: 4–5 (1984), pp. 36–48.

29 See V. N. Volosinov's concept of the 'multi-accentuality' of the sign in V. N. Volosinov, *Marxism and the Philosophy of Language*, Cambridge, Mass.: Harvard University Press, 1973, p. 23.

30 Jackie Stacey, *Star Gazing: Hollywood Cinema and Female Spectatorship*, London and New York: Routledge, 1994.

31 Pierre Bourdieu, *Distinction: A Social Critique of the Judgement of Taste*, London: Routledge, 1984.

32 *Distinction*, p. 28.

33 *Distinction*, pp. 26–8.

34 Meaghan Morris, 'Banality in Cultural Studies', *Block*, 14 (1986), p. 24.

35 See, as a sample of this kind of work, Barry King, 'Stardom as an Occupation', in Paul Kerr, ed., *The Hollywood Film Industry*, London and New York: Routledge and Kegan Paul, 1986; and Barry King, 'The Star and the Commodity: Notes Towards a Performance Theory of Stardom', *Cultural Studies*, 1: 2, pp. 145–61.

A Gremlin discusses Susan Sontag: references run riot for the media-savvy audiences of the post-classical film, *Gremlins 2* (1990).

Historical poetics

Poetics, derived from the Greek word *poiesis* (meaning 'active making'), represents one of the oldest approaches we have for analysing artistic production. A detailed history of the concept might trace it from Aristotle's *Poetics* (which dealt primarily with the epic and the tragedy as dominant forms of Greek literature) and into more contemporary times through the work of art historians such as Erwin Panofsky and E. H. Gombrich and literary scholars such as Mikhail Bakhtin and Viktor Shklovsky.[1] Poetics, broadly defined, focuses on the processes and conventions through which artworks are constructed and evaluated. Historically, poetics has included such areas as thematics (the study of motifs, iconography and themes around which artworks are constructed), constructive form (the study of larger organizational principles such as narrative) and stylistics (the study of basic aesthetic materials and patterns).[2] Poetics has encompassed both descriptive accounts (how artworks *have been* constructed) and prescriptive arguments (how artworks *should be* constructed).

Although critics accuse this formalist tradition of an apolitical fixation on art for art's sake and an ahistorical focus on the text to the exclusion of other social and economic practices, the best formalist essays situate aesthetic issues in broader contexts. Boris M. Ekenbaum's 'O. Henry and the Theory of the Short Story', for example, focuses on how the magazine market-place shaped the form and content of the American writer's short stories.[3] Bakhtin's *Rabelais and His World* links the French humorist's language and structure to the early history of the novel and to the medieval social climate, class hierarchy, and cultural practices.[4] Aesthetic form exists in social contexts, draws on contemporary social thought for its materials, and has social effects. The formalist tradition, however, believes that historical explanations must start with the work itself and move gradually towards its most immediate contexts rather than adopt global or transhistorical theories.

Historical poetics represents a contemporary inflection of this larger poetics tradition, one borrowing heavily from Russian and Slavic formalism, semiotics and structuralism, reader-response theory and cognitive psychology.[5] The historical poetics of the cinema has been most fully explored by David Bordwell and Kristin Thompson. According to Bordwell, historical poetics seeks to answer two general questions about cinema:

(1) What are the principles according to which films are constructed and by means of which they achieve particular effects?

(2) How and why have these principles arisen and changed in particular empirical circumstances?[6]

The first set of questions represent the traditional concerns of poetics with the artistic process and its conventions. The second set of questions insists on the centrality of history to our understanding of the affective and cognitive experience of the spectator and the rules, codes, and conventions governing film art.

Historical poetics may approach these questions on a highly specific level, as in Edward Branigan's detailed examination of Ozu's construction of space in *Equinox Flower* in relation to debates about Hollywood influences on Japanese film style.[7] Or writers in this tradition may sketch the dominant aesthetic principles of whole artistic movements, as in David Bordwell, Janet Staiger, and Kristin Thompson's *The Classical Hollywood Cinema*. The most complex and ambitious exploration of historical poetics to date, this book examines the norms and institutions which dominated the American cinema from 1915 to 1960.[8]

Aesthetic and historical investigation

Historical poetics is more interested in explanation than in interpretation. Much film criticism has sought to identify what films mean, with meaning understood either as originating in the world-view of a particular film-maker (as in the auteur theory) or as a product of dominant ideological assumptions in the culture at large (as in much contemporary criticism), as either implicitly present in the artwork or as visible through a close consideration of symptomatic moments of rupture or structuring absences. Historical poetics forestalls this search for meanings in order to ask other questions about how film narratives are organized, how films structure our visual and auditory experience, how films draw upon the previous knowledge and expectations of spectators. Historical poetics is primarily descriptive and explanatory, while other contemporary criticism is evaluative (in either an aesthetic or ideological sense) and interpretative.

Historical poetics is governed by an investigatory process or, as Bordwell describes it, historical poetics is 'problem-and-question-centered' and 'data-driven'. Aesthetic principles are understood as historic facts to be documented and interpreted in the larger contexts of the film's production, circulation, and reception. While such work necessarily draws on theoretical assumptions to explain and contextualize the 'data'

it gathers, researchers are ideally open to new discoveries which might test or refute their initial assumptions. As Boris Eichenbaum writes of the formal method, 'In our studies, we value a theory only as a working hypothesis to help us to discover and interpret facts ... We posit specific principles and adhere to them in so far as the material justifies them. If the material demands their refinement or change, we change or reform them.'[9]

Norms and institutions: the classical Hollywood cinema and beyond

What is perhaps most important about 'historical poetics' as an approach to aesthetic history is its movement away from great works and great authors towards a more broadly based survey of the aesthetic norms in place at a particular historical juncture. Stylistic choices are understood not simply as a means of individual expression by exceptional artists, but rather as grounded in institutional practices and larger aesthetic movements. Key to Bordwell's analysis is the conception of norms, which he derives from the work of Jan Mukarovsky.[10] Norms are not codified and inflexible rules but rather relatively flexible, common-sense assumptions artists bring to bear upon the production of artworks: 'Those norms constitute a determinant set of assumptions about how a movie should behave, about what stories it properly tells and how it should tell them, about the range and functions of film technique, and about the activities of the spectator.'[11] Artists' acceptance of the general logic underlying an aesthetic system encourages them to make certain choices from the larger vocabulary of available options. Adherence to those norms allows for the production of works which win easy approval both from the production system and from audience members. Yet disobedience of the norms is not necessarily a 'negative' act, since such formal transgressions often result in welcome artistic innovation or novelty. Any given work will be situated more or less comfortably in the dominant aesthetic tradition, though it may also borrow formal devices from outside that system as a basis for expanding the aesthetic vocabulary. The formalist tradition in historical poetics has particularly been interested in works which 'deform' or 'defamiliarize' the dominant aesthetic traditions within which they operate. Such artworks invite us to rethink our aesthetic perceptions and expectations, and through this process to look upon the world with fresh eyes.

The Classical Hollywood Cinema shows how a specific set of aesthetic norms emerged from early cinema's relationship to the well-made play and to the magazine short story, came to dominate American film production in the late silent period and held sway into the 1960s; the book suggests how these norms were structured into the Hollywood mode of production, articulated by trade press discourse and production manuals and understood by both film-makers and film-goers. Individual expression in the classical Hollywood cinema operated in the 'bounds of difference' demarcated by this system of norms. These norms included the Hollywood cinema's focus on the goal-governed protagonist as the organizing principle behind a causally structured narrative, the push towards closure or resolution, the insistence on immediate legibility and continuity, and the desire to subordinate aspects of visual and aural style to the demands of narrative exposition.

Others have expanded this mapping of classical norms into other aspects of film style, such as music, costumes, performance, or colour. Mary Beth Haralovich, for example, has investigated the conventions surrounding colour in the classical Hollywood cinema, looking both at the guidelines handed down by Technicolor and at the application of those principles in classically-constructed films.[12] This conventional understanding of colour forms a background against which she can explore Douglas Sirk's systematic and unconventional use of colour in *All that Heaven Allows*. Revising her account, John Kurton has identified several different Hollywood colour schemes, arguing that Sirk follows a less common but nevertheless conventional set of practices.[13] The norms can thus provide a baseline against which to understand the invention or innovation of individual works. Innovative film-makers can be seen as either as operating fully within the system (as in Jane Gaine's discussion of Edith Head's costume designs)[14] or as constituting a 'limited play' within and against dominant norms (as suggested in recent work on Dorothy Arzner or Oscar Micheaux). Such an account also shows how a non-Hollywood film-maker (Sergio Leone, John Woo or R. W. Fassbender) may rework the generic conventions and formal norms of the classical cinema for alternative political and aesthetic projects.

In the case of these and many other artists (post-1968 Godard for example), their political commitments help to define the conditions under which they operate and the aesthetic assumptions behind their work. In *Making Meaning*, Bordwell has called for a moratorium on interpretative criticism, yet such cases point to the murky space between formal and ideological analysis. Bordwell suggests, for example, that 'interpretation of individual films can be fruitfully renewed by a historical scholarship that seeks out the concrete and unfamiliar conditions under which all sorts of meaning can be made'.[15] Historical poetics can, in that sense, be seen as less about privileging form over ideology than promoting historical specificity over abstract theory.

Difference and the classical cinema

The Classical Hollywood Cinema is a monumental and intimidating book, focusing on the stability and continuity of classical norms rather than looking at the more localized and intrinsic norms associated with specific films, genres, periods or directors. Some criticize the book for its lack of interest in the 'differences' within the classical Hollywood system. At times, the studio era film becomes a monolithic structure so that the similarities between, say, *The Crowd*, *The Band Wagon* and *Touch of Evil* overwhelm their more distinctive qualities.[16]

However, the Bordwell–Staiger–Thompson model *does* talk about differences between Hollywood films. The absorption of alternative aesthetics or the introduction of a new technology into the Hollywood cinema necessarily involves periods of transition and experimentation before the system can fully stabilize itself around these changes. The early sound period represents one such important transitional point; film noir may be another. Even if the classical system can restabilize itself in the long term, this transitional phase generates some films which push against the margins of dominant screen practice. On one level of analysis, these works may still be classical films. On another, they suggest stress points in the classical system itself.

The acceptance of classical norms is uneven across the cinematic institution. Peter Kramer, for example, has shown how film comedy lagged behind most other genres in its adoption of the classical norms and traces this process of aesthetic resistance and assimilation in Buster Keaton's films.[17] Certain genres (the musical, pornography, comedian comedy) embraced show stopping performances at the expense of linear narrative or character consistency.[18] Since historical poetics does not see norms as rigid rules whose violation causes serious disruption or as codes which ascribe fixed meanings to formal devices, these formal discrepancies are typically understood as operating within the allowable space of 'transgression' established by the formal system itself.[19] Genres constitute their own norms, sometimes a subset of the classical system, sometimes borrowing more broadly from other aesthetic traditions, and therefore establish their own aesthetic goals and assumptions.

The differences between genres cannot, of course, be reduced to their formal norms. Genres also assume different social perspectives, different ways of structuring audience identification and cultural experience, though formal norms play a large role in defining what themes are appropriate to a particular genre and how they will be addressed. A sociological critic such as Andrew Bergman may read the Marx Brothers' *Duck Soup* as a direct expression of the social chaos of the early depression years, while an account grounded in historical poetics would stress how these political images are linked to disruptive and flamboyant tendencies in the vaudeville aesthetic which pits spontaneous protagonists against repressive antagonists.[20]

As a result of genres' intrinsic norms, a moment which might seem disruptive or disorientating in a docudrama may be accepted as more or less conventional in an animated cartoon. Even within a genre, one can distinguish between the classical realism of Disney animation (with its insistence on preserving the bodily integrity of its characters) and the more anarchic character and narrative construction associated with Chuck Jones and Tex Avery or the more abstracted and sometimes spatially disorientating visual style developed by UPA. Critics such as Donald Crafton[21] and Rick Altman[22] point towards other aesthetic logics, such as the paradigmatic focus of traditional melodrama or the comic spectacle of cinematic gags, which coexist and compete with the causality and continuity at the heart of the classical cinema. A nuanced account of these films would recognize how each operates in relation to systemic classical norms, generic conventions, aesthetic counter-traditions and their own intrinsic norms.

Similarly, historical poetics' consideration of authorship requires attention to the range of formal choices available to directors and the conditions under which authorial expression occurs. The European art cinema, for example, is understood as a formal system which strongly foregrounds the expressiveness of the film director as the source of the film's thematic and formal patterns. Other systems (such as Soviet Revolutionary cinema) seek to subordinate the director's voice to larger state interests or develop a 'group style' (such as the expressionistic look of Universal horror films or the reflexive mode of MGM musicals). Attention to formal norms can locate the competing voices which constitute the film's production (such as the ways that Stephanie Rothman

exploits the space provided her for feminist formal and thematic exploration in Roger Corman's exploitation cinema). At the same time, historical poetics may allow a closer consideration of the impact of filmic
conventions upon avant-garde or documentary film-makers generally
seen as free from the classical system.

A significant body of work has centred on pre-1915 cinema, trying to
understand its institutions, practices, and genres as distinct from the
classical period which followed it.[23] The pre-1915 cinema was long dismissed as a 'primitive' chapter in the 'evolution' of film form, as film-
makers such as Edwin S. Porter or D. W. Griffith discovered and
mastered the vocabulary of a new medium. As recent studies by Charles
Musser and Tom Gunning suggest, the works of even these canonical
figures have been misunderstood and misinterpreted, removed from the
context of cinema as a broader aesthetic institution, isolated from developments and practices of their lesser-known contemporaries, and cut off
from the different context of their production, exhibition, and reception.[24] Tom Gunning, for example, calls this period the 'cinema of
attractions', stressing its dramatically different relationship to the spectator and its closer adherence to vaudeville aesthetics. Gunning's work
locates an alternative set of norms which dominated film production
during this earlier period, one marked by showmanship rather than
effacement, spectacle rather than narrative causality, heterogeneity
rather than unity, openness rather than closure and fragmentation
rather than continuity.[25]

Rethinking aesthetic evaluation

A governing principle behind this line of enquiry has been the importance of suspending evaluation until one has fully mapped and understood the aesthetic norms appropriate to a particular group of film texts.
The privileging of classical norms as a basis for evaluating pre-1915
films blinded earlier film historians to the richness and complexity of
this period. Historical poetics rejects the notion that a universal standard, however constituted, can be applied to evaluating all artworks and
insists on more local assessments based upon a fuller historical understanding. This suspension of evaluative judgement liberates the study
of popular cinema, which has long been vexed by a priori assessments
that certain genres are inherently less worthy than those of high art.
Once all forms of cinema are understood to be both governed by artistic conventions and shaped by innovation or transgression, the tired dis-

tinction between the personal expression of high art and the conven-
tionality of popular cinema starts to break down.

For example, recent research into pornography as a genre has gained
benefit from the willingness of writers such as Linda Williams momen-
tarily to suspend the moral and ideological judgements which had
charged earlier discussions of adult cinema.[26] Instead, she traces the history of the pornographic film in terms of generic conventions (such as
the 'money shot' showing male ejaculation), formal practices (such as
camera placement or editing practices which fragment the woman's
body and present it as a visual spectacle) and plot structures (such as a
range of different relationships between sexual 'numbers' and larger
narrative developments). Williams replaces a monolithic conception of
pornography with a more diversified sense of the genre, ranging from
the voyeuristic spectacle of the early stag films through the narrative
integration of *The Opening of Misty Beethoven* to the feminist interven-
tions of Candida Royale and Annie Sprinkles.

Williams's work is not exclusively concerned with formal matters and
she, like some of the other writers discussed here, might resist being
included in the category of historical poetics. Her book is strongly influenced by the feminist psychoanalytic and Marxist ideological theory
which Bordwell and Thompson have often cast in opposition to their
own formalist project. Yet the strength of her approach has been a willingness to allow the exploration of formal principles and norms to challenge her own initial preconceptions about pornography. As other
writers have begun to examine this genre closely, broad theoretical concepts such as fetishization or objectification have been displaced or
supplemented by more nuanced attention to the role of editing, camer-
awork, and sound in the production and representation of cinematic
sexuality. Eithne Johnson, for example, has studied how the long takes
and fluid camera movements of Femme's new feminine and feminist
pornography contrasts with the disjointed, abrupt, and fragmented cutting of traditional male-made pornography.[27] The Femme style promotes a 'full body eroticism' that is dramatically different from the
obsessive display of genitals found in mainstream porn films.

This suspension of evaluation need not be permanent. A film aesthetics which precludes evaluation would be undesirable and unwork-
able. We all make evaluations all the time when we decide which films
belong on our syllabuses. We need a way to talk about the different ideological consequences of the various styles of pornographic representation Johnson identifies; we need the ability to recognize that some works

in a generic tradition make more sophisticated or innovative use of its formal vocabulary and thematic resources than others. The question isn't whether to evaluate or not, but rather what criteria allow us to evaluate a given text meaningfully. The task of historical poetics is to reconstruct *appropriate* aesthetic frameworks. A focus on content alone would ignore the fact that content has been worked upon, transformed or reshaped by formal practices and that form may set its own expectations about appropriate content. Historical poetics rejects a simple separation of form and content, seeing an understanding of form as essential to any consideration of content. By requiring us to spell out the underlying formal assumptions at work in a particular cinematic institution, historical poetics helps to denaturalize established cultural hierarchies. A scrupulous historical poetics demands a constant reassessment of canonical works as we come to understand them against new backgrounds and contexts, and a reappraisal of popular forms as we develop appropriate aesthetic frameworks.

Historical poetics and reception

Norms are seen as a shared framework of understanding between artists and consumers, both of which groups are situated in relation to formal systems and aesthetic institutions. Historical poetics offers two approaches to the question of spectatorship: one strategy foregrounds the way that textual features cue audience response, or films depend upon audience knowledge; and the other looks at intertextual and extratextual factors, studying interpretative communities to locate the conventions governing their activities.

Bordwell's *Narration in the Fiction Film* suggests the potential for a textually-based approach to film spectatorship. Here Bordwell combines a close attention to different modes of filmic narration (classical, historical–materialist, art cinema, parimeteric) and to cognitive-based models of narrative comprehension, inference, and hypothesis-testing.[28] Spectators draw upon norms and expectations from their previous film-viewing experience to make sense of the perceptual challenges posed by a new film narrative. While Bordwell's appeal to cognitive science to explain the 'viewer's activity' in textual consumption might suggest a universal model of the film-viewing experience, Bordwell opens a more explicit space for a historically and culturally situated viewer than does the subject-positioning model which dominates much contemporary film criticism. Film viewing for Bordwell is a 'dynamic psychological process' involving the interplay of perceptual capacities (such as the perception of motion or the recognition of colour and light patterns), the audience's prior knowledge and experience (which is biographically specific but which may also be intersubjective and common to many in a shared historical and cultural context) and the material and structure of the film itself ('cues, patterns, and gaps that shape the viewer's application of schemata and the testing of hypotheses'),[29] A close consideration of the formal structure of films identifies the various cues that spark cognitive, perceptual, and affective activity, while attention to broader historical movements shows the process by which spectators acquire and master the expectations governing their interpretations and inferences.

A related area of research considers the informational economy surrounding different modes of film practice. Roberta Pearson and William Uricchio have studied the place of literary adaptation in pre-1915 cinema, suggesting that films which reduce *Hamlet* or *Uncle Tom's Cabin* to a ten-minute or shorter series of silent vignettes and stock poses assume a high degree of audience knowledge. Pearson and Uricchio trace the intertextual grid (including the popularization of these works through picture postcards or burlesque house presentations) that allowed the contemporary spectator to fill in the gaps left by the story's textual presentation.[30] The inscription of meaning in early films was often carried by lecturers and showmen, such as Lyman Howe, who accompanied the films and structured them into an evening's entertainment.[31] Classical films, by contrast, are seen as more tightly structured and self-contained, depending upon a high degree of redundancy to ensure easy spectator comprehension. K. C. D'Alessandro has investigated the ways in which the genre-mixing characteristic of such contemporary science fiction films as *Gremlins*, *Robocop* and *Back to the Future* depends upon the 'mixed competencies' of viewers accustomed to reading multiple sets of expectations against one another in a tradition characterized by both an aesthetic and thematic of constant change.[32]

A contextual approach in historical poetics looks at the institutions which shape the reception of popularly circulating films. Janet Staiger's studies of the reception of such films as *Foolish Wives*, *Birth of a Nation*, *Zelig* and *Silence of the Lambs* or larger movements such as the European art cinema, draw on reader-response theory to explore the assumptions journalistic critics and popular viewers bring to the theatre with them.[33] She wants to understand the historical basis for differences in

interpretation, looking at how our responses are shaped by larger critical debates (such as those surrounding film authorship or nationalism)
and social commitments (such as the gay subcultural readings of Judy
Garland as a star performer). Working in this same tradition, Jeff
Sconce has looked at the reception community drawn to 'bad films',
such as the screen œuvre of Edward Wood (*Plan Nine from Outer Space*,
Glen or Glenda).[34] Sconce is interested both in the aesthetic features of
these films (mismatched cuts, poor continuity, wooden acting, inexplic-
able plots, narrative confusion, obvious 'movie talk',) and in the interpretative and evaluative criteria, the myths of authorship and the
notions of film style, that surface in fanzine criticism. Differing interpretative contexts shape not only what films mean (a characteristic concern of social historical or cultural studies approaches to film reception)
but what textual features seem most salient to those interpretations and
what aesthetic frameworks get adopted for evaluating such works (questions which are of especial importance to historical poetics).

Poetic politics

A politically-orientated historical poetics explores the potential relationship between aesthetic norms and broader cultural categories, such
as the taste distinctions which Pierre Bourdieu documents.[35] Taste distinctions, Bourdieu argues, are not idiosyncratic choices, natural facts,
or trivial details; rather, they emerge from specific socio-economic contexts, reflecting our relative access to educational and economic
resources, our early and prolonged exposure to differing aesthetic traditions. Taste distinctions are discriminatory, making choices between
available goods for consumption, marking distinctions between different social groups. Bourdieu describes the great divide which separates
the bourgeois and the popular aesthetics. The bourgeois aesthetic privileges contemplative distance, an aesthetic pleasure in formal experimentation and innovation, a connoisseur's eye focusing on what
distinguishes one artwork from another. The popular aesthetic is more
functionalist (rejecting style which blocks the easy comprehension of
narrative and content); the popular aesthetic also embraces a stronger
spectator identification and a more intense affective experience (more
bang for your bucks) rejected by the bourgeois tradition.[36]

Bourdieu's analysis is problematic: its transplantation from its original specifically French context to a consideration of American popular
cinema is more difficult than most of its advocates acknowledge; Bour-

dieu himself never succeeds in writing about the popular aesthetic in anything other than vaguely patronizing terms. Still, these broad distinctions (and the assumption that they originate in response to social and economic conditions) have proved useful in thinking about the historical poetics of the cinema. Writers on early cinema, for example, have traced a muting of the sensationalistic and spectacular qualities of the 'cinema of attractions' and a shift towards the deferred pleasures of narrative exposition as film-makers sought to appeal to middle class consumers as a potential-economic base for their productions.[37] Debates surrounding early comedy suggest strong tensions between the popular aesthetic of 'new humour' with its emphasis upon emotional immediacy and intensity (as displayed in vaudeville comic performances) and the more restrained and contemplative aesthetic of 'true comedy', as promoted by bourgeois magazines in turn-of-the-century America and embraced by advocates of the classical cinema.[38]

Bourdieu's work helps us to identify the political stakes in talking about popular cinema in aesthetic terms. Aesthetics is a discourse of power, claimed as the exclusive property of dominant classes as a club to use against the 'debased' tastes and preferences of the lower orders. Popular culture has often been discussed as a 'non-culture' which must be displaced by educating us in the proper models of cultural discrimination. Often, these distinctions have boiled down to a privileging of artworks that produce intellectual pleasure over those which are dominated by affective (comedy, melodrama) and bodily (horror, pornography) pleasures.[39] That historical poetics takes popular cinema seriously *as an aesthetic practice* presents a powerful challenge to this hierarchal account of artistic production. To map the aesthetics of an otherwise neglected form, then, constitutes a political act, helping to question the naturalness of the aesthetic norms separating high and low culture (and with them, the social distinctions they express and repress).

Such an assumption underlies much recent writing on black American cinema, for example, where the dominant culture's focus on sophisticated visual style has worked against our appreciation of film-makers who did not have access to the technological and economic resources of Hollywood.[40] Many critics have responded not by privileging black content over style but rather by trying to understand the ways that film-makers such as Oscar Micheaux developed their own aesthetic practices appropriate to their production and reception context. The category of the aesthetic, for these writers, is too important to ignore and too powerful to dismantle. Teshome H. Gabriel, for example, draws upon the political and cultural theories of Franz Fanon to account for the economic institutions and aesthetic practices characterizing various phases of post-colonial film-making.[41] He shows how choices in lighting style, camera placement, music, acting style, and narrative structure, which have led to a critical dismissal of third-world films as technically poor and aesthetically 'underdeveloped', reflect alternative cultural traditions. For Gabriel, these practices warrant respect on their own terms as central to the experience of third world cinema as a political and cultural force.

There is a danger, of course, that historical poetics' fascination with aesthetic defamiliarization may reconstruct hierarchical aesthetic distinctions. Some formalist accounts have tended to treat popular cinema as a baseline (a 'zero degree style') against which to read and appreciate the formal innovations of art cinema directors. Consider the hierarchical assumptions implicit within Kristin Thompson's statement that 'People who have been nurtured on an almost-exclusive diet of classical films may simply reject the notion that film viewing should be challenging and even difficult.'[42] Thompson's call to teach such viewers how to appreciate more 'difficult' and aesthetically 'satisfying' works, however well meaning, reinscribes the class distinctions that characterize the high art tradition. After all, as Thompson suggests in this same discussion, 'defamiliarization is thus an element of all artworks, but its means and degree will vary considerably and the defamiliarizing powers of a single work will change over history'. Defamiliarization is recognized against the background set of available conventions and the ability of film-makers such as Rothman, Royale, and others, to make changes in the dominant practices of popular genres may be as 'defamiliarizing', if not more so, than the ability of directors such as Bresson, Bergman or Fellini, operating within the institution of the art cinema, to surprise us with what can quickly become conventional challenges to the classical system. The concept of 'defamiliarization' does imply that the appreciative audience possesses certain knowledge or competency in film aesthetics and takes pleasure when a gifted artist twists or reshapes their expectations. Yet defamiliarization may involve a play with fan knowledge as easily as it involves a play with schoolroom knowledge, may reward the cultural competences associated with the popular aesthetic as easily as it does the cultural competence of more trained observers, and may lead to emotional intensification as readily as it does towards distanciation. The problem lies not with the concept of defamilarization so much as with our own willingness as college-educated academics to accept and appraise forms of knowledge and systems of evaluation which emerge in more popular contexts. Bourdieu himself speaks as if the appreciation of high art involves specialized knowledge while the appreciation of popular art can be taken for granted. In practice, an avid viewer of Japanese animation or reader of popular romances or fan of television soap opera must master a complex array of aesthetic and generic conventions and interpretative skills necessary for a full appreciation of these forms.

Case study: post-classical Hollywood cinema

The utility of historical poetics as an approach for talking about popular cinema may be illustrated by a more sustained example, looking at post-classical Hollywood cinema as an emergent set of aesthetic norms with a complex relationship to the classical tradition. Postmodernist critics have described a series of radical shifts in contemporary American film marked by a breakdown of classical storytelling conventions, a merger of previously separated genres, a fragmentation of linear narrative, a privileging of spectacle over causality, the odd juxtaposition of previously distinct emotional tones and aesthetic materials.[43] Some postmodern critics, most notably Fredric Jameson, see these shifts as symptomatic of the cultural logic of late capitalism, of the rising dominance of multinational corporations, the shift from a production-centred to an information-based, service-centred economy, and the fragmentation of social communities and disintegration of previously stable identities. The term postmodernism describes both a new aesthetic tradition, first identified in architecture, and later self-consciously or unconsciously developed in the other arts (what comes after realism and modernism), and a new socio-cultural logic tied to particular economic structures (what comes after pre-modern and modern societies).

The historical poetics tradition suggests another way of making sense of these formal shifts. Here the term 'post-classical' seems preferable to the terminological confusion posed by postmodernism, since it suggests both continuities and breaks with classical cinema. Adopting more immediate, middle-range explanations, such an account would see post-classical cinema as emerging from the breakdown of the studio system following the 1948 Paramount decision and the gradual dissolution of the dominance of the system of classical norms since 1960. The relationship of contemporary cinema to the group style described in *Classical Hollywood Cinema* is ambiguous. As the book's introduction suggests, its central argument is that 'between 1917 and 1960 a distinct and homogeneous style has dominated American studio film-making'.[44] This claim would suggest that something different, or at least less 'homogeneous', came after 1960 or that the dominance of the classical style was challenged in subsequent periods. In the book's concluding chapter, however, David Bordwell argues that 'the principles of classical film-making still hold sway' in contemporary Hollywood. Looking at such post-1960 films as *The China Syndrome* and *The Conversation*, Bordwell concludes they have more in common with the classical Hollywood cinema than such superficially similar art films as *Tout Va Bien* and *Blow-Up*. The contemporary cinema, he suggests, 'has absorbed narrational strategies of the art cinema while controlling them within a coherent genre framework'.[45] Bordwell's argument seems essentially correct. What is fascinating about the elliptical narratives, the abrupt cutting, the unusual camera angles and movements, the jarring juxtapositions of material found in recent films by Francis Ford Coppola, Robert Altman, William Friedkin, Bob Fosse, or Walter Hill (to name only a few obvious examples) is the ways in which these directors have taken formal devices which, in their original art cinema context, were used to establish distantiation and employ them to intensify our emotional experience of stock generic situations.

Bordwell's stress on the stability of the Hollywood system fails to acknowledge the necessary process of experimentation and accommodation which surrounds the adoption of alien aesthetic norms into the dominant classical system. Since the breakdown of the studio system, Hollywood has entered a period of prolonged and consistent formal experimentation and institutional flux with a media-savvy audience demanding consistent aesthetic novelty and difference. As a result, stylistic changes which might have unfolded over several decades under the studio system have occurred in a matter of a few years in contemporary Hollywood. In some ways, as Bordwell suggests, this experimentation has changed relatively little in the way Hollywood operates and how its films tell stories, continuing to place strong emphasis upon stars and genres as the primary appeals of commercial entertainment. In other ways, this experimentation changes everything about the informational economy and interpretative framework through which film-makers and viewers approach the contemporary cinema. A historical poetics of the cinema would want to trace the process by which the dominance of a stable set of aesthetic norms tolerated a surprisingly lengthy phase of stylistic experimentation, the process by which formal devices from the art cinema and the avant-garde were fitted to the demands of genre entertainment, and the uneven process by which critics and viewers have responded to these shifts.

The institutional structures which ensured the stability and consistency of the classical 'group style' collapsed. By treating film-makers as independent contractors, the new production system places particular emphasis on the development of an idiosyncratic style which helps to increase the market value of individual directors rather than treating them as interchangeable parts. Directors such as Steven Spielberg, David Lynch, Brian DePalma and David Cronenberg develop distinctive ways of structuring narratives, moving their camera, or cutting scenes which become known to film-goers and studio executives alike. The emergence of the auteur theory in the 1960s provided these directors with a way of articulating and defending these stylistic tendencies as uniquely valuable. Innovations by individual directors are soon duplicated industry-wide and become part of the intrinsic norms of specific genres (as has occurred with the lengthy, often unmarked subjective tracking shots characteristic of the slasher horror film).

As early as 1965, the American press spoke of a Hollywood 'New Wave', consisting of bright young directors who came to the cinema from television, including Norman Jewison, Arthur Penn, Sidney Lumet, John Frankenheimer, Stanley Kubrick, George Roy Hill, and Martin Ritt.[46] Their films, such as *The Boston Strangler*, *The Manchurian Candidate* or *The Thomas Crown Affair* were praised for their location shooting, improvisational acting, and self-conscious experimentation with swish pans, repeated actions, zooms, jumpcuts, over-amplified sounds, colour filters, extreme deep focus, intimate close-ups, freeze frames, hand-held camera, split screen, jazz scoring and sound-image mismatches, a grab-bag of devices borrowed from the European New Wave movements. This generation of film-makers was quickly displaced in the critical pantheon by the 'movie brats', film school graduates such as Spielberg, Brian De Palma, George Lucas, Francis Ford Coppola, Martin Scorsese and Paul Schrader, who came to Hollywood with a sophisticated grasp of film techniques. Later generations came to the commercial cinema from advertising and from MTV, traditions which freely borrowed from the visual vocabulary of the avant-garde. Each generation of new recruits brought new formal elements which further broadened the classical Hollywood cinema, increased their own market potential and satisfied a media-savvy audience's demands for novelty and innovation.

The viewers have watched MTV, too, not to mention endless hours of television storytelling and now the entire repertoire of the world cinema on video. It is not so much that these viewers have a short attention span, as critics protest, but rather that they know all the stories already and they are ready to shift their attention to other levels of the film presentation, to glossy colour schemes, rapid-fire editing, or dizzying camera movements which challenge their comprehension and intensify their emotional engagement. The narrative may be suggested, evoked, without having to be fully developed; narrative traditions can be merged, mixed and matched, played against each other as new hybrid forms of entertainment emerge.

The economic rationale of the new corporate conglomerates which control the film industry requires the cross-promotion and exploitation of story properties across multiple media.[47] This cross-media circulation of images further influences film aesthetics, resulting in what Justin Wyatt has described as a 'high concept' style of film-making – a focus on the surface iconography, on spectacle, rather than on narrative depth or complexity. Over time, these stylistic experiments get absorbed, so that the film remains fully comprehensible according to traditional classical criteria of causality, coherence and continuity, while adopting a range of stylistic options which would have been transgressive in the context of studio-era film-making. That this new, self-conscious style has so quickly become 'invisible' as it has moved from self-consciously auteurist films to the most mundane action flick suggests something about the stability of the classical norms and their ability to absorb innovations and borrowings from other aesthetic traditions.

Such an approach to the post-classical film may ultimately be compatible with the postmodern account of larger cultural and social shifts, but it seeks initial explanations in terms of cinematic institutions, formal practices and interpretative frameworks. As a historical poetics, it seeks to understand the relationship between this emergent film style and the shifting conditions of production, distribution and exhibition in contemporary Hollywood. Such an approach would map the aesthetic norms governing current film production and reception. Evaluative judgement should be withheld until we can develop new criteria for the meaningful critical assessment of these films. Yet at the same time, generational differences in taste (amplified by the shifting audience demographics of the post-classical cinema) might link these new formal norms with larger social and political contexts (such as changing assumptions about sexuality). Further investigation might explore the similarity and difference between this transitional phase and others in Hollywood history, such as the innovation of sound, the emergence of deep-focus cinematography, or the stylistic experimentation associated with film noir. A historical poetics would also look more closely at the different ways in which borrowed formal devices operate in post-classical cinema, the European art film, the avant-garde, music video and advertising and at the ways that the same narrative gets transformed as it moves across the new entertainment supersystem. Comparative study is a useful way to understand the interplay of aesthetics, commerce and ideology. Such a model provides appropriate backgrounds for examining specific films, genres, and film-makers who operate in the post-classical cinema, as well as addressing issues such as the aesthetic consequences of remakes, sequels and adaptations.

Notes:

1 For Gombrich's work, see especially E. H. Gombrich, *Art and Illusion: A Study in the Psychology of Pictorial Representation*, Princeton: Princeton University Press, 1969. For useful overviews of the Russian formalist tradition, see Landislav Matejka and Krystyna Pomorska, eds, *Readings in Russian Poetics: Formalist and Structuralist Views*, Cambridge: MIT Press, 1971; Lee T. Lemon and Marion J. Reis, eds, *Russian Formalist Criticism: Four Essays*, Lincoln: Nebraska University Press, 1965; Victor Erlich, *Russian Formalism: History–Doctrine*, The Hague: Mouton, 1969. On the Russian formalists' writings on cinematic poetics, see Herbert Eagle, ed., *Russian Formalist Film Theory*, Ann Arbor: University of Michigan Press, 1981 and Richard Tayler, ed., *The Poetics of Cinema, Russian Poetics in Translation*, no. 9, 1982. For Bakhtin, see especially Mikhail Bakhtin, *The Dialogic Imagination: Four Essays*, Austin: University of Texas Press, 1981; *Problems in Dostoevsky's Poetics*, Minneapolis: University of Minnesota Press, 1984; Mikhail Bakhtin and P. N. Medvedev, *The Formal Method in Literary Scholarship: An Introduction to Sociological Poetics*, Baltimore: The Johns Hopkins University Press, 1991.

2 See David Bordwell, 'Historical Poetics of Cinema', in Barton Palmer, ed., *The Cinematic Text: Methods and Approaches*, Atlanta: Georgia State University Press, 1988.

3 Boris M. Ejxenbaum [Ekenbaum], 'O. Henry and the Theory of the Short Story', in *Readings in Russian Poetics*, pp. 227–72.

4 Mikhail Bakhtin, *Rabelais and his World*, Bloomington: Indiana University Press, 1984.

5 The relationship between Bordwell's concept of historical poetics and

Kristin Thompson's notion of neoformalist criticism is a complex one which Bordwell addresses in the essays cited here. Thompson's own account of her approach can be found in *Breaking the Glass Armor: Neoformalist Film Analysis*, Princeton, Princeton University Press, 1988; and *Eisenstein's Ivan the Terrible: A Neoformalist Analysis*, Princeton: Princeton University Press, 1981. As a term, historical poetics has been adopted almost exclusively by Bordwell and a few other writers who have been closely associated with him. Bordwell goes to some trouble in his debate with Barry King to stress the 'differences' within the work of his University of Wisconsin students and colleagues. See Barry King, 'The Wisconsin Project', Screen, 27(6), 1986, pp. 74–88; Barry King, 'The Story Continues ...', *Screen*, 28(3), 1987, pp. 56–82; David Bordwell, 'Adventures in the Highlands of Theory', *Screen*, 29(1), 1988, pp. 72–97; Janet Staiger, 'Reading King's Reading', *Screen*, 29(1), 1988, pp. 54–70; Kristin Thompson, 'Wisconsin Project or King's Project', *Screen*, 29(1), 1988, pp. 48–53; Barry King, 'A Reply to Bordwell, Staiger and Thompson', *Screen*, 29(1), 1988, pp. 98–118. In 'Historical Poetics of the Cinema', Bordwell suggests that the concept of historical poetics can include critics as diverse as André Bazin, Raymond Bellour, Thiery Kuntzel, Roland Barthes, Nelson Goodman, and Noel Burch. In the conclusion to *Making Meaning: Inference and Rhetoric in the Interpretation of Cinema*, Cambridge, Mass.: Harvard University Press, 1989, Bordwell identifies Donald Crafton, André Gaudreault, Tom Gunning, Charles Musser, Janet Staiger, Charles Wolfe, Lea Jacobs and Richard Maltby as recent writers working loosely within the area of historical poetics. Following Bordwell's lead, I am choosing to include within this discussion many writers who may not conceptualize their work as historical poetics but who nevertheless observe some of its basic principles and assumptions.

6 'Historical Poetics of the Cinema'.

7 Edward Branigan, 'The Space of *Equinox Flower*', in Peter Lehman, ed., *Close Viewings: An Anthology of New Film Criticism*, Tallahassee: Florida State University Press, 1990, pp. 73–108. For other work on Ozu's use of space, a central question in the neoformalist tradition, see Kristin Thompson and David Bordwell, 'Space and Narrative in the Films of Ozu', *Screen*, 17(2), 1976, pp. 46–55; Noel Burch, *To the Distant Observer: Form and Meaning in Japanese Cinema*, Berkeley: University of California Press, 1979; Kristin Thompson, 'Notes on the Spatial System in Ozu's Early Films', *Wide Angle*, 1(4), 1977, pp. 8–17; and David Bordwell, *Ozu and the Poetics of Cinema*, Princeton: Princeton University Press, 1988.

8 David Bordwell, Janet Staiger and Kristin Thompson, *The Classical Hollywood Cinema: Film Style and Mode of Production to 1960*, New York: Columbia University Press, 1985.

9 Boris Eichenbaum [Ekenbaum], 'The Theory of the "Formal Method"', in *Russian Formalist Criticism: Four Essays*, pp. 102–3.

10 Jan Mukarovsky, 'The Aesthetic Norm', in John Burbank and Peter Steiner, eds. and trans., *Structure, Sign and Function*, New Haven: Yale University Press, 1977, pp. 49–54.

11 *The Classical Hollywood Cinema*, p. 3.

12 Mary Beth Haralovich, '*All That Heaven Allows:* Color, Narrative Space, and Melodrama', in Peter Lehman, ed., *Close Viewings: An Anthology of New Film Criticism*, Tallahassee: Florida State University Press, 1990.

13 John Kurton, 'Red, White and Hot Color: The Technicolor Canon', unpublished manuscript.

14 Jane Gaines, 'Costume and Narrative: How the Dress Tells the Woman's Story', in Jane Gaines and Charlotte Herzog, eds, *Fabrications*, New York: Routledge, 1991, pp. 180–211.

15 *Making Meanings*, p. 272. For an example of the kind of historically-informed interpretations Bordwell embraces, see Lea Jacobs, *Reforming Women: Censorship and the Feminine Ideal in Hollywood, 1929–1942*, Madison: University of Wisconsin Press, 1981.

16 See, for example, Andrew Britton, 'The Philosophy of the Pigeonhole: Wisconsin Formalism and "The Classical Style" ', *Cineaction*, 15, winter 1988/89, pp. 47–63.

17 Peter Kramer, 'Vitagraph, Slapstick and Early Cinema', *Screen*, spring 1988, pp. 99–104; Peter Kramer, 'Derailing the Honeymoon Express: Comicality and Narrative Closure in Buster Keaton's *The Blacksmith*', *The Velvet Light Trap*, spring 1989, pp. 101–16; Peter Kramer, 'The Making of a Comic Star: Buster Keaton and *The Saphead*' in Kristine Brunslova Karnack and Henry Jenkins, eds, *Classical Hollywood Comedy*, New York: Routledge, 1994. For a similar argument, see Tom Gunning, 'Crazy Machines in the Garden of Forking Paths: Mischief Gags and the Origins of the American Film Comedy', in *Classical Hollywood Comedy*.

18 Rick Altman, *The American Film Musical*, Bloomington: Indiana University Press, 1987; Jane Feuer, *The Hollywood Musical*, Bloomington: Indiana University Press, 1982; Linda Williams, *Hardcore: Power, Pleasure and the 'Frenzy of the Visible'*, Berkeley: University of California Press, 1992; Steve Seidman, *Comedian Comedy: A Tradition in Hollywood Film*, Ann Arbor: UMI Research, 1981; and Frank Krutnik, 'The Clown-Prints of Comedy', *Screen*, 4–5, pp. 50–9. Krutnik returns to this model in 'the Spanner in the Works?', in *Classical Hollywood Comedy*.

19 *The Classical Hollywood Cinema*, pp. 70–84. See also Henry Jenkins, *What Made Pistachio Nuts?: Early Sound Comedy and the Vaudeville Experience*, New York: Columbia University Press, 1992, especially chapter one, and the introductory essays in *Classical Hollywood Comedy*.

20 Andrew Bergman, *We're in the Money: Depression America and its Films*, New York: Harper and Row, 1971; and H. Jenkins, *What Made Pistachio Nuts?*

21 Donald Crafton, 'Pie and Chase: Gag and Narrative in Early Film Comedy', in *Classical Hollywood Comedy*.

22 Rick Altman, 'Dickens, Griffith and Film Theory Today', in Jane Gaines, ed., *Classical Hollywood Narrative: The Paradigm Wars*, Durham, NC: Duke University Press, 1992, pp. 9–48.

23 For overviews of this work, see Noel Burch, *Life to Those Shadows*, London: British Film Institute, 1990; Thomas Elsaesser, ed., *Early Cinema: Space, Frame and Narrative*, London: British Film Institute, 1990; John L. Fell, ed., *Film Before Griffith*, Berkeley: University of California Press, 1983; Charles Musser, *The Emergence of Cinema: The American Screen to 1907*, New York: Scribner/Macmillan, 1990. Research in this tradition is regularly featured in *Isis* and *Griffithana*.

24 Charles Musser, *Before the Nickelodeon: Edwin S. Porter and the Edison Manufacturing Company*, Berkeley: University of California Press, 1991; Tom Gunning, *D. W. Griffith and the Origins of the American Narrative Film: The Early Years at Biograph*, Chicago: University of Illinois Press, 1991.

25 Tom Gunning, 'The Cinema of Attractions: Early Film, its Spectator and the Avant-garde', in *Early Cinema: Space, Frame, Narrative*, p. 59. See also Tom Gunning, 'Non-Continuity, Continuity, Discontinuity: a Theory of Genres in Early Films' and 'Primitive Cinema: A Frame-up? Or, the Trick's on Us', in *Early Cinema: Space, Frame, Narrative*.

26 *Hardcore: Power, Pleasure and the 'Frenzy of the Visible'*.

27 Eithne Johnson, 'Excess and Ecstasy: Constructing Female Pleasure in Porn Movies', *The Velvet Light Trap*, forthcoming.

28 Some might claim that cognitive psychology can be read as being as much a 'doctrine' or 'dogma' as the psychoanalytic tradition Bordwell often criticizes. There are important differences, however, in the ways that these models inform their critical practice. Psychoanalytic models provide interpretative categories which get mapped on to formal devices. Cognitive psychology is interested in *how* things mean, not *what* they mean. It describes processes of perception, cognition and affect applicable to a range of different formal and ideological systems. This does not mean that cognitive psychology is 'doctrine-free', however. Cognitive accounts often adopt a functionalist, goal-driven and rationalistic conception of human nature which privileges cognition over affect as the central force in our reception of films. There has been little systematic critique of the ideological assumptions underpinning cognitive approaches.

29 *Narration in the Fiction Film*, pp. 32–3. For a useful overview of the potential contributions of cognitive models to film theory, see David Bordwell, 'A Case for Cognitivism', *Iris*, 5(2). Other works within this cognitive tradition would include Edward Branigan, *Narrative Comprehension and Film*, New York: Routledge, Chapman and Hall, 1992; Noel Carroll, *Mystifying*

Movies: Fads and Fallacies in Contemporary Film Theory, New York: Columbia University Press, 1988; and Noel Carroll, *The Philosophy of Horror: Paradoxes of the Heart*, New York: Routledge, 1990. See also the special issue of *Iris*, 5(2), devoted to 'Cinema and Cognitive Psychology'.

30 William Uricchio and Roberta E. Pearson, *Reframing Culture: The Case of the Vitagraph Quality Films*, Princeton: Princeton University Press, 1993.

31 Charles Musser and Carol Nelson, *High-Class Moving Pictures: Lyman H. Howe and the Forgotten Era of Travelling Exhibition*, Princeton: Princeton University Press, 1991.

32 Kathryn D'Alessandro, *Mixed Competence: The Tendency Toward Hybridization in Post-1976 Science Fiction Films*, unpublished Ph.D. dissertation, University of Wisconsin–Madison, 1992.

33 Janet Staiger, *Interpreting Films: Studies in the Historical Reception of American Cinema*, Princeton: Princeton University Press, 1992; Janet Staiger, 'Taboos and Totems: Cultural Meanings of *The Silence of the Lambs*', in *Film Theory Goes to the Movies*, New York: Routledge, 1993, pp. 142–54.

34 Jeffrey Allen Sconce, *Colonizing Cinematic History: The Cult of 'Bad' Cinema and the Textuality of the 'Badfilm'*, Master's Thesis, University of Texas–Austin, 1989.

35 Pierre Bourdieu, *Distinction: A Social Critique of the Judgement of Taste*, Cambridge, Mass.: Harvard University Press, 1979.

36 Bourdieu, p. 33. Following Bourdieu, then, a historical poetics of the popular cinema would want to explore which formal devices worked to intensify affective immediacy and audience identification, as well as to examine the critical categories by which popular audiences discussed and evaluated those aesthetic experiences.

37 See, for example, Tom Gunning, 'Weaving a Narrative: Style and Economic Background in Griffith's Biograph Films', in Elsaesser, pp. 336–47.

38 Jenkins, *Pistachio Nuts*, chapter two; and Charles J. Malland, *Chaplin and American Culture: The Evolution of a Star Image*, Princeton: Princeton University Press, 1989.

39 On this point, see Linda Williams, 'Film Bodies: Gender, Genre and Excess', *Film Quarterly*, vol. 44, no. 4 (1991), pp. 2–13.

40 See, for example, the essays contained in Manthia Diawara, ed., *Black American Cinema*, New York: Routledge, 1993; and Jim Pines and Paul Willeman, eds, *Questions of the Third Cinema*, London: British Film Institute, 1989.

41 Teshome H. Gabriel, 'Towards a Critical Theory of Third World Films', in *Questions of the Third Cinema*, pp. 30–52.

42 Thompson, *Glass Armour*, p. 33.

43 See, for example, Scott Bukatman, *Terminal Identity: The Virtual Subject in Postmodern Science Fiction*, Durham, NC: Duke University Press, 1993; James Collins, *Uncommon Cultures: Popular Culture and the Postmodern*,

New York: Routledge, 1989; Timothy Corrigan, *Cinema Without Walls: Movies and Culture After Vietnam*, New Brunswick: Rutgers University Press, 1991; Anne Friedberg, *Window Shopping: Cinema and the Postmodern*, Berkeley: University of California Press, 1993; and Fredric Jameson, *Signitures of the Visible*, New York: Routledge, 1990.

44 Bordwell, Staiger and Thompson, p. 3.

45 Bordwell, Staiger and Thompson, p. 377.

46 Peter Hart, 'New Breed Scans Horizons', *New York Times*, 10 January 1965.

47 Eileen Meehan, 'Holy Commodity Fetish, Batman!: The Political Economy of a Commercial Intertext', in Roberta E. Pearson and William Uricchio, eds, *The Many Lives of Batman: Critical Approaches to a Superhero and His Media*, New York: Routledge, 1991, pp. 47–65; Justin Wyatt, 'High Concept, Product Differentiation, and the Contemporary US Film Industry', *Current Research in Film*, 5, 1991, pp. 86–105; Justin Wyatt and R. L. Rutsky, 'High Concept: Abstracting the Postmodern', *Wide Angle*, 10: 4, 1988, pp. 42–9.

A passive object of male desire? Ripley (Sigourney Weaver) fights back in *Aliens* (1986)

Screen theory

As should be clear from previous chapters, screen theory[1] represented the summation of a series of debates. Grounded in a reaction against auteurism, it developed out of an attempt to move beyond the model of communication inherent in auteur theory, a model which placed the individual author at the centre of a film's meaning and significance, and simply saw film texts as a medium through which authors express themselves.

Like historical poetics, the ambitions of screen theory were global rather than local. Screen theory was not concerned with the analysis of one aspect of cinema (authorship, genre or stars), but with the form of cinema itself. It sought to discuss the formal features of film *as* film. It also differed from the earlier stages of genre theory, star studies and historical poetics through its claim that these approaches had not gone far enough in reformulating the model of communication inherent in auteurism. If auteurism had seen sign systems as a means of self-expression, it was claimed, genre theory, star studies and historical poetics still saw meaning as being embodied within the text itself.

In response, screen theory not only drew on Saussurian linguistics, but also on Althusarian Marxism and, particularly in its later stages, on Lacanian psychoanalysis to examine the way in which meaning is produced through the encounter between the text and the spectator. In doing so, it aimed

> first, to work towards a greater understanding of the relationship between viewer and film; second, to assess the ideological implications of this process; and third, to do so not so much in the interests of scientific accuracy or high scholarly endeavour but rather with the political aim to develop 'a new social practice of the cinema'...[2]

Implicit in this project are therefore two claims: first, that ideology is less a matter of particular opinions than of the ways in which people perceive themselves to be coherent individuals; and second, that existing cinema is somehow implicated in the maintenance of ideology and needs to be countered. These claims may not be problems in themselves, but the particular way in which they were formulated within screen theory did result in some difficulties.

In the case of the first claim, for example, screen theory asserted that it was less interested in the politics of representation – how things were represented – than in the politics of signification – the ideological effects of significatory processes. This has led to two major problems. First, despite their claim to discuss the formal features of texts and to be more interested in significatory processes than the particular ways in which issues are presented, many articles only allude to the former while actually concentrating on the latter. These articles often focus on narrative and character, rather than on cutting and editing. There is a sense in which screen theory tended to assume too quickly that its theoretical claims had been proved, and to make connections which needed far greater analysis. For example, its assumption that 'cinema contributed to the maintenance of capitalism; [or] from a more recent feminist perspective, [that] it performs the same service for patriarchy'[3] created immense problems which have never really been fully acknowledged. Too often screen theory seemed to fall into the very reductionist functionalism which it attacked elsewhere.

These factors all resulted in the second problem. Screen theory had a strong tendency to homogenize texts and to fail 'to do justice to the subtlety of individual films'.[4] Too often its global theories merely became templates or stencils through which individual films, or groups of films, were read, and this situation had the effect of ignoring or repressing that which did not fit. For example, the stress on signification rather than representation meant that films which espoused very different ideological positions (for example, pro- or anti-capitalist) were seen as being indistinguishable, because they could be fitted into a broader formal category, such as the 'classic realist text'.

It is here that the issue of the popular becomes most problematic. Screen theory tended to view popular film as an inherently ideological system. It is true that it often attacked certain varieties of art cinema, and in the case of McCabe's theory of the classic realist text, it has been argued that he 'avoids the charge of intellectual snobbery by spanning the high art/mass culture divide, "lumping together *The Grapes of Wrath* and *The Sound of Music*"'.[5] But such a claim is not entirely accurate. Screen theory may have seen popular and elite forms of film as often sharing certain formal features, but popular film was consigned to the realms of the ideological and conservative, almost without exception.[6] The opposition was not between high and low culture, it is true, but it was between the avant-garde and the non-avant-garde. This may have lumped some art cinema in with the popular, but it consigned the popular to the ideologically conservative.

What one finds is a distinction between the open and the closed text, or the text of pleasure and the text of bliss (or *jouissance*). The closed text, or the text of pleasure, is seen as an ideological text. It does not challenge the spectator's perceptions, and is therefore easily consum-

able. The open text, or the text of bliss, on the other hand, is associated with the radical and the avant-garde. It disrupts the reader's perceptions, and refuses to resolve ideological contradictions. As a result,
many screen theorists referred to Barthes's distinction between the
'readerly text' (the text of pleasure which is easy to consume) and the
'writerly text' (the text of bliss which forces the reader to 'write' the
text, or actively to engage with the text in the production of its meaning).[7] As a result, it is not surprising to find theorists claiming that a
popular film works 'in the service of pleasure ... a pleasure which
depends on the suppressing of conflicts and contradictions' because
they already know that this is 'a requirement of the mass audience
film'.[8] In this way, screen theory, for all its sophistication and complexity, ends up reproducing a theory of the popular which goes back
at least as far as mass culture theory.

From structural linguistics to Althusserian Marxism

As previously stated, screen theory's main objection to auteur theory
centred on its model of communication. Auteur theory, it was argued,
saw the auteur as an individual who used visual language to express his
or her world-view to the audience. The primary problem with this
model, for screen theory, was that it presented the auteur and the
viewer as essentially independent and autonomous individuals for
whom visual language was simply a medium of exchange. In contrast,
screen theory drew on Saussurian or structural linguistics to argue that
language is a system of structures, rules and codes which does not just
pre-exist individuals, but actually constitutes them.

For Saussure, the meaning of a particular sign (such as a word) is not
given by individuals who express themselves through it, but through its
place in the linguistic system.[9] It was argued that any sign was made up
of two components: the signifier (for example, the sounds or shapes
which make up a spoken or written word); and the signified, which is
the particular meaning associated with those sounds or shapes. However, just as the signifier 'cat' is only distinguished by its relations of
similarity and difference to other signifiers such as 'bat' or 'cart', the
signified (or the meaning associated with that signifier) is not defined
by its reference to some external object which exists in the world, but
though its relation to other signs.

While one may actually experience the world as though it were made
up of a series of discrete objects with particular meanings which one

simply names though the use of words, according to Saussurian linguistics, it is language which divides the world up into objects and gives them meaning. One may experience the world as containing classes of objects such as trees, bushes and shrubs, but there is in fact only a continuum which is divided up and distinguished by linguistic terms. Probably the most common example used to illustrate this point, despite evidence that this example may not be accurate, is the comparison between European and Eskimo cultures. In most European languages there is only one word for ice – it is our only category – but in Eskimo cultures there are many different words for ice. Eskimos do not have one object – ice – but a whole series of different objects which have quite different meanings.

Saussure also drew a distinction between the paradigmatic and the syntagmatic structures of language. The paradigmatic refers to the relationship between words which are similar but different: for example, feline is an alternative for cat. The syntagmatic, on the other hand, refers to issues of syntax or the way in which words are put together, in a sentence, for example. One does not just string words together, but obeys certain rules which govern the ways in which words can combine to produce meaning. For example, the simpliest combination is that of subject, verb and object, as in the sentence: I (subject) hit (verb) the wall (object).

These theories have major implications. Not only do they imply that language structures the ways in which one thinks, but also that one's very sense of identity (who one is) is a product of language. For structuralists, language not only structures one's perceptions of the world, but also one's sense of being a independent and autonomous self which exists in relation to an external world. For example, let us take the sentence, 'I hit the wall'. It is the structures of language which make one think that there is a subject (I) which performs an action (hit) upon an external object (the wall). The same is true if one reverses the sentence and suggests that, in fact, the wall hit me. It is for this reason that structuralists are given to saying that the self is a 'function' of language. In using language, one is positioned either as the subject or the object of an action; either as an independent and autonomous being which performs an action upon an equally independent object, or as an independent and autonomous being which is acted upon by another.

This theoretical basis was developed by screen theory in two interrelated ways. First, it was pointed out that one of the main features of most cinematic forms were that they were narratives. This situation, it was stressed, was not natural or necessary; there was no reason why cinema should have developed in this way. It was also emphasized that narrative is a particular way of structuring and ordering material, that it has its own structures, rules and codes. Most obviously, a narrative will have a beginning, a middle and an end. This relates to the second development, a critique of realism. Just as Saussure had argued that signs do not simply refer to pre-existing objects, screen theorists pointed out that texts do not simply refer to a pre-existing reality. The narrative structure of beginning, middle and end, for example, may appear to be realistic, but it is a particular way of structuring the world which selects material and orders it in particular ways. For example, many film-goers jokingly comment on the fact that it is unusual for films to show their main characters sleeping for eight hours a night, or even show them going to the toilet (unless of course this has a specific narrative motivation). It is for this reason that film narratives do not occur in 'real time'. A two-hour film may cover fifty years, while it selects only those elements which are deemed important to the narrative. Such selection is important if a narrative is to organize a central issue which can be resolved and so establish an ending.

These concerns underpin Colin McCabe's theory of the classic realist text. For McCabe, the classic realist text works to produce the 'illusion' of realism, an illusion which has certain ideological implications. The classic realist text denies contradiction within the social world; it may present many different points of view, and even needs to include conflicts between them, but ultimately it works to repress or disqualify these difference by providing a privileged point of view.

McCabe's work starts out from an analysis of the nineteenth-century novel, but also applies its positions to film. In the case of the novel, it is argued, this privileged point of view is usually provided by an omniscient narrator, a narrator who knows all – even the private thoughts of characters within the novel. This narrator is presented as 'the voice of truth', and is able to interpret, disqualify or guarantee the views and perceptions of characters within the narrative.

Film, however, seems somewhat different. There is rarely an omniscient narrator. Instead, it appears, the audience is simply presented with a series of different points of view as the camera angles change. However, McCabe claims that the camera itself becomes a guarantor of truth, and he uses the example of *Klute* to illustrate this point. While the audience may hear the main character, Bree Daniels, express doubts over her relationship with John Klute, the camera shows her packing up and leaving with him at the end and so establishes her real desires.

According to McCabe, not only does this form effectively deny all social contradictions, and present the social world as one which can ultimately be mastered and understood, but it also has specific ideological effects on the viewer. The viewers of the classic realist text are presented with an apparently direct assess to the truth which discourages them from thinking for themselves (a position which seems remarkably similar to mass culture theory's concept of the 'Built-In Reaction' which was discussed in chapter one). In the process, they also have their sense of themselves as independent and autonomous individuals reaffirmed. The viewers are situated 'outside the realm of contradiction and action – outside of production'.[10] They relate to the film as though they are outside it, as though they were independent and autonomous beings witnessing an equally autonomous and independent social world.

This position draws directly upon Althusser's theory of ideology in which he claims that ideology does not function through the indoctrination of particular ideas and opinions, but through the 'interpellation' of the subject.[11] Although a Marxist, Althusser drew heavily on the structuralist ideas of his period (the 1960s), and he claimed that ideology was a system by which individuals came to see themselves as independent and autonomous beings who existed not as the effect of social structures, but rather as their cause.

This situation was achieved, according to Althusser, by the ways in which individuals were interpellated by society, 'interpellation' meaning to be hailed or addressed. In this way, this theory relates to the claim of Saussurian linguistics that the subject is a function of language. Just as when one is addressed as 'you', one is positioned as the subject or the object of the sentence, so, for Althusser, subjects are addressed by society. One takes up positions in society which are defined by the social structure. These positions are not natural and inherent to individuals, but individuals 'misrecognize' or mistake these positions as being natural and inherent to themselves.

In this way Althusser attempted to provide a critique of individualism, an ideology in which society is mistakenly seen as simply the interaction between independent and autonomous beings, rather than a structure which produces subjects for itself. However, Althusser's position is not simply that this misrecognition is an illusion, although in many ways he overstated his difference from theories of false consciousness. On the contrary, as Stuart Hall has argued in relation to the capitalist market 'The market of course, *really exists*. It is not the figment of anyone's imagination. It is a *mediation* which enables one kind of relation (social) to appear (i.e. *really* to appear) as another kind of relation (individual)."[12] Society is organized as though it were made up of autonomous and independent beings, but such a situation disguises the fact that it is actually a social structure within which subjects are positioned.

Indeed, Althusser's theory of ideology has been used to point out that narratives are fundamentally subject-centred in their organization. They are usually the story of a central character whose concerns are privileged. This mode of organization, it is argued, acts to individualize social conflicts and so legitimate the existing social structure. This is related to McCabe's claim that the classic realist text cannot deal with the social world as contradictory.

The pleasure offered by narrative, it has been argued, is based upon the process of narrative closure within which conflicts and contradictions are resolved. As has been stated, narratives are said to set out from a situation of order (beginning), to move through a period of disorder and conflict (middle), and finally to reach a point of closure and completion in which disruptive elements are contained or destroyed, and the original order is re-established. The viewer's pleasure is supposed to depend upon the expectation that the narrative will reach this particular type of conclusion, and the eventual fulfilment of this expectation. Narrative closure is supposed not only to give the viewer a sense of mastery and coherence, but also to legitimate the existing social system.

Conflict and struggle are therefore necessary to narrative, but they are not presented as the product of inherent contradictions within the social structure. Rather they are individualized and presented as the result of individual error or morality. As a subject-centred form, it is argued, narrative cannot deal with social structures as anything more than the product of individual action, and ultimately presents all social problems as capable of resolution within the terms of the existing social system. As a result, the claim is that narrative structures suggest that there is nothing inherently wrong with existing social structures that cannot be dealt with through individual action, and hence no reason fundamentally to change the ways in which we live our lives as a society.[13]

McCabe's point is therefore that the text 'positions the subject in ideology' through its mode of address. As has been argued, this may seem difficult to establish in the case of film, but it is argued that the classic realist text is structured in such a way that spectators are addressed by the film to the extent that they occupy the position in which all the different points of view cohere and become meaningful.

McCabe's position is also that this process is ideological in so far as it privileges one point of view over others and so makes this point of view seem transparent or obvious – it is presented as the truth, rather than as a particular point of view. However, there are severe problems with McCabe's theory which, at least in part, relate back to his reliance on Althusser's theory of ideology. Althusser's theory is not simply a theory of bourgeois ideology, but one of 'Ideology-in-general'. He claimed that while there may be different ideologies, 'Ideology-in-general' was 'eternal' and 'universal'. It was the basic structure which all socially-specific ideologies must share, and would continue even after a communist revolution. Every society requires an ideology, if it is to position subjects within itself.

However, the concentration on 'Ideology-in-general' has made it difficult for Althusserian Marxists to distinguish between different, and even competing, ideologies. Thus, while many Althusserians, such as McCabe, argued that they were interested in the form of cinema, rather than its content, they ran the risk of claiming that any text which conforms to their definition of 'Ideology-in-general' will have the same effect; it will reproduce the dominant order. (In fact, many Althusserians, including McCabe, explicitly state this at times.) The problem with McCabe's work is that its concentration on the form of ideology, rather than on its content, means that texts with radically different ideological agendas (say, anti- or pro-capitalist) would be seen as having the same effect of reproducing capitalist relations.

Also like Althusser's theory of 'Ideology-in-general' which in many ways seems to be merely a critique of a historically specific ideology, bourgeois individualism, McCabe's theory of realism ignores the notion that forms of realism change. Indeed, the theory of the classic realist text, at least as McCabe describes it, does not seem to refer to a transhistorical structure, but rather to a form of fiction which only developed in the late eighteenth century, and even then mainly in Europe. The application of this concept to forms from other periods or cultural traditions seems questionable, to say the least.

These problems become particularly clear when one considers the alternatives to the classic realist text which are offered by McCabe. He refers to the first two alternatives as the progressive and the subversive text. The progressive text, it is argued, conforms to the model of the classic realist text, but privileges a point of view which is at odds with the dominant order; for example, a film such as *Salt of the Earth* which is told from the point of view of striking workers. The subversive text, on the other hand, breaks with the classic realist text to the extent that it refuses to privilege any one point of view and so refuses to resolve its warring points of view. However, neither of these alternatives was really seen as particularly radical or significant. For McCabe, it was only the revolutionary text (as exemplified by James Joyce in literature and Godard in film) which was seen as a real alternative. Only this form, it was argued, took issue with the structures of 'Ideology-in-general' to any great degree. As should be clear, McCabe was not able to resolve the problem of the difference between 'Ideology-in-general' and historically specific ideologies.

However, McCabe's concern with the text as an attempt to secure mastery and coherence remained central to later developments which were to extend, or take issue with, his formulations. Unfortunately, the problem of distinguishing between 'Ideology-in-general' and historically specific ideologies was to remain a major problem.

From Althusserian Marxism to Lacanian psychoanalysis

The Althusserian theory of 'Ideology-in-general', on which McCabe's theories were based, relied heavily on Lacanian psychoanalysis. Althusser's theory of interpellation draws upon Lacan's theory of the mirror stage, a stage of child development. However, the film theories which followed McCabe increasingly turned back to Lacan in an attempt to rectify some of the problems which they identified in Althusser. These problems were identified in two main areas. First, it was argued that while Althusser's theory of ideology was an attempt to explain the formation of the subject, its theory of interpellation actually assumed the existence of that which it sought to explain. To put it another way, the concept of interpellation attempted to explain how the individual came to see itself as an autonomous and independent being, but this theory already required an individual which could recognize itself as being addressed by the social structure. As a result, many of those who turned to Lacanian psychoanalysis to resolve the problems of Althusserian Marxism eventually claimed that the former offered a better account of the construction of the subject, and of subjectivity in general, than was available in Althusser's theory of ideology.[14]

Second, it was claimed that McCabe's theory of the classic realist text was altogether too static. The viewer was simply presented with an omniscient point of view. As a result, later work was more concerned with the process by which positions of mastery and coherence were produced by the processes through which the subject encounters the forms of the film.

Related to these developments was a third major transition. For many feminists, Lacan's psychoanalytic preoccupation with sexuality and sexual difference provided not just a better account of the construction of the subject, but also one which explained the construction of gendered subjects.[15] Lacanian psychoanalysis was seen as a description of the processes through which patriarchy reproduced itself, and as the debate moved on, the rhetoric of film criticism changed from one of Marxism to one of feminism; from a critique of capitalism to a critique of patriarchy. However, there are several problems with the application of psychoanalysis to feminism (see chapter seven).

The work of Jean-Louis Baudry is a useful place to start when trying to understand these transitions. Like McCabe, Baudry was concerned with the way in which the film constructs a sense of mastery and coherence for the subject, but unlike McCabe, he saw this construction as a far more dynamic process which involved the spectator in specific activities. In his article 'Ideological Effects of the Basic Cinematographic Apparatus',[16] for example, he argued that the camera lens was designed to produce the same ideological effects as the system of perspective in Renaissance painting. It organizes the world in relation to the spectator's vision, and so establishes the spectator as the centre of the world.[17] However, Baudry also noted that film is not composed of a single point of view, but of constant intercutting between points of view. Far from destroying the spectator's sense of mastery and coherence, he argued, this process actually enhances the spectator's sense of mastery over the world of the film. It frees his or her vision from a sense of its location and particularity, and gives it a sense of total mastery and omnipotence. The spectator's vision appears to be omnipresent and hence godlike. As a result, the confirmation of the subject's mastery and coherence is achieved through the process of watching the film, from the interrelation between shots and the ways in which they are put together. However, Baudry also pointed out that this sense of mastery is a misrecognition in which subjects perceive themselves to be the centre of the text's meaning when they are only an effect of its operations.

The influence of Lacan prompted theorists to take this concern with the relationship between shots somewhat further, and in this endeavour, the Lacanian concept of 'suture' became central. This term originally referred to the surgical process of stitching a wound back together, but it was used by Lacan to refer to a far more complex psychological process.

For Lacan, the subject was not only a product of language, but was fundamentally divided or split. He explains this situation through an account of the subject's development, in which it is claimed that the 'child is born into the experience of lack'.[18] It exists in a state which Lacan refers to as the *manque à être*, or the 'want to be'.[19] The child yearns for a condition of completion and wholeness which will bring an end to its experience of lack, and it various stages of development are seen as successive attempts to overcome this state of lack, attempts which can never ultimately be successful.

One of the troubles with Lacan's account is that he is never clear whether his account of these various stages is a description of actual moments of development, the subject's interpretation of earlier stages (what it believes and needs to believe about its origins), or merely a 'useful' fiction developed by psychoanalysis itself. For example, the child's relationship with its mother is claimed to be interpreted, in retrospect, as a blissful state of completeness in which the mother completes the child and the child completes the mother. In this state, the child makes no distinctions between itself and its world – it has no sense of self.

However, in later stages, this sense of wholeness is disrupted and the child (and later the adult) spends its time trying to recapture this sense of wholeness. The subject is continually in search of that which will bring an end to lack. For Lacan, the object of this search is referred to as *l'objet petit a* ('little object a'). However, it is not a real object which exists in the world. It is a substitute for the missing mother. People may believe that they would feel satisfied and complete if only they had that lover, or that car, or that job, but such beliefs are illusory; they are simply the result of the ways in which subjects project their own desires on to objects, objects which are only substitutes for that which is lacking and missing.

The subject is therefore 'caught in a bind'. It desires that which is ultimately non-existent, and tries to compensate for this situation through 'imaginary' solutions which provide idealized images through which it perceives itself to be whole and complete. However, the word 'imaginary' is complex and potentially misleading here, and to understand its use it is necessary to examine Lacan's discussion of the various stages of child development which follow on from its state of blissful unity with its mother.

Lacan's account of child development involves three main stages: the mirror phase in which the child acquires a sense of self; the *fort/da* game in which it acquires language; and the Oedipus complex in which it is forced to accept the laws of sexual difference. In the mirror phase (which occurs between six and eighteen months of age), the child first comes to see itself as separate from its world. Lacan uses the image of the mirror to illustrate this process, though it also occurs through the child's identification with the bodies of others. In seeing its image in the mirror, the child perceives an image of completeness and unity which it identifies as itself. This also occurs when it identifies with the bodies of others. This sense of its own body as complete and unified is essential for the child to develop motor co-ordination, but it has a fundamental problem.

The identification with the image involves misrecognition and hence self-division. The mirror image has a peculiar quality; it is both identical and different. In saying of the mirror image, 'that's me', the child is also identifying itself as something which is separate and distinct, something which is elsewhere. As a result, the child becomes a split subject which is on both sides of the mirror. Furthermore, it only gains a sense of self in so far as that sense of self is sanctioned by another; by the image in the mirror, or by the mother who points out the mirror-image and says 'that's you'. As a result, from the moment at which the child derives a sense of self, that self is split and divided.

In the *fort/da* game, the child seeks compensation for its separation from its mother (achieved through the mirror phase) through its mastery of language. The term '*fort/da* game' is drawn from an incident Freud discussed in which he witnessed his grandson playing with a cotton reel. The young boy was throwing the cotton reel away and then retrieving it while uttering sounds which Freud interpreted as the words *fort* ('gone') and *da* ('here'). Freud interpreted this game as a means by which the child came to terms with the loss of its mother through a re-enactment of this traumatic moment. The child converted its feelings of abandonment, he claimed, into one of mastery by pretending that it had control over that which was present and that which was absent. It converted the feeling of abandonment *by* the mother into one of mastery, the act of abandoning the mother. Lacan read this game slightly differently. He emphasized that the child was using a symbol (a cotton reel) to stand in for that which was absent (the mother). As a result, the child's acquisition of language is seen as another means of compensating for lack. Linguistic terms do not stand for that which is present, but for that which is absent; and as such, they are ways of denying or disavowing absence and lack.

As a result, while language allows the child to voice its demands, it also raises problems. Language always pre-exists the child, and in accepting its terms, the child must always define its desires through terms which pre-exist it. If, as we have seen, Lacan argued that desire can never be fulfilled, this situation is only intensified with the acquisition of language. The terms in which desire is voiced can only be those of language and thus desire becomes determined not by the self, but by the Other (language). However, for Lacan, language can never fully express the subject's desire. There will always be some element of exclusion, and it is that which is excluded by language which Lacan describes as the 'unconscious'; the 'unconscious' is that which is in excess of, and cannot be represented by, language. Language also intensifies the sense of self-division found in the mirror stage. When one refers to the self, there is always a difference between the self who speaks (the subject of enunciation) and the self of whom one speaks (the subject of the enunciated). In this way, language and subjectivity (consciousness, self-hood) necessarily entail the unconscious for Lacan. They always create further self-division.

The third major stage of child development is the Oedipus complex, when the child encounters sexual difference. If, as Lacan claims, the child overcame its terror of dependence upon its mother by believing that it was indispensable to her, the figure of the father threatens this sense of security. Initially, the child believes that it is what the mother lacks, and Lacan refers to this as the phallus. However, the presence of the father challenges this happy arrangement. When the child recognizes that its mother desires its father, the child is also forced to recognize that it cannot be the phallus (that which the mother lacks), and it assumes that the father must possess the phallus. As should be clear, for Lacan, the phallus and the penis are not the same, but the child comes to see sexual difference as the sign of possession or non-possession of the phallus (that which will make up for absence or lack). Possession of the penis is equated with wholeness, completeness and mastery, while its absence is equated with incompleteness and lack. The child is thus forced to acquire a sexual identity, and one which it cannot choose. It must either represent lack (female) or completeness (male).

As a result, the boy must identify with an idealized image of the father as the figure who is supposed to be in possession of the phallus. Again this move will ultimately end in failure as the male can never escape either self-division or the unconscious. The girl, on the other hand, must learn to identify with the mother in the hope of winning the love of a male (one whom she believes to have possession of the phallus). Much debate exists within psychoanalysis over the precise character of female sexuality, but it is generally agreed that the female's position is even more problematic than that of the male. She must define herself in terms of a symbolic order (language/society/culture) in which she is merely defined in terms of males. She either represents lack, or that which will make good males' sense of lack. She is an object either of fear or of desire, but cannot define herself as a subject. As a result, it is claimed, women have a problematic relationship to the symbolic order in so far as they are excluded by it, rather than from it. They are defined by their difference from males (what they are not) rather than in their own terms (what they are).

One of the problems here is that Lacan also claims that all terms are relational (their meanings are only determined through their difference from, or opposition to, other terms), and hence it is difficult to see how the position of women is substantially different from that of men within the terms of this theory. Men can only define themselves in terms of their difference from women, and if men are also unable finally to overcome absence, the precise way in which the situation of males differs from that of females remains essentially unclear. In fact, numerous problems have been raised with regard to psychoanalytic accounts of female sexuality, and even defenders of psychoanalysis such as Lapsley and Westlake claim that the 'absence within psychoanalysis of a satisfactory explanation of female sexuality was ... severely to restrict its value in understanding the exchange between film and women spectators'.[20]

The concept of suture needs to be understood within this context. As we have seen, the Lacanian subject is split and divided, but attempts to produce or maintain a sense of unity, coherence and mastery. This sense of self-division is a condition of the subject's place within the symbolic in which there is always division between the self which speaks and the self of which one speaks. The sense of unity, on the other hand, is a product of the subject's 'imaginary' in which it identifies with an idealized self as in the mirror phase. Suture is the process by which the subject tries to repair the divisions within the self, to fill the gaps, and to impose order and uniformity on the conflicting and contradictory elements of the unconscious. The concept of suture is therefore centrally about the subject's relationship to language, particularly the relationship between the subject and meaning.

Psychoanalytic film theory

In film studies this concept was appropriated as a way of discussing the spectator's relationship to the intercutting between camera shots. Jean Pierre Oudart, for example, claims that the intercutting between shots is necessary to maintain the spectator's sense of mastery and coherence.[21] Initially, he claims, the spectator sees the image as offering an 'imaginary' completeness, but the frame or edge of the image always threatens this promise. The frame only emphasizes that which is absent (that which is out of the picture), and hence threatens to reveal that the image is not just there, but is there for someone; that it is not complete, but only a particular point of view. For Oudart, it is the use of the shot/reverse shot system which overcomes this problem. This system involves a technique, often used in the representation of conversations, in which the film cuts between shots taken from the perspective of one character and shots taken from the perspective of another character. This system, it is argued, presents the first shot as the point of view of a character and so overcomes the sense of incompleteness inherent within it.

A similar position was also argued by Daniel Dayan who claimed that the shot/reverse shot system was a means by which the text disguised its own operations and so created the appearance of transparency.[22] It was the means by which the text disguised its own status as representation. Instead of presenting the image as the product of a system of signification, the image was defined as part of the diegesis (the fictional world of the film). It was not presented as the product of ideology, but simply as the point of view of a narrative character. This position seems very close to McCabe and Baudry in so far as it argues that the ideological effect of the film was to render itself transparent, to present a particular ideological position as though it were 'truth'. Where it differs from McCabe is through its concern with the way in which this effect is produced through the process of viewing, through the way in which the viewer ties together different shots, rather than through McCabe's more static model of spectatorship.

As a result, the concept of suture is about the way in which the process of viewing involves the stitching together not only of different shots, but also of the conflicting tendencies of the imaginary (the identification with an idealized image of unity and coherence) and the symbolic (the systems of language which force the subject to acknowledge his or her determination by culture). None the less, a number of problems have been raised in relation to this work. For example, as Barry Salt has pointed out, the shot/reverse shot system does not represent the majority of shots used in Hollywood films.[23] As a result, Stephen Heath has argued that suture is better understood as the effect of cutting in general, and he describes this process as the continual oscillation between presence and absence which is the subject's condition within the symbolic.[24]

These concerns with cutting and editing (as well as the system of shot/reverse shot) have also been discussed by Raymond Bellour, but in this case he is more concerned with the ways in which systems of symmetry and asymmetry are organized so as to create a sense of unity and coherence within narrative. For example, in his discussion of a sequence from *The Big Sleep*, he discusses the ways in which camera angles, framing and other codes are used over the course of twelve individual shots. This work is close to other work on narrative in so far as it examines the ways in which narrative is ordered to create a series of oppositions which can be given coherence and resolution, but it does so through an analysis of the ways in which these are developed through the interplay between different camera shots.[25]

However, this work also drew out further implications from psychoanalysis. In his analysis of *The Birds*, for example, Bellour also discusses the way in which the narrative intercutting of different shots involves issues of identification and sexual difference.[26] Heath also deals with many of these issues, but he does so by returning to the concept of suture.[27] As he claims, the subject and the meaning of language are always mutually dependent. The subject produces the meaning by constantly stitching together different shots, but it is also produced by the text as it does so. There is no subject without language, but language also requires a subject. Suture is therefore a way of denying lack or absence, and it is in this sense that Heath connects suture with narrative. For Heath, narrative is concerned with the subject's sense of lack and is an attempt to compensate for this absence.

As Terry Eagleton has claimed, the *fort/da* game 'is perhaps the shortest story we can imagine: an object is lost, and then recovered'.[28] Narrative concerns the loss of a sense of wholeness (the disruption of order); the search for that which is lacking (the process of disorder); and finally the recovery of that which was lost (narrative resolution). However, it should be pointed out that just as, for Lacan, the sense of lack can never be filled, so narrative is ultimately unable to achieve complete resolution. The text provides substitutes for the missing object, but can never finally portray the moment of wholeness and completion. It must end as the lovers embrace, or the Nazis are conquered, but cannot show what comes afterwards, for any such material will always be a disappointment. It will always reawaken a sense of lack.

While many defenders of psychoanalysis claim that it is this concern with process which distinguishes Lacanian theory from Althusserian Marxism, there are problems with this claim. It is argued that Althusserian Marxism only concentrated on the 'imaginary' identifications which gave the subject an illusion of mastery and coherence, and that it ignored the processes of the symbolic which created division and the unconscious. Thus it is claimed that psychoanalysis provided a far more dynamic account of the processes of viewing texts than the more static theory of interpellation available in Althusserianism. Unfortunately for such defenders of psychoanalysis, not only did Althusserian Marxism offer accounts of narrative processes which were similar to those of psychoanalysis,[29] but the most influential uses of psychoanalysis were those of Metz and Mulvey, uses which even Lapsley and Westlake acknowledge are more concerned with the imaginary than the symbolic, with interpellation rather than suture.

This situation can be seen clearly in the subtitle of Metz's book, *Psychoanalysis and Cinema: The Imaginary Signifier*. For Metz, the cinematic institution is made up of two 'machines': the first was the industrial processes of production and reproduction; and the second was the psychic processes of the subject's production and reproduction. But it is the analysis of this latter 'machine' which primarily concerns Metz, and he argues that it is bound up with three processes: identification, voyeurism and fetishism. For Metz, cinema was not like other art-forms. It addressed more of the senses (sight and hearing) than was common, and unlike those art-forms which did address the same senses (forms such as theatre and opera), cinema was a record of that which was absent. In the theatre, the performers and the audience occupy the same time and place – they are present to one another – but in the cinema the spectator is presented with images of a world which exists (or existed) elsewhere. As a result, he argues that the cinema is necessarily of the 'imaginary'. It offers the spectator images of wholeness and completion which are fundamentally illusory.

However, unlike the mirror in the mirror phase, the screen does not present the spectator with an image of his or her own body, and is necessarily bound up with the symbolic. As a result, Metz denies that the primary form of imaginary identification is with the characters of the narrative. Instead, he claims that the spectator identifies 'with himself [*sic*] as a pure act of perception'.[30] This involves two features: first, spectators are conscious that they are placed outside the action presented on the screen and that they exist in a position of omnipotence and mastery over the narrative world; and second, they recognize that the film exists for them, that it has no purpose without them. As a result, spectators identify with 'the *position* of the spectator' which involves the illusion of mastery and coherence. However, like other theorists, Metz argued that this position is itself a misrecognition in which spectators perceive themselves as the cause rather than the effect of the text.

For Metz, the absence of the performers presented in films from the same time and space as the spectator is also related to the voyeurism inherent in the cinematic institution. Not only does sight require a distance from the object of vision, but the absence of that which is presented on the screen only increases this sense of distance. The performer has no relationship to the spectators, and cannot know their reactions. As a result, there is an illicit quality to the viewing of films, one that is intensified by the spectator's situation; the spectator sits in the dark and is so freed from the surveillance of those on the screen and of other members of the audience. Thus cinema spectatorship has something of a 'peep-show' quality in which the spectator derives a sadistic pleasure of control over the image.

Finally, Metz argued that the absence of the objects presented on the screen was also related to the concept of fetishism. For Lacan, the recognition of sexual difference, and the association of the female with lack, are both fundamentally traumatic. They raise the issue of absence and have to be disavowed or denied. This process of disavowal involved the process of fetishizing parts of the female body, or investing them with virtually magical, erotic powers which act as a means of compensating for, and drawing attention away from, the lack represented by the female genitals. This process involves the subject in both knowing and denying what the female represents. They know that she is lacking, but choose not to believe so. In much the same way, Metz argues, spectators watching a film know that they are watching that which is absent, but choose to believe that it is present. As a result, the cinematic signifier is 'imaginary' in so far as it presents an illusory image of whole-ness and completion though a process of denying the fundamental absence on which it is founded.

If Metz's influence was substantial, Laura Mulvey's article 'Visual Pleasure and Narrative Cinema' is probably the most republished and referenced work within Anglo–American film studies. Like Metz, her argument is essentially bound up with theories of interpellation, but unlike Metz's work, its concern is not primarily with the politics of signification. Instead its main influence has been its concern with the politics of representation; particularly, how women are represented within narrative cinema.[31] Mulvey's work was part of an attempt to appropriate Lacanian psychoanalysis for feminism, a project which was fraught with problems but which was also to become the primary justification for psychoanalysis as a mode of criticism. It is important to note that Lacan was in no sense a feminist, nor had he any such poli-tics in mind when he developed his theories. In fact, the feminist appro-priation of psychoanalysis had to stress that the Oedipus complex was not a necessary and inevitable stage of child development, but rather the product of patriarchy; hence the common tendency to conflate the symbolic order with patriarchy.

For Mulvey, the forward drive of narrative and the static image which had to be ordered by the narrative were gendered in a manner that reproduced 'a world ordered by sexual imbalance'.[32] It was the male who was defined as the active subject of the narrative; it was he who made things happen and so propelled the narrative forward. In this way, despite their presence as images, males did not become the objects of the audience's gaze, but became points of 'imaginary' identification. They gave the spectators an image of coherence and mastery with which they identified. Women, on the other hand, were presented as essen-tially passive sexual spectacles who existed as the objects of the audi-ences gaze. They were defined as peripheral to the narrative, except as objects to be fought over and won by men.

However, while the male image becomes a point of identification for the spectator, the image of the female body is a problem which always threatens to re-evoke the memory of that which it represents – lack and absence. For Mulvey, there are two main techniques which are used to deal with this problem. The first is voyeurism, which is related to a 'preoccupation with the re-enactment of the original trauma (investi-gating the woman, demystifying her mystery) counterbalanced by the devaluation, punishment or saving of the guilty object'.[33] In this case, woman's situation as a representation of absence is read as a difference from the male norm of patriarchal culture. The woman is presented as a deviant who is blamed for her state, as though it were a crime. This reaffirms the male's sense of mastery and coherence through a sadistic control over woman in which he is presented as having the privilege of punishing woman for her difference or forgiving her for her deviance. In either case, the male is defined as the norm, and so given a sense of dominance and control.

Indeed, it is often argued by feminist psychoanalysis that women, and female sexuality in particular, are frequently represented as the threatening and disruptive forces which must be contained or destroyed in order for the narrative to reach resolution and closure. For example, while many films may appear to be about defeating the Nazis or solving a murder, these elements are often bound up with and inextricably linked to issues of gender and sexuality. At the end of *Casablanca*, it is perhaps less important that Rick has outwitted the Nazis than that he has won Ilsa's love. The problem of the narrative is therefore the control of female sexuality, and by the end of the narrative it is argued that women must either learn to subjugate themselves to men or else be punished.

The second way of dealing with the problem presented by the image of the female's body, according to Mulvey, is fetishism. As we have already seen, this process involves a denial or disavowal of the absence which women represent, and it is achieved by investing some part of the female body with a magical, erotic power in order to compensate for, and distract attention from, that which is seen as lacking elsewhere. The most commonly cited examples are usually Marilyn Monroe's breasts, Betty Grable's leg's and Rita Hayworth's shoulders.

In this way, the woman's body is presented as an object of desire for men. It simultaneously defends the male subject against the trauma of castration anxiety, and defines the female as an object for his satisfaction. Women are defined as the object of the narrative rather than its subject; women are acted upon, rather active; women are desired, rather than desiring. So film manages to repress and contain the threat of female sexuality and define women in terms of men.

However, it is important to emphasize that Mulvey claims that these features are the condition of all mainstream cinema, not just some films. These features are a product of 'the way the unconscious of patriarchal society has structured film form'.[34] Thus, while one might recognize that her claims might apply to some films, the question remains whether they necessarily apply to all mainstream films. If this is not the case, her theory is seriously undermined. One problem which might be raised is the case of films – often 'women's pictures' – which feature a central female character. In fact, many of these films bear the names of their central female characters as titles (films such as *Stella Dallas*, *Mildred Pierce*). In these cases, the argument often used by psychoanalytic feminists is that while these women may be the central characters, they are not defined as the active subjects of the narrative, or, if they are, they are punished for this by the end of the narrative. These narratives are supposed to concern what happens to these female characters, not how they make things happen.[35] Such claims are questionable, but they seem to be even less applicable in the case of films such as *Thelma and Louise*, and most particularly, *Aliens* where women do seem to motivate the narrative.[36]

Mulvey's position provides other problems. Most importantly, it has been pointed out that Mulvey assumes a male, heterosexual spectator, but this assumption raises questions about how women watch films and gain pleasure from them. Mulvey suggests two alternatives: either women must learn to identify with the male protagonist through a sort of transsexual identification; or else they must identify with the woman and assume the position of passive sexual object. Such conclusions seem highly pessimistic, and assume that most women simply accept subordinate positions. If, as Mulvey argues, her intention is to destroy the pleasures upon which mainstream cinema depends, one also needs to ask what she proposes as an alternative. Unsurprisingly, this alternative is the avant-garde.

Criticism and conclusions

In fact, screen theory, as we have seen, seems to work around a central opposition between the mainstream and the avant-garde, and this is best described by Barthes's opposition between the text of pleasure (mainstream cinema) and the text of bliss or *jouissance* (the avant-garde):

> Text of pleasure: the text that contents, fills, grants euphoria; the text that comes from culture and does not break with it, is linked to a *comfortable* practice of reading. The text of bliss (*jouissance*): the text that imposes a state of loss, the text that discomforts (perhaps to the point of boredom), unsettles the reader's historical, cultural, psychological assumptions, the consistency of his tastes, values, memories, brings to a crisis his relationship with language.[37]

As we have seen, this opposition not only consigns the popular, almost without exception, to the status of the ideologically conservative; it also tends to homogenize the range of popular forms. It results in an either/or politics which is necessarily reductive. Once again, popular film becomes an essentially repetitive and formulaic system which reproduces the dominant ideology.

Screen theorists like Stephen Neale may claim that mainstream or popular films are not all the same, and that 'difference is essential to the economy' of popular film, but he does so only to claim that individual films need to be different only in so far as they need to attract people back to the cinema. Despite the apparent differences between popular films, for screen theorists such as Neale each film will still repeat the same processes of containment and repression which reproduce the dominant ideology.[38]

There are exceptions to this rule, but these films are not presented as radical in themselves. Instead it is argued that some films (though it is never explained quite why), while still conforming to the ideological project of mainstream cinema, fail to resolve their contradictions and allow the gaps and contradictions to become apparent.[39] As a result, the discussion of these films does not lead to a re-evaluation of popular film, but defines these films as being of value exactly because they do not perform the functions associated with the popular. It is also rather odd to find that a film's value should be based on its failure to achieve its aims.

This homogenization of popular texts also makes screen theory essentially ahistorical. It may allude to 'epochal' structures such as capitalism and patriarchy, but it has little conception of the struggles and changes which take place within these abstract structures.[40] Indeed, like Althusserian Marxism, psychoanalytic theory is less interested in specific systems of language than with 'Language-in-general', and less interested in socially specific constructions of subjectivity than in 'Subjectivity-in-general'. As Stuart Hall claims of psychoanalytic criticism, 'the manner in which this "subject" of culture is conceptualized is of a trans-historical and "universal" character; it addresses the subject-in-general, not historically determinant social subjects, or socially determinant particular languages'.[41]

Indeed one of the problems with feminist appropriations of Lacanian psychoanalysis is that, within its terms, the end of patriarchy will not bring about the end of the divided subject or the unconscious. For Lacan, these are eternal human conditions, not the products of a specific culture. They are a necessary product of the subject's relationship to 'Language-in-general'.

Indeed the psychoanalytic account of the construction of subjectivity is no more satisfying as an explanation of this process than Althusserian Marxism. From the first, it presupposes one who 'wants to be', and even all of Lacan's three main stages of development (the mirror phase, the *fort/da* game, and the Oedipus complex) presuppose a subject that has already acquired language. In the mirror phase, the child needs to understand what its mother means when she says 'that's you'. It also needs to be able to distinguish its own image as separate from the world. The Oedipus complex is even more of a problem. The child needs already to understand the meaning of sexual difference in order to associate the phallus with the penis. The question is why this form of difference – sexual difference – is read as that which signifies possession or non-possession of the phallus, rather than some other marker of difference, such as hair-colour or smell.

It is also the case that, as Jane Gallop has pointed out, the distinction between the phallus and the penis in psychoanalytic theory is nowhere near as clear as its defenders claim.[42] The two are continually being conflated, and it has been pointed out that rather than offering an anti-essentialist account of gender differences (one which defines these differences as cultural rather than natural in origin), psychoanalytic criticism frequently essentializes both masculinity and femininity.

As a result, screen theory has swung between two poles, an emphasis on the politics of signification and an emphasis on the politics of representation. Both these tendencies remain highly abstract in their presentation, but it is also the case that they tend to work against one another. The feminist emphasis is on the politics of representation, and while it may try to address the politics of signification, it cannot go too far down this road without ultimately finding that it removes the grounds for any conception of feminism. The politics of representation allows for some sense of social change, but the politics of signification is only concerned with the eternal problem of the subject's relationship to language, a problem for which only the end of language, culture and the subject can provide a solution. Some feminists have tried to go down this road, but have yet to clarify what such a solution could possibly mean.

Indeed, not only do screen theory's abstractions tend to erase differences between popular forms, they also tend to produce the very sense of mastery and complete truth which they deny elsewhere. Most of its models seem to produce such closed, self-justifying systems that they have even been open to attack from within psychoanalytic criticism itself.[43] Unfortunately for screen theory, it is still unclear how it gets out of such a situation. Indeed, so self-justifying are many of its arguments that they seem to close off all possibilities, and seem entirely circular in their logic. For example, it is common to find that not only do women signify lack, but lack signifies women. In her account of horror, to refer to one particular case, Barbara Creed claims that it is women who are ultimately defined as monstrous within the genre. She cites numerous examples of films where the monster is clearly defined as female. However, when she finds cases where the monster is clearly defined as male, she argues that its status as a monster identifies it with lack, and hence defines it as feminized.[44] It is difficult to see what would not fit this kind of logic.

It is this problem which Andrew Tudor raises in his discussion of psychoanalytic criticism. He claims that the most worrying problem with psychoanalysis is that it is ultimately unfalsifiable. Indeed, he claims that it has an in-built tendency to produce 'esoteric readings'.[45] The psychoanalytic concern with the unconscious (that which the subject must deny or repress) means that psychoanalysis must be opposed to people's experiences of film texts. That which is conscious must be, of necessity, inadequate or even contrary to the 'truth'. As a result, any response made in opposition to psychoanalytic claims can simply and easily be dismissed by psychoanalysis as the product of repression or resistance. For this reason, psychoanalytic criticism has an inherent tendency to produce theories and interpretations which not only bear no relation to one's experience of a text, but positively contradict those experiences.

Notes:

1 Screen theory is named after the British film journal *Screen*, through which many pieces were published. It should be borne in mind, as I hope this chapter demonstrates, that this approach was not a completely monolithic entity, but emerged out of a series of theoretical debates. It should also be noted that many of the key positions were drawn from articles originally published in France, but not self-consciously produced within screen theory.

2 Pam Cook, *The Cinema Book*, London: British Film Institute, 1985, p. 242.

3 Robert Lapsley and Mike Westlake, *Film Theory: An Introduction*, Manchester: Manchester University Press, 1988, p. vii. This book provides a

useful and detailed introduction to many of the debates, but one that is both difficult and supportive of psychoanalytic criticism.

4 *The Cinema Book*, p. 243.

5 *The Cinema Book*, p. 243.

6 Some popular films have been praised, but these are usually seen as those which fail to achieve the ideological project of popular film. They fail to resolve ideological contradictions. However, such a position still presents popular film as inherently conservative. See, for example, *Cahiers du Cinéma* editorial board, 'John Ford's *Young Mr Lincoln*' in *Screen*, 13: 3 (autumn 1972), and some of the articles in Christine Gledhill, ed., *Home is Where the Heart Is: Studies in Melodrama and the Women's Film*, London: British Film Institute, 1987.

7 Roland Barthes, *The Pleasure of the Text*, London: Jonathan Cape, 1975.

8 Constance Penley, 'Time Travel, Primal Scene, and the Critical Dystopia (on *The Terminator* and *La Jetée*)', in *The Future of an Illusion: Film, Feminism, and Psychoanalysis*, London: Routledge, 1989, p. 129.

9 Ferdinand de Saussure, *Course in General Linguistics*, London: Fontana, 1974.

10 Colin McCabe, 'Realism and the Cinema: Notes on Some Brechtian Theses', *Screen*, 15: 2 (summer 1974), pp. 21–7.

11 Louis Althusser, 'Ideology and Ideological State Apparatuses: Notes Towards and Investigation', in *Lenin and Philosophy and Other Essays*, London: Verso, 1971.

12 Stuart Hall, 'Culture, the Media and the "Ideological Effect"', in *Mass Communications and Society*, James Curran *et al.*, eds, London: Edward Arnold, 1977, p. 323.

13 See, for example, *The Pleasure in the Text*; Roland Barthes, 'Introduction to the Structural Analysis of Narative', in *Image–Music–Text* (Selected and Translated by Stephen Heath), London: Fontana, 1977; and Pierre Machery, *A Theory of Literary Production*, London: Routledge, 1978.

14 See, for example, Rosalind Coward and John Ellis, *Language and Materialism: Developments in Semiology and the Theory of the Subject*, London: Routledge and Kegan Paul, 1977.

15 See, for example, Juliet Mitchell, *Feminism and Psychoanalysis*, London: Penguin, 1975.

16 Jean-Louis Baudry, 'Ideological Effects of the Basic Cinematographic Apparatus', in Bill Nichols, *Movies and Methods Volume II*, Berkeley: University of California Press, 1985.

17 For a discussion of perspective in Renaissance painting, see John Berger, *Ways of Seeing*, Harmondsworth: Penguin, 1972.

18 *Film Theory: An Introduction*, p. 67.

19 Jacques Lacan, *Ecrits: A Selection*, London: Tavistock Press, 1977.

20 *Film Theory: An Introduction*, p. 75.

21 Jean Pierre Oudart, 'Cinema and Suture', *Screen*, 18: 1 (winter, 1977/78).

22 Daniel Dayan, 'The Tutor Code of Classical Cinema', in Bill Nichols, ed., *Movies and Methods Volume I*, Berkeley: University of California Press, 1976.

23 Barry Salt, 'Film Style and Techonology in the Forties', *Film Quarterly*, (fall 1977).

24 Stephen Heath, *Questions of Cinema*, London: Macmillan, 1981.

25 Raymond Bellour, 'The Obvious and the Code', *Screen*, 15: 4 (winter 1974/75).

26 Raymond Bellour, '*The Birds* – Analysis of a Sequence', London: British Film Institute, 1972.

27 *Questions of Cinema*; and Stephen Heath, 'Narrative Space', *Screen*, 17: 3 (autumn 1976).

28 Terry Eagleton, *Literary Theory: An Introduction*, Oxford: Basil Blackwell, 1983, p. 185.

29 For example, Roland Barthes's *The Pleasure of the Text* was used in both Althusserian and psychoanalytic accounts. Indeed, the two approaches are much closer than is often claimed. It is merely a question of the rhetoric used by critics using these ideas.

30 Christian Metz, *Psychoanalysis and Cinema: The Imaginary Signifier*, London: Macmillan, 1982, p. 49.

31 As Lapsley and Westlake suggest, 'one might say that Mulvey's concern was with the cinematic signified and Metz's with the cinematic signifier' (*Film Theory: An Introduction*, p. 84).

32 Laura Mulvey, 'Visual Pleasure and Narrative Cinema', in *Movies and Methods Volume II*, p. 309.

33 'Visual Pleasure and Narrative Cinema', p. 311.

34 'Visual Pleasure and Narrative Cinema', p. 305.

35 See, for example, Christine Gledhill, *Home is Where the Heart Is: Studies in Melodrama and the Women's Film*.

36 Both these films have caused enormous debate within psychoanalytic feminism. However, the case of *Aliens* is particularly interesting. Both Constance Penley and Barbara Creed have found reasons for arguing that it ultimately conforms to patriarchal constructions of gender. However, while Penley argues that this is because Ripley is defined as maternal, Creed has claimed it is because she performs the male role in which the maternal is repressed through her conflict with the Alien mother. Nor would the fact that the film could be read as refusing to confine Ripley within these constructions be seen as necessarily radical. It could still be argued, within psycholanalytic terms, that the film is therefore trying to resolve contradictions; that it wants to eat its cake and have it. It is difficult to see how one can get out of this kind of logic. See Barbara Creed, *The Monstrous–Feminine: Film, Feminism, Psychoanalysis*, London: Routledge, 1993; and Constance Penley,

'Time Travel, Primal Scene and the Critical Distopia'.

37 Roland Barthes, *The Pleasure in the Text*, p. 14.

38 Stephen Neale, *Genre*, London: British Film Institute, 1980.

39 See 'John Ford's *Young Mr Lincoln*' and *Home is Where the Heart Is*.

40 Raymond Williams, *Marxism and Literature*, Oxford: Oxford University Press, 1977.

41 Stuart Hall, 'Cultural Studies: Two Paradigms', in Richard Collins *et al.*, eds, *Media, Culture and Society: A Reader*, London: Sage, 1986, p. 46.

42 Jane Gallop, 'Phallus/Penis: Same Difference', in *Men by Women, Women and Literature II*, Janet Todd, ed., New York and London: Holmes and Meier, 1981.

43 See, for example, Constance Penley, 'Feminism, Film Theory and the Bachelor Machines', in *The Future of An Illusion: Film, Feminism, and Psychoanalysis*.

44 *The Monstrous–Feminine: Film, Feminism and Psychoanalysis*.

45 Andrew Tudor, *Monsters and Mad Scientists: A Cultural History of the Horror Movie*, Oxford: Blackwell, 1989, p. 3.

New femininities: reconstructing women's history in A League of Their Own (1992)

From psychoanalytic feminism to popular feminism

If one's encounter with feminism had been through film theory alone, one could be forgiven for thinking that psychoanalysis was the only feminist position open to women who seek to transform sexual politics. But outside the field of film studies there is a variety of feminist approaches which do not accept the terms of psychoanalytic discourse, or which employ different theoretical perspectives and methodologies, approaches which are useful in reassessing the sexual politics of popular cinema.

Feminism and psychoanalysis

Feminist film theory has been largely dominated by psychoanalytic theory since the mid-1970s. Laura Mulvey's influential article 'Visual Pleasure and Narrative Cinema',[1] which appeared in *Screen* in 1975, greatly influenced feminist film theorists and critics. It was part of a general theoretical attempt to use the work of Freud and Lacan for the analysis of mainstream cinema.

In her piece, Mulvey claims that psychoanalytic theory can be 'appropriated ... as a political weapon'.[2] She argues that it offers a causal analysis of women's oppression under patriarchy which can provide the foundation for political action and social change. Concerned with the relationship between the gendered spectator, the cinematic image and the pleasures of dominant cinema, Mulvey asserts that mainstream cinema organizes the spectator in a gender-specific way. She argues that the visual pleasures of popular film are associated with fetishistic and voyeuristic ways of looking. These looks are organized so that the spectator has no choice but to identify with the narrative's male protagonist and thus becomes complicit with his objectification of female characters. Women, according to Mulvey's article, are theorized as the passive 'sexual Spectacle',[3] at the mercy of the active male gaze. In popular film, Mulvey argues, men look and women are looked at; men act and women are acted upon. This claim may emphasize male control, but it tends to obscure differences between definitions of masculinity and femininity within society. It also, and perhaps most worryingly, tends to emphasize domination rather than struggle, contestation or resistance. In this way, it tends to reproduce the very ideas of women as victims which many feminists have criticized so vehemently.

Challenging the essentialism of the male gaze

Many feminist film theorists in the 1980s have questioned Mulvey's use of psychoanalytic discourse as a viable and effective form of feminist analysis.[4] For example, in the introduction to *The Female Gaze: Women as Viewers of Popular Culture*, Lorraine Gamman and Margaret Marshment call for a radical reassessment of 'the notion of a "male gaze" as dominant in all mainstream genres' which, they argue, had become 'something of an orthodoxy' in the 1980s.[5] In the process, they pose some important questions:

> is it true that the gaze is always male? And if it isn't – if it is merely 'dominant' – how do we analyse the exceptions? Mulvey assumes a (heterosexual) male protagonist and a (heterosexual) male spectator. What happens when the protagonist is a woman as in *A Woman of Substance?*; or when there is a range of female looks – as in *Cagney and Lacey* or *Lace?* What happens when there is nothing for us to look at but men, whether actively forwarding the narrative as in war films or Westerns, or more obviously coded for erotic appeal ...? What about the representation of gay relationships (now not absent from the mainstream)? And what about spectators who are not male or not heterosexual?[6]

Such questions pose a challenge to Mulvey's essentialist assumption that voyeurism is inherently masculine. Mulvey's theory also fails, as Gamman and Marshment suggest, to take into account the role of audiences in the activities of textual consumption. The construction of textual meaning is not simply an *effect* of the text, it is also dependent on differences of gender, race, class and sexuality within specific audiences.

Jackie Stacey, in her article 'Desperately Seeking Difference', claims that there is a need for feminists to move away from the theory of the masculine spectator. She asks, 'What is the place of women's desire towards women within this analysis of narrative cinema?'[7] For Stacey, a psychoanalytic framework is problematic because it theorizes active desire between women as necessarily masculine, thereby precluding the 'pleasures of looking between women in narrative cinema available to all women in the audience'.[8] Using *All about Eve* (1950) and *Desperately Seeking Susan* (1984) as examples, she argues that the leading female character in each of the films constructs the narrative gaze through an active fascination with, and desire to be like, another female character. In this way, these characters actively control the look.

However, psychoanalysis has problems with these ways of looking. Its assumption that the active control of the look is a male position means that it tends to define active female desire – and particularly lesbian desire – as somehow 'masculine', and perhaps even 'unnatural'. Psychoanalytic feminism finds it difficult to describe or even imagine relationships which fall outside a simple dichotomy between the masculine, active controller of the gaze and the female, passive, object of the gaze. If the look in films such as *All About Eve* and *Desperately Seeking Susan* does not conform to Mulvey's model of the controlling male gaze, which defines women as objects of male desire, Stacey also suggests that it is not necessarily a look of pure identification either. While Mulvey claimed that the position of the spectator was organized so as to objectify women, she also claimed that it was organized so that the spectator came to identify with the central male protagonist who becomes an idealized male self for the spectator. But rather than conforming to this look of pure identification, Stacey argues that, in the films which she is discussing, the look is one of a pleasurable 'interchange of feminine fascinations'.[9] The audience watches a woman who not only actively desires, but is herself watching another woman who is presented as the embodiment of an exciting, powerful and alternative femininity.

In *Desperately Seeking Susan*, for example, Roberta (Rosanna Arquette) wishes to be transformed into a woman more like Susan (Madonna), the women she idolizes. But the film constantly avoids the idea that they simply swap identities. Instead, as Stacey argues, it repeatedly plays on the differences between the women. In this way, Stacey analyses the desire of the female spectator outside a psychoanalytic framework. She argues that the psychoanalytic model cannot account for the pleasures which fall outside 'the rigid distinction between *either* desire *or* identification'.[10]

However, while Stacey argues that the 'pleasures of looking' might be made available to 'all women in the audience',[11] her article does not include any analysis of how black female spectators relate to mainstream cinema. bell hooks, in *Black Looks: race and representation* argues that Mulvey's conception of the active male look and consequent passive female objectification has never applied to black women because the female spectacle of dominant cinema has historically been white. Black women, hooks argues, have turned away from dominant cinema because there are no positive representations of black womanhood to be seen. Recognizing the racism which has systematically excluded black women from films, hooks argues that black women in the United States have learned to bring an 'oppositional gaze' to the cinema:

black women were able to critically assess the cinema's construction of white womanhood as object of phallocentric gaze and choose not to identify with either the victim or the perpetrator. Black female spectators, who refused to identify with white womanhood, who would not take on the phallocentric gaze of desire and possession, created a critical space where the binary opposition Mulvey posits of 'women as image, man as bearer of the look' was continually deconstructed.[12]

Just as Mulvey's article omits any consideration of the relationship of the black female spectator to Hollywood cinema, much feminist film theory in the years that followed remained silent about the specific oppression black women have experienced while viewing mainstream cinema. Feminist film theory, at the time of writing, still remains largely silent on the issue of black female spectatorship (although there are notable exceptions.)[13] hooks is therefore quite justified in claiming that 'Mainstream feminist film criticism in no way acknowledges black female spectatorship.'[14]

Thus, while Stacey challenged Mulvey's claim about the workings of film texts, hooks challenges Mulvey's claims about the activities of spectators. Problematically, hooks still accepts Mulvey's claims about the ideological workings of Hollywood cinema even ·if she qualifies it with reference to issues of race and the activities of audiences. Moreover, she contradicts herself by claiming that black women have both turned away from Hollywood cinema, and developed an 'oppositional gaze'. This sweeping claim, which would seem to speak on behalf of all black American women, risks essentializing black femininity. hooks remains silent on why black women would want to view Hollywood film, what they specifically watch, and how they watch it.

None the less hook's argument exposes the fact that feminist film theorists have tended to rely on a transhistorical psychoanalytic model which takes only sexual difference into account, consequently erasing its relation to issues of racial difference. In this type of analysis, the experience of white middle-class college-educated women tends to be taken as the norm and, as a result, perpetuates a lack of discussion about the representation of black women in cinema. While providing a critical feminist intervention into film theory, white feminists have assumed that their analysis addresses all women, when in fact it has tended only to take the political concerns of white middle-class women into account. Yet if feminists are to devise politically effective strategies which might potentially change women's relationship to film theory and cinematic practice, the concerns of black and working-class women must be included in such programmes of change.

Feminism and social history

Not only has psychoanalytic feminism been criticized in more recent work on popular film, it actually displaced earlier feminist approaches to cinema. In the early 1970s feminist film critics in the United States, arguing from a broadly sociological perspective, claimed that women's relationship to the cinema was an important ideological arena for feminists to examine and contest. They also argued that representations of women in Hollywood up until the 1970s were, in fact, 'misrepresentations', distorted and 'unreal' images of women's lives. The most important texts from this moment of feminist film criticism are Marjorie Rosen's *Popcorn Venus: Women, Movies and the American Dream*[15] and Molly Haskell's *From Reverence to Rape: The Treatment of Women in the Movies.*[16] Jackie Byars, in *All that Hollywood Allows,*[17] provides an account of feminist film studies, and contends that as psychoanalytic feminism displaced sociological criticism, film theory became exclusively concerned with 'significatory processes' at the expense of socio-historical factors.[18] But the specificity of these socio-historical factors is crucial for an adequate understanding of the relationship between film texts and the ways in which readers construct meaning. However, sociological works such as those by Rosen and Haskell were dismissed as hopelessly naive because they failed to focus on the 'formalist concerns' that the proponents of psychoanalytic feminism had chosen as their area of consideration. In doing so, some of the valuable aspects of these sociological approaches were lost.

Rosen and Haskell examine the images, roles and stereotypes of women presented in popular films from the 1920s to the early 1970s. Both of these texts assume a reflectional relationship between cinema and society; that is, that films simply reflect the values and beliefs of the culture in which they are produced. As Haskell argues, cinema is 'one of the clearest and most accessible of looking glasses into the past'.[19] However, they emphasized that at specific historical moments there were disparities between the norms and values reflected in films and the reality of women's position in society. At such moments 'the industry held a warped mirror up to life'.[20] For example, in the 1920s, Rosen argues, Hollywood focused on women who worked in blue-collar occupations thereby creating the impression that women were nonachievers, yet Rosen cites examples of women who did hold important societal positions, women such as the female zoologist Delia Akeley. Rosen and Haskell argue that the relationship between text and context must be analysed. This idea is politically important and worth preserving: the representation of femininity cannot be theorized outside specific historical moments.

Furthermore, Rosen and Haskell were also concerned to construct a history of women who worked in the film industry. However, in so doing, they simply charted particular moments at which *individual* women gained power within the male-dominated Hollywood industry. While psychoanalytic feminists have expressed disdain for this kind of analysis, they too have focused on individual practitioners such as Dorothy Arzner. Interestingly though, in psychoanalytic feminist work, little or no interest is shown in the position of women film-makers such as Arzner within the film industry. Instead they concentrate on texts produced by 'women'. By contrast, Rosen celebrates the scriptwriter Anita Loos who produced 105 scene plots from 1912 to 1915, 101 of which were realized in cinema releases.[21] Dorothy Arzner, who directed seventeen feature films between the years 1927 and 1943, featuring some of the industry's most prominent female stars, is also foregrounded as an important figure in women's film history.[22] Haskell cites the achievements of Mary Pickford, who co-founded United Artists in 1920, and whose various contributions to the industry mark her out as a female role model: 'Long before she became her own producer ... she was choosing her own scripts and directing her own directors. She was thus in a unique position among American actresses: she played whatever roles she wished and she shaped her own image.'[23]

The authors argue that these women made significant impacts on the industry by winning equal access to some of the key production roles in Hollywood, and mark the most progressive moments in women's cinematic history. As Haskell explicitly argues, 'I see history and cinema and art in terms of individuals rather than groups.'[24] Haskell's refusal to consider women's experience of domination as a group has, rightly, incited some feminist critics to question the validity of the sociological label given to her work. Instead one critic has chosen to call her position 'quasi-sociological'.[25] An adequate feminist history of women's involvement in the cinema must acknowledge that, as a group, women carry less social power than men in our culture.

This kind of historical work has been conducted by a variety of socialist feminists. Unfortunately, their work on women's social

activism and collective political resistance has not only had little impact
on studies of women in the film industry; its frequent hostility to psychoanalytic feminism has either been ignored or dismissed within film
studies. One of the most famous, influential and striking examples of
this kind of work is Sheila Rowbotham's *Hidden from History*.[26] This
book attempts to reclaim a 'forgotten' history of women's political
activism. It seeks to counter the tendency of historians to write women
out of history and present them either as unimportant, or as simple victims of historical processes. For example, Rowbotham cites evidence
from *The Leeds Mercury* which reported in May 1832 that 1,500 women
took part in a cardsetters' strike. She also references to the existence of
'female radical associations' which were reported in the Chartist news-
paper *The Northern Star* in 1837.[27] Rowbotham charts the active role
women played in the trade unions in the 1880s, citing instances where
they organized strikes in Dewsbury, Heckmondwike and Nottingham
for improved conditions of service. Such examples are used to frame
her argument that women have a history of radical political activism,
that they have acted to counteract class oppression; and that they have
recognized the need for women to form separate groups which
specifically served women's interests.

Socialist feminist writers who published in the *History Workshop*
journal have also sought to reveal particular historical moments at
which women have posed a challenge to existing power relations. Jan
Lambertz, in 'Sexual Harassment in the Nineteenth-Century English
Cotton Industry',[28] examines the historical documentation surrounding
three case studies of sexual intimidation which occurred in 1887, 1891
and 1913 in Lancashire and the West Riding of Yorkshire. In each of
these cases women and their male counterparts collectively sought to
contest this form of male domination in the workplace.

Therefore, the work of socialist feminist historians challenges the liberal position adopted by Haskell and Rosen. Its stress upon the importance of collective social activism as a means of transforming the
material power structures which oppress women is crucial if such
change is ever to be realized. Its emphasis on historical specificity might
usefully be appropriated to produce a more politicized feminist analysis of women's involvement in the production of mainstream cinema. It
is also an important strategy for showing the social construction of gendered subjectivity and, as a result, why femininity takes various forms
in particular contexts. For example, the documentary film *The Life and
Times of Rosie the Riveter*, made by Connie Field in 1980, explores the

construction of femininity in the United States during World War II. Historically specific, this text shows the way in which women were urged to take on what had previously been defined as male occupations and modes of being in order to serve the interests of the state. Using this approach, film texts can act as historical documents in which the representation of femininity is shown to be changeable at historical moments and open to radical transformation.

Socialist feminist strategies of rewriting women's political history challenge other accounts of history in which women have been marginalized and locate specific historical moments at which women have resisted oppressive forms of male power. In doing so, they show that patriarchal power relations are not total or all-encompassing, but are unstable and responsive to organised social resistance.

Audiences, Consumption and resistance

The tendency within psychoanalytic feminism to see culture as an inherently patriarchal structure which gives women little or no position outside those areas prescribed by 'patriarchal ideology' is also contested by some feminists working on women's reading of romantic fiction. Rather than seeing women who read this fiction as immobilized victims of patriarchy, these feminists have sought to show how the activity of reading such fiction (even if it is 'ideological' in its form) may function as a form of resistance to specific power relations.

For example, Helen Taylor, in *Scarlett's Women: Gone With the Wind and its Female Fans*,[29] invited the women whom she targeted through various magazines and newspapers in 1986 to complete a questionnaire. This questionnaire was compiled with the specific aim of eliciting memories and readings which would detail how each respondent had used *Gone With the Wind* as both novel and film. This study is concerned with the different meanings *Gone With the Wind* had for British and American female fans, from the time it was first screened to the time Taylor began her research. It was also an attempt to investigate how respondents from different social contexts produce differing readings of a single text.

Taylor chronicles the readings her correspondents made of particular aspects of the film: the representation of white Southern womanhood embodied in Scarlett; the film's historical accuracy; the representation of black Southerners and the way in which masculinity is portrayed in the film. As a result, Taylor received markedly divergent responses from the members of her sample group on every aspect of the film. For example, her respondents' reactions to the representation of the black mammy and the black character Prissy in the film were numerous. One woman, who saw the film in the early 1940s, claimed she had never seen a black person and she therefore accepted the portrayal of black characters unquestioningly.[30] Another woman was shocked at the 'childlike, dependent, rather stupid' way in which they were shown.[31] Taylor's black female correspondents, not surprisingly, were critical of the 'one-sided and patronizing' black roles in the film.[32] Taylor therefore illustrates that race, class, age and sexuality are factors which heavily impinge on the meanings audiences produce from texts.

She also stresses that meaning emerges from the relationship between specific audiences and the text, rather than existing as a single, unified object which resides in the text, and waits to be revealed by an individual with enough skill to gain access to it. This emphasis on how readers construct meaning from the text also allows Taylor to discover potentially resistant readings made by the women with whom she corresponded. For some of the women in Taylor's sample group, Scarlett is regarded as a feminist figure. As Taylor documents:

> [Scarlett was seen as] an early feminist – 'a premature women's libber', as one put it. This is expressed in different ways, and often by women over the age of fifty in terms of bravery and 'guts'. One woman commented on the 'egalitarian nature' of Scarlett's relationship with Rhett, and her 'ability to succeed in a man's world' – both elements other women observe with approval. A great many note with considerable envy the fact that Scarlett knows what she wants, and then goes ahead and gets it.[33]

Taylor also argues that many of the fans felt they could identify with Scarlett's fictional characterization because they viewed her as a woman who, despite experiencing a great deal of loss in life, managed to survive. Taylor uses the example of a Jewish woman, Anne Karpf, whose parents survived the Holocaust, and whose experience of the loss of family, home and land was acute. Taylor cites the way in which she utilized *Gone With the Wind* by quoting her directly: 'the way in which her life was so sharply divided into two mirrors my parent's lives, pre-war and post-war. The loss of Scarlett's privileged life and home, the rupture of the family – these are the *Gone With the Wind* stories that really spoke to me.'[34] Examples such as these illustrate the fact that women clearly use fictional texts as a way of recognizing and voicing their own interests and aspirations.

Janice Radway, in her book *Reading the Romance: Women, Patriarchy and Popular Literature*,[35] also used ethnography in order to research the specific social and contextual factors which influenced the consumption of romantic fiction by a group of women from Smithton, Ohio. While this text shares the focus on the contextual factors which influence readings dealt with in Taylor's text, it also argues that particular forms of consumption have the potential to act as part of a wider challenge to patriarchal power relations. Radway worked closely with Dorothy Evans, a middle-class wife and mother who, at the time of Radway's research, was a bookstore worker and resident expert-adviser to her regular female customers. It was through Dot that Radway was able to set up a group of forty-two women who were prepared to help her with her research on how they used romantic novels.

When Radway began to investigate the reading habits of the Smithton women, she found that this sample of educated, economically comfortable women had an 'intense reliance' on these novels.[36] This dependence manifested itself in several ways: a sizeable proportion of the women read every day; the group devoted large amounts of time to their reading, often compressing it around extremely heavy domestic schedules; and they often found it impossible to abandon a text before finishing it. Radway's findings show that 55 per cent of the women managed to consume between one and four novels per week.[37] Radway's interpretation of the way in which these texts were consumed also shows that these women were quite aware of what ingredients the most intensely pleasurable romance must contain. For example, a happy ending was crucial. As a result of studying the consumption of these texts, Radway argued that they provided emotional nourishment which helped these women to shore up the lack which they experienced as a result of the patriarchal power relations which structures their daily lives.

It is Radway's study of the Smithton women's reading of romantic fiction in the context of the home, however, which produced some of the most interesting findings. The context of the home was precisely that in which the pressures of family and domestic life were most acute, and Radway found that the activity of reading within this context often served as a type of resistance. For example, she quotes Dot's account of her customers' thoughts: "'Hey", they say, "this is what I want to do and I'm gonna do it. This is for me. I'm doin' for you all the time. Now leave me, just leave me alone. Let me have my time, my space.

Let me do what I want to do.'" Romantic fiction, Radway argues, gave these women the opportunity to resist the demands made upon them in the home while they 'vicariously attend to their own requirements as independent individuals who require emotional sustenance and solicitude'.[39] Radway's group also claimed that their reading actually changed their sense of themselves quite dramatically. The women's reading of what they termed 'bad' romances – that is romances which contain passive and weak heroines – made them question their own lives:

> Dot explained, the readers 'are thinking they're "nerds". And they begin to re-evaluate. "Am I acting like that?"' They begin to say to themselves, she added, ' Hey wait a minute – my old man kinda tends to do this.' And then, 'because women are capable of learning from what they read', they begin 'to express what they want and sometimes refuse to be ordered around any longer'.[40]

The Smithton women's favourite heroines were both intelligent and independent. The pleasure they derived from identifying with these heroines is also claimed to have had an effect upon their lives. Many women claimed that by identifying with these heroines, they became more assertive. As a result, while Radway has some reservations about romantic fiction – for example she is worried by the generic representations of rape[41] – she still maintains that a text-based approach would miss the fact that romance reading can be a resistant activity. As Radway argues, 'the significance of the act of reading itself might, under some conditions, contradict, undercut, or qualify the significance of producing a particular kind of story'.[42] This shift of emphasis is relevant for the study of popular film. Film studies tends to remain focused on an analysis of the film text and needs to consider the historical and cultural conditions of consumption.

Rather than simply identifying conservative ideologies within texts or groups of texts, film studies needs to consider the significance and meaning of different forms of consumption. Just as the reading of romantic fiction may be used to resist the demands made upon women in the home, so might the activity of watching particular types of films on television, video or at the cinema. On the other hand, the choice between watching a video or going to the cinema may also have a significant implication. A trip to the cinema, for example, may give women the opportunity to escape the constraints and demands of everyday life within the home. As Helen Taylor has argued in her work on *Gone With the Wind*, cinema-going can have the status of an 'event' which may also provide an opportunity for female friends to get together on their own. The example of melodrama is particularly relevant here. While film studies has debated its ideological significance, it has largely failed to discuss how melodrama is used within women's daily lives. This does not invalidate textual analysis itself, but requires a consideration of the social conditions of textual production and consumption. Without such a consideration, a proper understanding of the role of film in women's lives is virtually impossible and film studies will continue to concentrate on how women are dominated, rather than on how they might resist domination.

Pornography and popular film

Probably no area of popular film has been seen as so entirely male-dominated and ideologically oppressive in relation to women than pornography. At the centre of the feminist debate about pornography is the issue of female sexuality and the objectification of women. During the 1980s, in both Britain and the United States, this led to feminist calls for the censorship of pornographic materials. Recently, however, certain feminists have begun to challenge these assumptions about pornography, assumptions which had virtually acquired the status of feminist orthodoxy. The proposals put forward by these anti-censorship feminists have implications not only for feminist approaches to pornography, but also for the analysis of the sexual politics of popular films.

At the opening of her article 'Does Pornography Cause Violence? The Search for Evidence'[43] Lynne Segal argues that there are three opposing positions on the issue: '*liberal, moral right* and *feminist*'.[44] However, as Segal herself acknowledges in her piece, feminist positions have been split since the late 1970s between those who are anti-pornography and those who are anti-censorship.

The anti-pornography feminists, most notably Andrea Dworkin, Susan Griffin, Catherine Mackinnon and Robin Morgan, several of whom have been active in the radical feminist movement, have historically campaigned for a separatist women's culture. These feminists argue that pornography not only justifies sexual violence against women, but ultimately acts as a theoretical incitement to rape. As Andrew Ross argues, the feminists in this camp believe that all men are essentially 'rapacious and gynocidal'.[45] According to this position, the insatiable and destructive elements of male sexuality, supposedly exemplified by pornography, are violence against the integrity of women's sexuality and bodies. For this group, as Carol Clover argues, pornography 'is a *meaningful text about* the sexual acts it represents'.[46] It is presented as a transparent medium which reveals the 'truth' about masculinity. As a result the only possible course of effective action is to eradicate pornography, which is identified as the causal factor which incites male violence.

However, there are problems with the assumption that there is a direct causal link between pornography and sexual violence. Ethnographic and empirical research on the effects of pornography conducted in the 1960s and 1970s found no evidence to suggest that such a connection exists.[47] More recently, Donnerstein, Linz and Penrod in *The Question of Pornography: Research Findings and Policy Implications*[48] found that male subjects who were shown pornographic material including violence admitted to feelings of arousal upon which they might act. However, the authors found that similar results were produced when subjects were shown non-sexually explicit material which contained violence to women. This evidence led the authors to conclude that it was the *violence* which was the significant element in relation to these aggressive responses.

Segal also argues that laboratory research in itself is highly problematic and unreliable. Its 'highly artificial conditions … may not involve behaviour which is in any way generalisable'.[49] Moreover, this research, conducted outside the context in which these materials are generally consumed, ignores the factor which Segal regards as crucial to the debate, 'the complex question of the relationship between fantasy and reality, between psychic arousal and behaviour'.[50] The engagement in sexual fantasy need not necessarily be realized.

Gillian Rodgerson and Elizabeth Wilson in their book *Pornography and Feminism: The Case Against Censorship* refute the behaviourist assumptions of the anti-pornography feminists:

> Some feminists … argued that male violence, especially the sexual violence with which they were particularly concerned, was the result of direct example … Yet this theoretical cocktail of biologism and behaviourism is lethal. To see men as naturally programmed for violence is to endorse the most conservative views on human nature, and to see it as unchanging and unchangeable.[51]

To assume that masculinity is fixed or closed to historical and social change would effectively mean that the feminist challenge to male violence was doomed from the outset.

Moreover, the anti-pornography feminists, in joining with the moral right over the issue of pornography, have tended to ally themselves with a politics which embraces the traditional, reactionary gender and familial roles which feminists have traditionally sought to question and challenge. This alliance also turned to the state to legislate against pornography, a tactic which had numerous problems. First, it made feminists dependent upon the state to act on their behalf, whereas they had previously challenged and criticized the state's role in maintaining sexual inequality. Second, this situation made it more likely that the sexual material which was traditionally defined as 'deviant', such as that dealing with gay and lesbian relationships, would find itself increasingly under attack. There was a danger that traditional sexual relationships and family structures would be privileged, while the very alternatives feminists had fought to defend or promote would be outlawed. As a result, anti-pornography feminists allied themselves with interests which were in many ways contrary to the political concerns which feminists had traditionally sought to protect and defend.

The anti-pornography feminists also tended to reproduce a fairly traditional and essentialist notion of male and female sexuality. Men were violent, aggressive and genitally-centred, while women's sexuality was more caring, loving and less focused on the genitals. As a result, these feminists were less concerned to promote alternative sexualities and sexual relationships than to restrict and control existing ones. Men's violent and aggressive sexuality had to be contained in order to protect women. This position, however, has been criticized by many anti-censorship feminists who point out that it also tends to oppress women. It tends to be 'normative'. It legislates between legitimate and illegitimate sexualities, and it does not create greater sexual freedom. Instead it requires adherence to specific norms. For example, women who might desire penetrative genital sex have been condemned as 'brainwashed', 'male-identified', and even 'gender-traitors'.[52]

A related problem is the tendency of the anti-pornography feminists to see pornography and male power as a virtually all-pervasive and impenetrable monolith which is unchanging in its essential characteristics. But such a position only emphasizes the conception of women as powerless victims, a characterization which Linda Williams criticizes in her book, *Hardcore*: 'As long as we emphasise woman's role as the absolute victim of male sadism, we only perpetuate the supposedly essential nature of women's powerlessness.'[53]

The anti-censorship feminists, on the other hand, present a far more politically useful analysis. They argue that sexual images are not inherently meaningful or transparent representations of real sexual relations. Instead their forms are seen as far more various than the anti-pornography feminists suggest, and their effects are seen as far more dependent upon the context of their use. This group of feminists has also challenged monolithic conceptions of pornography by exploring its contradictions: some pornography contains dominatrix scenarios which represent men as women's sexual slaves; and there are many kinds of pornography with images which challenge dominant assumptions about male–female sexual relations.

Feminists in this camp have asked what pornography might have to offer women, and there is increasing evidence to suggest that women find gratification through some forms of pornography. Andrew Ross claims that 'Forty per cent of the adult videos in the US are rented by women … Cable programmers, moreover, report that most single women choose to pay extra for the adult entertainment option on a cable package.'[55] Ross also documents a relatively fresh presence in the pornography market of products directly aimed at women and heterosexual couples. Referring to a film which was produced and directed by Candida Royalle, *Christine's Secret*, Ross describes the film as 'a new kind of porn film, made by women, that is organised in a non-phallic way'.[56] Women are, therefore, actively producing alternative representations which serve their interests and give them pleasure.

However, this focus on activity and desire does not mean that male power and its exploitative constraints can be ignored. Carol Vance, in her opening speech at the Barnard conference *Toward a Politics of Sexuality*, argued:

> To focus on pleasure and gratification ignores the patriarchal structure in which women act, yet to speak only of sexual violence and oppression ignores women's experience with sexual agency and choice and unwittingly increases the sexual terror and despair in which women live.'[57]

Rodgerson and Wilson, mindful of the 'patriarchal structure', argue that pornography plays a relatively minor role in the wider regime of sexist practices pervading women's lives. The more worrying examples of pornography are merely symptoms of women's oppression, rather than its cause. Indeed, they argue that the exclusive focus on pornography has distracted feminist attention away from a whole range of other, potentially more urgent, issues: 'And all the while the real battle is elsewhere: it is the battle against unequal pay structures, against a lack of opportunities for girls and women.' [58] It is these issues and structures which provide the conditions within which pornography in particular, and popular film in general, are produced and consumed. They are what is at stake in feminist struggles and that which shapes women's experiences of everyday life. But such inequality does not define women solely as victims of power. It is vital to recognize that women are not simply the passive objects of a monolithic 'patriarchal ideology', but are actively engaged in resistances and struggles within their everyday lives.

Popular feminism in contemporary Hollywood cinema

Penny Marshall is a contemporary female director who has made significant and interesting contributions to Hollywood's film output, and her film *A League of their Own* (1992) illustrates that both film-makers and film critics share a common culture. Film critics presuppose a sense of distance from their object of study which may be insupportable. Many film-makers have been through film school and have been trained in feminist criticism, while others may read feminist writings and even be active in feminist movements themselves. As a result, Marshall's film is not simply open to feminist readings, but clearly develops out of many of the feminist traditions and concerns discussed previously.

Marshall's *A League of their Own* seeks to construct a history of women's baseball in the United States during World War II. Focusing on a particular set of women who are plucked from their varied backgrounds to join a women's baseball league, the film charts the ups and downs of their progression through the league's championship. Significantly, the film is careful to include scenes where the central female players are shown to be highly-skilled baseball players (either physically competent athletes or skilful strategists) in their home community *before* they are chosen and trained for league games. This serves as a pointer to their genuine, but so far only provincially realized, talent. In this way, the film can be seen to work within the socialist feminist strategy of reconstructing the sport's history.

The film shows how the women in the baseball team, the Rockford Peaches, are forced to operate within patriarchal constraints and documents the feared masculinization of female players involving themselves in a sport previously defined as a male preserve. In order to make baseball played by women palatable to spectators, the women are forced to wear impractical, scanty uniforms which clearly signpost the unmistakable femininity of their bodies. But while the Rockford Peaches agree to comply with some of the terms laid down for them by the team's manager – for example, they agree to wear a short-skirted uniform – the female collective is also shown to turn management terms around to suit its own objectives. The team agrees to 'perform' for publicity shots when audience figures decline, but they do so in order to continue their fight to play baseball. Moreover, providing 'performances' also affords these players the opportunity to show that they can perform both the 'masculine' and the 'feminine' roles. For example, the leading female character and star player, Dottie Hinson (Geena Davis), is shown 'doing the splits' in order to catch the ball, a move which testifies to her extra-ordinary skill. This team earns respect because the women in it are accomplished players who literally knock down those who try to humiliate them. During an early match, as a male member of the audience jeers at the notion of a women's team, Ellen Sue Gotlander (Freddie Simpson) throws the baseball with such incredible force of strength that the audience turns to laugh at the sexist and are jolted into the recognition that they are in the presence of truly talented female players.

This women-centred film also portrays Dottie's decision to terminate her baseball career, so that she can begin a family with her husband who returns from the war, as a tragic and regrettable sacrifice. The implications of Dottie's decision not to pursue a lifetime career opportunity and a re-entry into female comradeship, is emphasised further when she attends a baseball reunion towards the end of the film. At this important and moving event, which celebrates the opening of an exhibition documenting the history of women's baseball, Dottie's regret that she did not continue her career is poignantly sharpened. In this way, the film shows the problems women encountered in post-war American society; Dottie cannot reconcile her desire to be a successful baseball star with her desire to be a wife and mother. Dottie's decision to return home is shown to be a way in which this character deals with the contradictions of women's identity. She is shown to insist at several moments in the film that she can't remain in the team because of her desire to begin a family. The pressures for her to behave appropriately as a wife are shown to override her other aspirations, because she has internalized certain definitions of what it means to be a good wife. *A League of their Own* shows that women did not return home merely because they were forced to; they did so because they responded to the social construction of femininity in circulation in post-war America.

The experience of membership in an all-female team is shown to be positive and powerful. Doris Murphy (Rosie O'Donnell) gains a sense of personal confidence as she realizes that her love of baseball does not make her strange and unfeminine, a realization which persuades her to terminate her relationship with an abusive boyfriend. Kit Keller (Lori Petty) learns to value her contribution to baseball as different from, but as important as, her sister Dottie's, and finds a place outside her shadow. Marla Hooch (Megan Cavanagh) learns to stop regarding herself as ugly and discovers her sexuality; and Mae Mordabito (Madonna) teaches Shirley Baker (Ann Cusack) to read. The feeling of self-worth, the result of working in a collective, is a positive and nurturing experience for the whole team. Moreover, the experience of being in the team is shown to have been one of the most important periods of these women's lives, thereby making the women's meeting all the more moving and poignant.

A League of their Own is a film which actively appropriates the feminist concerns previously discussed, but is not only concerned with white women's interests. The plight of black American women, and an awareness of their exclusion from women's baseball, is also referenced in the film. At one moment in the film the baseball lands outside the pitch during a league game and a black women in the crowd throws the ball back. She does so with great force and the look she exchanges with Dottie clearly suggests that she too has the skill to be a team member. As a result, the text emphasizes that just as the white women ball players had previously been excluded from baseball history, their story also excluded the black women who were not allowed to play at all. As a result, in this film women are not simply objects of male desire, nor characters motivated by men, but rather active subjects who control the narrative. The film opens with Dottie's personal journey to the Doubleday Field reunion, and her memories recall how the women struggled to keep the sport alive for women.

A League of their Own attempts to rediscover the history of women's baseball in a manner that can be politically empowering for female spectators. The film highlights the patriarchal constraints with which these women had to contend, but it also, most importantly, seeks to celebrate women's history as one of active resistance and collective struggle.

Notes:

1 Laura Mulvey, 'Visual Pleasure and Narrative Cinema', in Screen Editorial Collective, *The Sexual Subject: A Screen Reader in Sexuality*, London: Routledge, 1991, pp. 22–33.

2 *Ibid.*, p. 22.
3 Jackie Stacey, 'Desperately Seeking Difference' in Lorraine Gamman and Margaret Marshment, eds, *The Female Gaze: Women as Viewers of Popular Culture*, London: The Women's Press, 1988, p. 116.
4 See, for example, Suzanne Moore, 'Here's Looking at You Kid!', in *The Female Gaze*, pp. 44–59; and Jacqui Roach and Petal Felix, 'Black Looks', in *The Female Gaze*, pp. 130–42.
5 *The Female Gaze*, p. 5.
6 *Ibid.*
7 'Desperately Seeking Difference', p.11
8 *Ibid.*, p. 133.
9 *Ibid.*, p. 115.
10 *Ibid.*, p. 129.
11 *Ibid.*, p. 113.
12 bell hooks, *Black Looks: Race and Representation*, London: Turnaround, 1992, pp. 122–3.
13 See, for example, Jacqueline Bobo, '*The Colour Purple*: Black Women as Cultural Readers', in Deirdre Pribram, ed, *Female Spectators: Looking at Film and Television*, London: Verso, 1990, pp. 90–109.
14 *Black Looks*, p. 124.
15 Marjorie Rosen, *Popcorn Venus: Women, Movies and the American Dream*, New York: Avon, 1973.
16 Molly Haskell, *From Reverence to Rape: The Treatment of Women in the Movies*, London: University of Chicago Press, 1987.
17 Jackie Byars, *All That Hollywood Allows: Re-Reading Gender in 1950s Melodrama*, London: Routledge, 1991.
18 *Ibid.*, p. 27.
19 Molly Haskell quoted in *All that Hollywood Allows*, p. 68.
20 *Popcorn Venus*, p. 81.
21 *Ibid.*, p. 390.
22 *Ibid.*, p. 397.
23 *From Reverence to Rape*, p. 59.
24 *Ibid.*, p. 40.
25 Annette Kuhn, *Women's Pictures: Feminism and Cinema*, London: Routledge and Kegan Paul, 1982, p. 75.
26 Sheila Rowbotham, *Hidden From History: 300 Years of Women's Oppression and the Fight Against it*, London: Pluto Press, 1973.
27 *Ibid.*, p. 34.
28 Jan Lambertz, 'Sexual Harassment in the Nineteenth-Century English Cotton Industry', *History Workshop Journal*, No. 19 (spring 1985), pp. 28–61.
29 Helen Taylor, *Scarlett's Women: Gone With the Wind and its Female Fans*, London: Virago, 1989.

30 *Ibid.*, p. 192.
31 *Ibid.*, p. 193.
32 *Ibid.*
33 *Ibid.*, p. 103.
34 *Ibid.*, p. 100.
35 Janice Radway, *Reading the Romance: Women, Patriarchy and Popular Literature*, London: Verso, 1987.
36 *Ibid.*, p. 59.
37 *Ibid.*, p. 60.
38 *Ibid.*, p. 92.
39 *Ibid.*, p. 93.
40 *Ibid.*, p. 102.
41 *Ibid.*, p. 216.
42 *Ibid.*, p. 210.
43 Lynne Segal, 'Does Pornography cause Violence? The Search for Evidence', in Pamela Church Gibson and Roma Gibson, eds, *Dirty Looks: Women, Pornography and Power*, London: British Film Institute, 1993, pp. 5–21.
44 *Ibid.*, p. 6.
45 Andrew Ross, *No Respect: Intellectuals and Popular Culture*, London: Routledge, 1991, p. 186.
46 Carol Clover, 'Introduction', in *Dirty Looks*, p. 186.
47 'Does Pornography Cause Violence?', p. 12.
48 E. Donnerstein, D. Linz and S. Penrod, *The Question of Pornography: Research Findings and Policy Implications*, London: Collier Macmillan, 1987.
49 'Does Pornography cause Violence?', p. 13.
50 *Ibid.*
51 Gillian Rodgerson and Elizabeth Wilson, *Feminism and Pornography: the Case against Censorship*, London: Lawrence and Wishart, 1991, p. 36.
52 See Ellen Willis, 'Sexual Politics', in Ian Angus and Sut Jhally, eds, *Cultural Politics in Contemporary America*, London: Routledge, 1989, pp. 167–81.
53 Linda Williams, *Hardcore: Power, Pleasure and the 'Frenzy of the Visible'*, London: Paladin, 1990, p. 22.
54 See Anne McClintock, 'Maid to Order: Commercial S/M and Gender Power', in *Dirty Looks*, pp. 207–31.
55 *No Respect*, p. 173.
56 *Ibid.*, p. 171.
57 Quoted in *No Respect*, p. 190.
58 *Feminism and Pornography*, p. 75.

Popular culture or film art? Norman Bates ponders the contradictions of *Psycho* (1960)

Cultural studies
and popular film

Cultural studies emerged in Britain during the 1970s – the same period as screen theory – and was closely associated at this time with work generated at the Centre for Contemporary Cultural Studies (CCCS) in Birmingham. In fact, both 'screen theory' and cultural studies developed, at least initially, through a process of dialogue and debate with one another. The conclusion to David Morley's classic cultural studies text, *The 'Nationwide' Audience*,[1] for example, clearly situates its position in relation to certain tendencies in screen theory. However, screen theory and cultural studies were not mutually exclusive. Many of the figures associated with cultural studies were published in *Screen*, and there was a constant interchange of ideas between the two approaches. As a result, the main feature which came to distinguish cultural studies from screen theory in the 1970s was that while the latter tended to see popular film as a form of ideological domination, cultural studies tended to see the 'popular' as a site of struggle between groups, rather than the property or expression of any specific group's interests. For this reason, cultural studies did not rely upon a simple opposition between a conservative popular culture and a radical avant-garde, but tended to be far more historical in its focus. It was concerned with the ways in which cultural forms developed through a process of conflict and struggle between social groups.

Work within cultural studies was also critical of the way in which screen theory tended to neglect the social conditions within which the consumption of cultural texts took place. Screen theory was preoccupied with textual analysis, and tended to deduce the ideological effect of texts from an analysis of their formal features. However, this form of analysis, as has frequently been pointed out, tends to ignore the activities of audiences. It implies a 'hypodermic' model of media effects in which audiences are seen as little more than a 'passive mass' who are acted upon by the text and have little or no means of resistance. For example, *The Cinema Book*,[2] a text which claims to provide a comprehensive summary of the major areas in film studies, gives very little space to the discussion of audiences. Even in the section entitled 'Narrative and the Audience', the analysis of audiences remains abstract. It is concerned with the ways in which texts construct the position of the spectator, not with the ways in which actual audiences make sense of texts. Although it is briefly acknowledged that social factors may affect interpretation, and that, as a result, the position of the spectator constructed by the text might not coincide with the position of 'empirical spectators' (actual social subjects), the implications of this observation are not drawn out. If social factors do affect interpretation, and if this does mean that the position of the spectator as constructed by the text does not necessarily coincide with that of 'empirical spectators', then one cannot simply deduce the ideological effect of a text from an analysis of its formal features.

As a result, some sort of investigation into the social conditions of the audience is essential if one is to understand the meaning and significance of popular film. However, this kind of work has largely been conducted within the field of media and cultural studies, rather than film studies; and usually in relation to television and popular fiction, rather than film.

None the less, the cultural studies approach can be applied to the analysis of popular film, and its strength is that it avoids the tendency either to celebrate or to condemn popular forms. It allows one to study how distinctions between popular film and more legitimate areas of cinema are produced and reproduced, and the ways in which such distinctions act to legitimate the tastes of dominant social groups. Furthermore, as the introduction suggested, many of the critics associated with cultural studies have questioned what is at stake in different definitions of 'the popular'.

The emergence of cultural studies

Cultural studies has emerged and developed over the past twenty-five years, most notably in Britain, Australia, the USA and Canada. It emerged out of a dialogue among different academic disciplines, most notably literature, history and sociology. Each of these disciplines offered different approaches to their area of study, and it was the ways in which cultural studies sought to bring these approaches together and relate them to one another which justified its claim to interdisciplinarity. This interdisciplinarity, coupled with the rapid expansion of work in the area, has made it difficult to define exactly what cultural studies is. Different institutions and practitioners seem to have very different ideas about what the area is or could be. But this difficulty in pinning cultural studies down also remains its greatest asset. It offers the possibility of developing different ways of analysising and understanding which can be applied to diverse areas of study.

None the less, it is widely accepted that the roots of what was to become cultural studies lie in the work of three British writers: Richard

Hoggart, Raymond Williams and E. P. Thompson. During the late 1950s and the 1960s, these critics were responsible for extending the meaning of the word culture. Instead of equating 'culture' with a 'canon' of great works of art as many previous critics had done, these writers used it in a quite different sense. They tended to use culture in its social or anthropological sense to refer to the institutions, activities and beliefs which define a social group's particular way of life. It was for this reason that Williams claimed that culture was 'ordinary'.[3] He acknowledged that the word 'culture' had come to mean 'the outward and emphatically visible sign of a special kind of people, cultivated people',[4] but he argued there was another meaning. For Williams, culture was not the property of social elites, but was also 'a particular way of life, which expresses certain meanings and values not only in art and learning but also in institutions and ordinary behaviour'. This emphasis on ordinary behaviour was central and it opened up the possibility of taking the study of working-class or popular culture seriously.

Hoggart's *The Uses of Literacy*[5] made a valuable contribution to this project. Rather than using his literary training simply to analyse and privilege official literary masterpieces, Hoggart turned his attention to working-class cultural forms such as pubs, working men's clubs, sports, popular songs, etc. In so doing, he sought to evoke the complex relations which distinguished this culture in order to portray it as a 'full rich life'. Whereas earlier critics had opposed a cultured minority to an uncultured working-class majority, Hoggart's analysis demonstrated that the working class had a rich and complex cultural tradition of its own. However, unlike Williams, he argued that this traditional working-class culture was being threatened and corrupted by a 'brash' and inauthentic mass culture. The working-class culture which he valued was presented as a traditional organic community, but one which was already located in a past associated with his own nostalgic memories of childhood. The popular music, television, fiction and film which were so important to the working-class culture of the 1950s and 1960s were therefore seen merely to corrupt and debase this earlier form of working class culture, and replace its richness and complexity with superficiality and artificiality.

Williams, on the other hand, became fascinated with these new media and the analysis of these forms was to become 'the central plank of the new field of cultural studies'.[6] Like Hoggart, Williams wanted to extend the analysis of culture beyond the realm of high culture to include the patterns of working-class life. But in his attempt to study 'the characteristic forms through which members of society communicate',[7] he was willing to take the new systems of 'communications' seriously, rather than seeing them simply as a threat to 'authenticity'. Whatever the problems with Williams's analysis of communications, its strength was that it sought to acknowledge their importance in cultural life and to develop modes of analysis which were appropriate to them. Although this included an analysis of media institutions and modes of production, Williams' examination of the cultural industries rejected the assumptions associated with mass culture theory in which high cultural forms were privileged as if they were somehow free of specific institutions and modes of production.

At this stage, however, Williams was still concerned to analyse 'the culture of a whole society', and it was this approach which E. P. Thompson criticized in his review of Williams's *The Long Revolution*. Thompson was both a historian and a Marxist, and as a Marxist he took issue with Williams's definition of culture as 'a whole way of life'. For Thompson, culture was better described as 'a whole way of conflict'.[8] He wanted to present culture as the product of struggles between *different* ways of life. Working-class culture was not simply different from middle-class culture, but was a specific form of opposition to it. For Thompson, working-class culture did not simply arise out of the shared meanings and values of a particular class at a specific moment in history; it was central to the emergence of a class. It was the specific means by which its members assembled themselves as a class 'for itself' and so resisted their exploitation by other classes.[9]

In this way, Thompson was reacting against specific forms of Marxism - specifically Althusserian or structural Marxism – which maintained that classes were simply defined by their relationship to the means of production. In contrast, Thompson argued that culture was essential to the formation of any class. Cultural concerns were not secondary to class politics, but were the specific realm within which resistance was articulated and practised. As a result, he not only claimed that working-class resistance took place through popular culture, he also emphasized that issues of domination, resistance and contestation were central to popular forms.

Because culturalists such as Hoggart celebrated working-class cultural production as an authentic expression of working-class interests, they tended to be critical of mass cultural forms such as cinema which they believed were imposed on the working-class community from the outside. The importance of film as a popular form was either ignored

or seen as a sign of inauthenticity and superficiality. In this way, this
work often reproduced some of the oppositions that had structured
debates about the popular in mass culture theory. Nevertheless, it has
also been pointed out that the cinema was an important institution in
the working-class community, and cinema-going an important practice.[10] Furthermore, it is possible to see a 'fit' between some films and
working-class cultural values and practices. For example, as Chambers
argues, Ealing comedies in the 1940s and 1950s emphasized 'the subal-
tern world and values of the street community, the pub, the Corona-
tion cup, fading sepia photographs on the parlour mantelpiece, the
virtues of working and sticking together'.[11] However, as Chambers
notes, this fails to exlain why, on the whole, British working-class audiences have tended to prefer American films. For early critics like Hoggart this could only be interpreted as a sign of the power of mass culture
and the ways in which Americanization was 'unbending the springs of
action' of the British working class. Alternatively, as Miles and Smith
have suggested in their work on 1930s cinema, American films may have
'fitted' more closely with the values of a British working-class audience
than British films.

Hegemony, dialogue and taste

By the 1970s, cultural studies was beginning to establish itself as a vital
and important area within academic life, and, in this period, much of
the work that helped shape it was associated with the Centre for Contemporary Cultural Studies (CCCS) at the University of Birmingham.
Under the directorship of Stuart Hall, the work of the Centre was still
clearly indebted to Hoggart, Williams and Thompson, but it was also
influenced by an alternative theoretical tradition, French structuralism.
In fact, Hall has claimed that it was the tensions between culturalism
and structuralism which were decisive in the formation of cultural
studies.[12] For example, while culturalists such as Hoggart, Williams and
Thompson had emphasized the creativity of ordinary people in the production of their own culture, structuralism tended to stress determinism. Rather than seeing culture as the product of human activity,
structuralism tended to see human activity as the product of culture.

The importance of structuralism to the Centre was that it offered a
theory of ideology which was a necessary antidote to culturalism's
overemphasis on the radicalism of working-class popular culture.
Although structuralism may have overemphasized ideological domina-

tion and provided little real space for struggle, it did offer some explanation of how cultural reproduction was brought about and how ordinary working people came to accept or even support the inequalities of the existing social system. However, cultural studies was far more critical of structuralism than was screen theory. (For an outline of this position, see chapter six.) As Hall pointed out, structuralism had functionalist tendencies which made it almost impossible for those working within this theoretical framework to conceive of 'ideologies which are not, by definition, "dominant"', nor could it broach 'the concept of struggle' in anything but a gestural way.[13] Ultimately Hall argues that just as the weaknesses of culturalism were answered by structuralism, the weaknesses of structuralism were answered by culturalism. As he noted, culturalism 'insisted, correctly, on the affirmative moment of the development of conscious struggle and organization as a necessary element in the analysis of history, ideology and consciousness'.[14]

The Centre found a way of overcoming the tensions between culturalism and structuralism in the work of Antonio Gramsci, an Italian neo-Marxist. However, the way out of the impasse between these two previous positions also depended on the influence of the Russian linguist, V. N. Volosinov, and in a far less explicit way, the French cultural analyst, Pierre Bourdieu.

The importance of Gramsci's work was that it enabled the Centre to address the issue of cultural domination without conceptualizing subordinate groups as merely passive 'effects' of ideology. Gramsci's central concept of 'hegemony' (or leadership) offered an explanation of how certain classes and social groups come to establish and maintain a position of dominance over other classes and groups. Rather than simply imposing its own will upon subordinate groups through the use of ideological or physical coercion, Gramsci argued that a class can only attain dominance by 'winning' the right to rule over others. It must present itself as the group which is best able to fulfil the interests and aspirations of other classes or social groups. As a result, he claimed that a class or group can only achieve and maintain dominance over others if it is able to gain the *consent* of other classes or groups by addressing their interests and aspirations and making concessions to them.[15]

However, Gramsci also stressed that hegemony is inherently unstable. Dominant classes can never finally satisfy the demands of subordinate classes. The dominance of one depends on the subordination of the other. For example, as Marx had argued, the interests of the bourgeoisie and the proletariat are necessarily at odds with one another. The dom-

inance of the former depends upon its exploitation of the latter. A bourgeoisie cannot exist without a proletariat to exploit. As a result, there
will always be challenges to dominant classes (so long as there continues to be a dominant class) and such challenges will continually require
the dominant class to reform itself in order to pacify and appease them.
As Stuart Hall argues:

> Hegemony ... is not universal and 'given' to the continuing rule of a par-
> ticular class. It has to be won, reproduced, sustained. Hegemony is, as
> Gramsci said, a 'moving equilibrium' containing relations of forces
> favourable and unfavourable to this or that tendency.[16]

Therefore, by using Gramsci's concept of hegemony the Centre was
able to analyse culture in a way which was, in Raymond Williams'
terms, 'historical' rather than 'epochal'.[17] Rather than understanding
'capitalist' or 'patriarchal' culture as essentially fixed and unchanging
systems, the 'turn to Gramsci' allowed the Centre to address the historical processes through which these systems changed and developed.
For example, the work of the Centre demonstrated that while the political configuration generally referred to as 'Thatcherism' may have been
an example of a capitalist culture, it was significantly different from –
and even opposed to – the post-war welfare capitalism which preceded
it.

Through the concept of hegemony, the Centre was also able not only
to acknowledge the interests and aspirations of different classes and
social groups within a given society at a specific historical moment, it
was also able to illustrate how these interests and aspirations were the
product of struggles between them. In this way, it offers a way out of
the oppositions which had dominated the discussion of popular forms
such as popular film. It enabled one to present an analysis of popular
films which neither celebrated nor condemned them, but examined how
they were produced in relation to the struggles between dominant and
subordinate groups. In this way, as Tony Bennett has argued,

> the critical spirit of Gramsci's work, totally shunning the intolerable con-
> descension of the mass culture critic while simultaneously avoiding any
> tendency towards a celebratory populism, both avoids and disqualifies
> the bipolar alternatives of structuralism and culturalism.[18]

As a result, popular film could no longer be seen as an ideological form
which was simply imposed upon subordinate groups. Instead it was recognized that popular films have to address the interests and aspirations

of their target audiences, even if a particular film may seek to contain those interests and aspirations within specific terms. As a result, popular films will always attempt to resolve contradictory ideologies, rather than simply to promote a specific ideological position.

Gramsci's work also offered a way of rethinking cultural politics so that 'foreign' influences need no longer be seen as a threat to national political struggles. Gramsci's 'project for a radical and political sense of culture did not exclude commercial or American-inspired forms'.[19] This creates space to re-evaluate the relationship between British audiences and Hollywood cinema. If, as Gramsci suggests, national cultural traditions are often implicated in the maintenance of a cultural conservatism, then, as Chambers argues, 'foreign' influences might offer radical alternatives. Indeed, Hollywood might 'represent a more significant challenge to a native cultural hegemony than more local forms of opposition based on more traditional affiliations'.[20]

For example, as Miles and Smith's work demonstrates, British working-class audiences in the 1930s responded to the morality and class-bound character of British cinema by voting with their feet. Rejecting British films as boring, these audiences found that Hollywood offered sexy and strong heroes and heroines in contrast to the puritanism of British cinema. Furthermore, Hollywood offered a vision of a vibrant society that was apparently classless, a world in which change seemed possible. In this way, although Hollywood cinema may not be more democratic than British cinema, it offered British audiences 'a more extensive and imaginative sense of the possible'.[21]

Volosinov's importance was that his work enabled the Centre to develop and apply this approach in terms of language and textuality, terms which were necessary for the analysis of literary, televisual or film texts. While structuralism had seen the meanings of signs as solely the product of their relations to other signs, Volosinov argued that the meanings of signs were always in a process of change and development as different classes or groups struggled over these meanings. For example, the word 'freedom' does not simply gain its meaning from its relation to other signs, but is continually being fought over by different sections of society whose interests and aspirations lead them to define it in different ways. Similarly, words such as 'black' and 'queer' have been used to denigrate certain groups, but they have also been appropriated by these groups and invested with alternative meanings and significance. As Volosinov argued,

> Class does not coincide with the sign community, i.e. with the totality of
> users of the same set of signs of ideological communication. Thus vari-
> ous different classes will use one and the same language. As a result, dif-
> ferently oriented accents intersect in every ideological sign. Sign becomes
> an arena of the class struggle.[22]

As a result, the meanings of signs are always changing as they become
the site of dialogue and debate between different classes and groups.

This position was also applied to 'utterances' or texts. Each text uses
a language which pre-exists it, but reaccents that language. It is part of
a process of dialogue and debate, and as such, each text is shaped
through its response to other texts. Just as Gramsci's work argued that
the dominant group can only win the consent of subordinate groups by
addressing their interests and aspirations, Volosinov's work suggested
that any text must include alternative positions if it is to respond to
other texts. This situation means that no text is ever purely radical or
conservative. Whatever its political ideology, it is always produced
within conditions of power, and as such it must address alternative
interests and aspirations if it is to present its own position as a solution
to them.

For example, *Philadelphia*, the first mainstream Hollywood AIDS
movie, attempts to portray a gay man with AIDS sympathetically and
as a victim of prejudice and dicrimination rather than the disease. In
order to achieve this, it has to engage with and answer other 'utterances'
about gay men and AIDS. For example, the film counters the New
Right's claims that both gays and AIDS are a threat to family values by
continually locating the protagonist, Andrew Beckett, within a strong,
supportive and caring family. The film engages with homophobia not
only through the narrative, but by presenting the homophobic views of
Beckett's attorney and showing how these views can be transformed. In
this way, the film seeks to win support for its case that discrimination
against gays is wrong. It achieves this both by engaging with, and
attempting to displace, the homophobic views that underpin this discrimination and New Right definitions of 'family values'.

Popular films must not only address the interests and aspirations of
their target audience (even if they seek to counter or contain their political implications), they also take elements of other films reworking
them in different ways and so giving them different political inflections.
This latter process is particularly clear in the case of film genres where
similar narrative patterns and figures are reworked with very different

political accents.[23]

For example, after the ways in which the film *Rambo*, became the object of violent criticism, action movies had to distance themselves carefully from associations with this film. For example, in *Die Hard*, the hero, John McClane (Bruce Willis), is taunted by the villain who accuses him of being 'an orphan of a bankrupt culture' and thinks he's 'Rambo'. McClane carefully deflects this association by choosing to identify himself with Roy Rogers, a self-effacing gesture which is able to distance his status as a male action hero from the negative associations of Rambo. In fact, even Sylvester Stallone has had to renegotiate his image in similar ways. In the film *Tango and Cash*, for example, not only does he carry a very small gun (one which is played off against the giant rocket-launcher which he carried on the poster for *Rambo*), but when one character associates him with the character of John Rambo, Stallone's character pointedly rejects the association.[24]

However, Volosinov's arguments about the multi-accentuality of the sign not only means that there will be differences between popular texts, it also means that audiences can respond to texts in different ways. It is here that the influence of Pierre Bourdieu is most pronounced, though it is often not explicitly acknowledged in the work from the Centre. For example, David Morley's work on television audiences is deeply dependent on Bourdieu's study of cultural competences and dispositions.

Bourdieu's analysis of cultural competences and dispositions was an attempt to explain how and why different classes and social groups consumed different cultural forms in different ways.[25] As was noted in chapter four, for Bourdieu, just as class differences are the product of differential access to economic capital, they are also produced through the unequal distribution of cultural capital. It is the amount and type of cultural capital which is possessed by a class which produces specific competences and dispositions. Cultural competences refer to the forms of skill and knowledge which enable one to make sense of certain types of material. For example, some groups may have the competence necessary for an understanding and appreciation of modernist art, but they may lack the competences necessary to make sense of Martial Arts movies. The differential distribution of cultural capital also means that different classes and social groups will have different dispositions; certain groups will be more disposed towards the consumption of avant-garde films and others will be more disposed towards the consumption of popular forms such as 'Carry On' films, action movies, or 'weepies'.

It is these dispositions which make people see certain types of film as 'for me' and other forms as 'not my sort of thing'.

As a result, Bourdieu does not see these differences as the result of individual tastes, but as the product of the ways in which people are socialized within specific classes, particularly through the agency of the family. While we may see our tastes as personal, natural and inherent to ourselves, Bourdieu argues that they are the product of wider (usually class-based) taste formations. (Bourdieu also suggests that the distribution of competences and dispositions is gendered, a point expanded upon in the work of critics such as Angela Partington and Ann Gray.)[26]

However, it is important to stress that Bourdieu is not simply arguing that subordinate sections of society are deprived of access to 'superior' forms of culture, quite the reverse. He is attempting to explain how and why different sections of society engage in different forms of cultural consumption, and the ways in which these differences are both the product of certain power relations and can also help to reproduce and justify those relations. Not only do different sections of society have different forms of cultural consumption, but these different forms of consumption are used to distinguish one group from another. For example, dominant groups often justify their dominance over others by reference to their 'superior' tastes, while subordinate groups will often reject these supposedly 'superior' tastes as 'arty-farty'. As Bourdieu puts it, bourgeois taste is usually defined through its rejection of popular tastes, while popular tastes are usually defined though a rejection of that rejection. As a result, taste formations are not simply produced out of the interests of a specific class or social group, but out of the struggles *between* classes and groups.

Audiences, interpretations and the activities of cultural consumption

As a result of the influence of Gramsci, Volosinov and Bourdieu, many of those associated with the Centre argued that one cannot deduce a particular ideological effect from an analysis of the formal features of a text or group of texts. Instead they stressed that different audiences make different responses on the basis of their specific cultural competences and dispositions. As many critics from the Centre have pointed out, the problem with much work on popular culture is not only that it obscures differences between texts, but also that it tends to present the audience as a homogeneous and passive mass. However, members of a film audience, for example, have a history which has constructed them as social subjects prior to their encounter with a particular film, and they will have attitudes and opinions which have been shaped by this history. As a result, while a film might have a 'preferred reading' which seeks to elicit certain responses from its audience, real audiences are not compelled to respond in this way. They may accept the film's ideological position, but they may also qualify or even reject that position.

For example, in his highly influential article 'Encoding/Decoding', Hall outlines three categories of audience responses: 'dominant', 'negotiated' and 'oppositional' readings.[27] The dominant reading, it is argued, uncritically accepts the text's 'preferred meaning'. (At this stage, it was still assumed that media texts necessarily presented dominant or hegemonic ideological positions.) People who produce the oppositional reading, Hall argues, challenge the positions presented by the text and articulate their opposition to these positions. The negotiated reading, on the other hand, is claimed to be the most common, and, it is argued, falls somewhere between the other two readings. While not always completely opposed to the dominant ideological positions present in the text, it does not simply accept them either. Negotiated readings may acknowledge contradictory evidence, which may be the product of the viewer's own experience, but define such evidence as merely an exception to the rule. For example, a viewer who has been harassed by a policeman may watch a news report which praises the police and denies that they harass people. In such a situation, he might accept the news report and believe that his own experience was simply the result of 'one bad apple'.

Although the Centre acknowledged the importance of the audiences, it did not reject textual analysis. This is illustrated by David Morley and Charlotte Brunsdon's *Everyday Television* which uses semiotics to analyse the television programme *Nationwide*. However, for Morley and Brunsdon this semiotic analysis was not used to provide a definitive reading of the text and its effects upon its audience. Instead it was simply seen as 'a base line against which differential readings might be posed'.[28] In other words, it was a first stage in a research process which would include an interrogation of the readings which specific audience groups made of this text. This did not mean that Morley and Brunsdon thought that any text could be read in any way. On the contrary, they argued that texts did have preferred readings, but that the social history of audience members will affect their interpretation of, and responses to, these preferred readings. Therefore, Morley and Bruns-don rejected the assumption within screen theory that the dominant ideology was guaranteed simply because a viewer watching a film was being 'positioned by the text'. Instead, they argued that it was also a matter of what position the text presented, and how the viewer responded to that position. As Morley puts it, domination is not secured solely through 'the successful positioning of the subject in the signifying process (the same signification or position is compatible with different ideological problematics; successful positioning in the chain of signification is not a guarantee of dominant decodings); but also because of the acceptance of what is said.'[29]

However, the different ways in which audiences interpret or decode a text are not just a result of whether they accept or reject a text's ideological position. As Morley argues, the relevance/irrelevance and comprehension/incomprehension of specific types of material must also be taken into account.[30] In this way, the effect of a text is also related to whether or not people choose to view these texts, and whether or not they are able to make sense of them. For example, an avant-garde film will not have the effect which many film theorists identify as the product of its formal features unless one is familiar with the theories and conventions of avant-garde cinema. But, in the same way, familiarity with the avant-garde will not equip one to make sense of popular cinema.

This may also help to explain why people so often find the tastes of others so incomprehensible. They literally do not comprehend what others see in the texts which they choose to consume. This sense of incomprehension is also related to whether or not people view a film as relevant to them or not. If they do not believe that it 'speaks to them', they may not only refuse to see the film, but also be hostile in their interpretation of it if they do see it. This not only applies to people who may justifiably feel that art-house films are 'not for people like me', but also relates to issues such as genre. It has often been claimed that different genres appeal to different genders, and while such gendered divisions are never absolute, there are good reasons why women may tend to see war films as irrelevant to their lives, or men tend to see domestic dramas as irrelevant to them. In such a situation, even if the power relations involved in such divisions do not produce a hostile response, a film's irrelevance to the viewer will make it unlikely that its ideological concerns will have much purchase or impact upon the viewer.

However, cultural studies has not simply been concerned with the competences and dispositions of audiences. As Morley has pointed out, the social situation of the viewer may also affect decoding and interpretation in other ways. For example, he felt dissatisfied with *The 'Nationwide' Audience* because he had not been able to examine the different responses which might be made by the same people within the different contexts of the workplace and the home. As a result, by the time he published *Family Television* he claimed that his 'focus of interest [had] shifted from the analysis of the patterns of differential "readings" of particular programme materials, to the analysis of the domestic viewing context itself – as the framework within which "readings" of programmes are (ordinarily) made.'[31] His point was that the meaning of cultural consumption cannot be limited to the interpretation or decoding of particular texts. For this reason he refers to Janice Radway who has suggested that whether the genre of romantic fiction is ideologically conservative or not, the activity of reading romantic fiction is often a form of resistance through which women are able to escape the demands made upon them in the domestic sphere. As Radway has argued, 'The significance of the act of reading itself might, under some conditions, contradict, undercut, or qualify the significance of producing a particular kind of story.'[32] As a result, Morley has argued that one of the problems which film studies faces has been its tendency to concentrate on the 'object viewed' rather than the 'context of viewing'; the film rather than, say, the 'picture palace'. As he puts it,

> There is more to cinema-going than seeing films. There is going out at night and the sense of relaxation combined with the sense of fun and excitement. The very name 'picture palace', by which cinemas were known for a long time, captures an important part of that experience. Rather than selling individual films, cinema is best understood as having sold a habit, a certain type of socialized experience ... Any analysis of the film subject which does not take on board these issues of the context within which the film is consumed is, to my mind, insufficient. Unfortunately a great deal of film theory has operated without reference to these issues, given the effect of the literary tradition in prioritizing the status of the text itself abstracted from the viewing context.[33]

This point seems central given that films are now viewed in so many different contexts: at the cinema; on network television; via satellite or cable; and on video. The meaning of any of these different contexts may well be very different.

However, Morley also suggests other ways of thinking about the context of consumption. People go to the cinema on dates, for a night out with the gang, or to fill a free afternoon. Couples may watch a film together as a way of winding down before sleep. All these contexts have different meanings which will affect the viewer's decoding, but which is not determined by that decoding.

The transition from *The 'Nationwide' Audience* to *Family Television* also marks another transition in the work associated with the Centre. Its initial work on the media had tended to concentrate on the sphere of news and current affairs programmes, but by the 1980s there was a growing interest in popular fictional programming. This transition was the product of changing conceptions of politics within the period. In the early stage, news and current affairs programming were seen as dealing with 'serious' political and ideological struggles. They were about government, labour disputes, and the policing of society. They also provided a useful way of examining the relationships between media institutions and the state. The influence of feminist work at the Centre helped to shift this focus. This work often refused the definition of the 'political' which limited politics to the public sphere, and in contrast it emphasized the political nature of the personal and domestic sphere. As a result, popular fictional programming was not seen as a distraction from 'real' politics but became a way of investigating the ways in which 'the contradictions of everyday life and popular experience' were worked through in relation to popular media.

These transitions were also related to a third transition. Despite the importance of Gramsci during the 1970s, the Centre had still tended to assume that the popular texts produced by media industries such as broadcasting, publishing and the film industry necessarily reproduced the dominant ideology – even if they stressed that they must include oppositional elements and could be resisted or challenged by audiences. The influence of feminism in particular tended to challenge this assumption. Instead of identifying media texts as an expression of the dominant ideology, later work from the Centre tended to reject this simple formulation.

In fact, as Hall points out, there is no actual fixed content of popular culture. It is not a series of objects whose status is fixed and unchanging, but rather the manner in which objects are defined and consumed. For example, a text which in one historical period was seen as popular may later be redefined as an example of high art. The case of Shakespeare is often used here, but it also applies to many more recent texts. For example, the melodramas of Douglas Sirk were often dismissed by critics during the period in which they were produced.

They were seen as displaying the clichéd and formulaic features associated with popular film. But during the 1970s auteur critics and psychoanalytic feminists appropriated and virtually 'canonized' these texts. Instead of clichéd and formulaic examples of popular culture, they were redefined as subtle and radical films which took the supposedly conservative forms of popular melodrama, and through the stylistic techniques of irony and distanciation, subverted their ideological project. In this way, Sirk's films were no longer seen as sharing the formal features associated with a conservative popular culture, but as texts whose formal features established their difference and distinction from popular film.[34]

Indeed, a text may even have different readerships at the same moment. This is illustrated by the case of *Psycho*. Initially it was derided as a sick and degraded work of popular horror, but it was very quickly appropriated within film studies as a major work of great aesthetic significance. None the less, it has continued to occupy an important space within popular culture as is shown by the number of sequels, imitations and allusions to it which have been made over the years. It has therefore acquired contradictory and opposed meanings within culture. It has been seen by some as an exemplary instance of all that is right or wrong with popular film, but in much the same way as Sirk's films, it has also been seen as an example of film 'art' which is defined by its difference and distinction from popular film.

Conclusion

So the simple distinction between popular film and the avant-garde found in much writing on film becomes untenable. The meaning and political significance of texts are not simply inscribed in their formal features, but are defined through their appropriation or rejection by different groups. The distinction between popular film and the avant-garde is not simply a property of individual texts or groups of texts. It is a product of the cultural distinctions through which the tastes of certain groups are rejected and the tastes of others acquire authority. As a result, texts can be deployed and redeployed in different ways. They can be appropriated or rejected, but the same text may at different moments be identified as displaying the textual features of a radical avant-garde or a conservative popular culture.

This critique of the distinction between a radical avant-garde and an ideologically conservative popular culture is important to the study of popular film because film studies has been so dependent on this kind of distinction. In fact, as Bourdieu's work suggests, the distinction between the popular and the avant-garde is itself a product of economic and cultural power. The idea that popular culture is ideological and conservative is necessary so that dominant social groups can define their own tastes as 'superior' and so win authority over others.

Notes:

1 David Morley, *The 'Nationwide' Audience*, London: British Film Institute, 1980.
2 Pam Cook, *The Cinema Book*, London: British Film Institute, 1985.
3 Raymond Williams, 'Culture is Ordinary' in Ann Gray and Jim McGuigan, eds, *Studying Culture: An Introductory Reader*, London: Edward Arnold, 1993, pp. 5–14.
4 'Culture is Ordinary', p. 7.
5 Richard Hoggart, *The Uses of Literacy*, Harmondsworth: Penguin, 1958.
6 Stuart Laing, *Representations of Working Class Life, 1959–64*, London: Macmillan, 1986, p. 217.
7 Raymond Williams, *The Long Revolution*, Harmondsworth: Penguin, 1965, p. 58.
8 E. P. Thompson, '"The Long Revolution" Part 1', *New Left Review*, nos. 9–10 (1961).
9 E. P. Thompson, *The Making of the English Working Class*, Harmondsworth: Penguin, 1963.
10 See Peter Miles and Malcolm Smith, *Cinema, Literature and Society*, London: Croom Helm, 1987.
11 Iain Chambers, *Border Dialogues: Journeys in Postmodernity*, London: Routledge, 1990, p. 40–1.
12 Stuart Hall, 'Cultural Studies: Two Paradigms', in Richard Collins *et al.*, eds, *Media, Culture and Society: A Reader*, London: Sage, 1986, pp. 33–48.
13 'Cultural Studies: Two Paradigms', p. 45.
14 'Cultural Studies: Two Paradigms', p. 45.
15 See Antonio Gramsci, *Selections from the Prison Notebooks*, London: Lawrence and Wishart, 1971.
16 Stuart Hall *et al.*, *Resistance through Rituals*, London: Hutchinson, 1976.
17 Raymond Williams, *Marxism and Literature*, Oxford: Oxford University Press, 1977.
18 Tony Bennett, 'Introduction: Popular Culture and "the Turn to Gramsci"' in Tony Bennett *et al.*, *Popular Culture and Social Relations*, Milton Keynes: Open University Press, 1986, p. xiii.
19 *Border Dialogues*, p. 44.
20 *Border Dialogues*, p. 44.

21 *Border Dialogues*, p. 42.
22 V. N. Volosinov, *Marxism and the Philosophy of Language*, (originally published 1929), Seminar Press, 1973, p. 23.
23 See, for example, Mark Jancovich, *Horror*, London: Batsford, 1992.
24 For discussions of masculinity in the action genre, see Yvonne Tasker, *Spectacular Bodies: Gender, Genre and the Action Movie*, London: Routledge, 1993; and Andy Willis, *Jean Claude Van Damme: A Study of Masculinity, the Male Body and Martial Arts Cinema*, M.A. dissertation, Thames Valley University, 1994.
25 Pierre Bourdieu, *Distinction: A Social Critique of the Judgement of Taste*, London: Routledge, 1984.
26 Ann Gray, *Video Playtime: The Gendering of a Communication Technology*, London: Routledge, 1992; and Angela Partington, 'Melodrama's Gendered Audience', in *Off-Centre: Feminism and Cultural Studies*, London: HarperCollins, 1991, pp. 49–68.
27 Stuart Hall, 'Encoding/Decoding', in Stuart Hall *et al.*, eds, *Culture, Media, Language*, London: Unwin Hyman, 1980, pp. 128–38.
28 David Morley and Charlotte Brunsdon, *Everyday Television: Nationwide*, London: British Film Institute, 1978, p. v.
29 *The 'Nationwide' Audience*, p. 153.
30 David Morley, *Family Television: Cultural Power and Domestic Leisure*, London: Comedia, 1986.
31 *Family Television*, p. 14.
32 Janice Radway, *Reading the Romance: Women, Patriarchy and Popular Literature*, London: Verso, 1987, p. 210.
33 David Morley, *Television, Audience and Cultural Studies*, London: Routledge, 1992, pp. 157–8.
34 See Christine Gledhill, ed., *Home is Where the Heart Is: Studies in Melodrama and the Women's Film*, London: British Film Institute, 1987.

Guide to further reading

Mass culture theory

Adorno, T.W., and M. Horkheimer, The Culture Industry: Enlightenment as Mass Deception, in *The Dialectic of Enlightenment* (London, Verso, 1979): also published in J. Curran et al (eds), *Mass Communication and Society* (London, Edward Arnold, 1977).

Brookeman, C., *American Culture and Society Since the 1930s* (London, Macmillan, 1984).

MacDonald, D., Masscult and Midcult, in *Against the American Grain* (London, Victor Gollancz, 1963).

MacDonald, D., *Dwight MacDonald on Movies* (Englewood Cliffs, N.J., Prentice-Hall, 1969).

Rosenberg, B. and D. Manning White (eds), *Mass Culture: the Popular Arts in America* (New York, Free Press, 1957).

Ross, A., *No Respect: Intellectuals and Popular Culture* (New York, Routledge, 1989), chapters 1 and 2.

Political economy

Blaug, M. (ed.), *The Economics of the Arts* (London, Martin Robinson, 1976).

Collins, R. et al, *Media, Culture and Society: a reader* (London, Sage, 1986).

Garnham, N., *Capitalism and Communication: Global Culture and the Economics of Information* (London, Sage, 1990).

Golding, P. and G. Murdock, For a Political Economy of Mass Communications, *Socialist Register*, 1973, pp. 205–34.

The film industry

Balio, T.(ed.), *The American Film Industry* (Madison, Wisconsin, University of

Wisconsin Press, 1976).

Balio, T. (ed.), *Hollywood in the Age of Television* (Cambridge, Mass., Unwin Hyman, 1990).

Gomery, D., *The Hollywood Studio System* (London, Macmillan/British Film Institute, 1986).

Hillier, J., *The New Hollywood* (London, Studio Vista, 1992)

Kerr, P. (ed.), *The Hollywood Film Industry: a Reader* (London, Routledge/British Film Institute, 1986).

Schatz, T., *Old Hollywood/New Hollywood: Ritual, Art and Industry* (Ann Arbor, Mich., UMI Research Press, 1983).

Schatz, T., *The Genius of the System: Hollywood Filmmaking in the Studio Era* (London, Simon and Schuster, 1989).

Schatz, T., The New Hollywood, in J. Collins et al (eds), *Film Theory Goes to the Movies* (New York, Routledge, 1993).

Sklar, R., *Movie-Made America: A Cultural History of American Movies* (New York, Random House, 1975).

Auteurism and Film Authorship Theory

Brookeman, C., Coming to Terms with Hollywood: From Mass Culture to Auteur Theory, in *American Culture and Society Since the 1930s* (London, Macmillan, 1984).

Caughie, J. (ed.), *Theories of Authorship* (London, Routledge, 1981).

Cook, P., Authorship and Cinema, in *The Cinema Book* (London, British Film Institute, 1985).

Hillier, J. (ed.), *Cahiers du Cinéma: the 1950s* (London, Routledge, 1985).

Hillier, J. (ed.), *Cahiers du Cinéma Vol. II: the 1960s* (London, Routledge, 1986).

Lapsley, R. and M. Westlake, Authorship, in *Film Theory: an Introduction* (Manchester, Manchester University Press, 1988).

Sarris, A., *The American Cinema: Directors and Directions 1929–1968* (New York, Dutton, 1968).

Wollen, P., *Signs and Meanings in the Cinema* (London, Secker and Warburg, 1972).

Genre

Alloway, L., *Violent America: The Movies, 1946–64* (New York, Museum of Modern Art, 1971).

Bazin, A., *What is Cinema: Volume II* (Berkeley, University of California Press, 1971).

Cook, P., Genre, in *The Cinema Book* (London, British Film Institute, 1985).

Grant, B.K., *The Film Genre Reader* (Austin, University of Texas Press, 1986).

Kitses, J., *Horizons West* (London, Thames and Hudson/British Film Institute, 1969).

Neale, S., *Genre* (London, British Film Institute, 1980).

Neale, S., Questions of Genre, *Screen*, 31(1), spring 1990, pp. 45–66.

Warshow, R., *The Immediate Experience: Movies, Comics, Theatre and Other Aspects of Popular Culture* (New York, Atheneum, 1971).

Wright, W., *Sixguns and Society: a Structural Study of the Western* (Berkeley, University of California Press, 1975).

Star studies

Dyer, R., *Stars* (London, British Institute, 1979).

Dyer, R., *Heavenly Bodies* (London, British Film Institute, 1987).

Ellis, J., *Visible Fictions* (London, Routledge, 1982).

Gledhill, C. (ed.), *Stardom: Industry of Desire* (London, Routledge, 1991).

King, B., Stardom as an Occupation, in P. Kerr (ed.), *The Hollywood Film Industry* (London, Routledge, 1986).

King, B., The Star and the Commodity: Notes Towards a Performance Theory of Stardom, *Cultural Studies*, 1(2), pp. 145–61.

Stacey, J. *Star Gazing: Hollywood Cinema and Female Spectatorship* (London, Routledge, 1994).

Historical poetics

Bordwell, D., J. Staiger and K. Thompson, *The Classical Hollywood Cinema: Film Style and Mode of Production to 1960* (New York, Columbia University Press, 1985).

Bordwell, D. and K. Thompson, *Film Art: An Introduction* (New York, McGraw-Hill, 1990).

Bordwell, D. and K. Thompson, *Film History: An Introduction* (NewYork, McGraw-Hill, 1994).

Bordwell, D., *Narration and the Fiction Film* (Madison, University of Wisconsin Press, 1985).

Bordwell, D., *Making Meaning: Inference and Rhetoric in the Interpretation of Cinema* (Cambridge, Harvard University Press, 1989).

Karnack, B. and H. Jenkins (eds), *Classical Hollywood Comedy* (New York, Routledge, 1994).

Schatz, T., *The Genius of the System: Hollywood Filmmaking in the Studio Era* (London, Simon and Schuster, 1989).

Schatz, T., *Old Hollywood/New Hollywood: Ritual, Art and Industry* (Ann Arbor, Mich., UMI Research Press, 1983).

Staiger, J., *Interpreting Films: Studies in the Historical Reception of American Cinema* (Princeton, Princeton University Press, 1992).

Screen theory

Cahiers du Cinéma Editorial Board, John Ford's *Young Mr Lincoln, Screen,* 13(3), autumn 1972.

Cook, P., Narrative and the Structuralist Controversy, in *The Cinema Book* (London, British Film Institute, 1985).

Heath, S., *Questions of Cinema* (London, Macmillan, 1981).

Lapsley, R. and M. Westlake, *Film Theory: an Introduction* (Manchester, Manchester University Press, 1988).

Metz, C., *Psychoanalysis and the Cinema: the Imaginary Signifier* (London, Macmillan, 1982).

Neale, S., Genre (London, British Film Institute, 1980).

Nichols, B.(ed.), *Movies and Methods Volumes 1 & 2*, (Berkeley, University of California, 1976 and 1985).

Penley, C. (ed.), *Feminism and Film Theory* (London, Routledge, 1988).

Screen Editorial Collective (ed.), *The Sexual Subject: a 'Screen' Reader in Sexuality* (London, Routledge, 1991).

Feminisms

Gamman L. and M. Marshment, *The Female Gaze: Women as Viewers of Popular Culture* (London, Women's Press, 1988).

Gibson, P. Church, and R. Gibson (eds), *Dirty Looks: Women, Pornography and Power* (London, British Film Institute, 1993).

Haskell, M., *From Reverence to Rape: the Treatment of Women in the Movies* (Chicago, University of Chicago Press, 1987).

Hooks, B., *Black Looks: Race and Representation* (London, Turnaround, 1992).

Pribram, D. (ed.), *Female Spectators: Looking at Film and Television* (London, Verso, 1990).

Radway, J., *Reading the Romance: Women, Patriarchy and Popular Literature* (London, Verso, 1987).

Rodgerson, G. and E. Wilson, *Feminism and Pornography: the Case against Censorship* (London, Lawrence and Wishart, 1991).

Rosen, M., *Popcorn Venus: Women, Movies and the American Dream* (New York, Avon, 1973).

Rowbotham, S., *Hidden from History: 300 Years of Women's Oppression and the Fight Against it* (London, Pluto, 1973).

Stacey, J., *Star Gazing: Hollywood Cinema and Female Spectatorship* (London, Routledge, 1994).

Taylor, H., *Scarlett's Women: 'Gone with the Wind' and its Female Fans* (London, Virago, 1989).

Williams, L., *Hardcore: Power, Pleasure and the 'Frenzy of the Visible'* (London, Paladin, 1990).

Cultural studies

Bennett, T. et al (eds), *Culture, Ideology and Social Process* (London, Batsford, 1981).

Bennett, T. et al (eds), *Popular Culture and Social Relations* (Milton Keynes, Open University Press, 1986).

Bourdieu, P., *Distinction: a Social Critique of the Judgement of Taste* (London, Routledge, 1984).

Franklin, S. et al (eds), *Off-Centre: Feminism and Cultural Studies* (London, Harper Collins, 1991)

Gray, A. and J. McGuigan (eds), *Studying Culture: an Introductory Reader* (London, Edward Arnold, 1993).

Hall, S., Encoding/Decoding, in S. Hall et al (eds), *Culture, Media, Language* (London, Unwin Hyman, 1980).

Hall, S., Notes on Deconstructing the Popular, in R. Samuel (ed.), *People's History and Socialist Theory* (London, Routledge, 1981).

Jenkins, H., *Textual Poachers: Television, Fans and Participatory Culture* (New York, Routledge, 1992).

Morley, D., *Television, Audiences and Cultural Studies* (London, Routledge, 1992).

Turner, G., *British Cultural Studies: an Introduction* (London, Unwin Hyman, 1990).

Index